Michael Garella, s.j.

The Virgin Text

Oklahoma Project for
Discourse and Theory

The Virgin Text

Fiction, Sexuality, and Ideology

BY JON STRATTON

Lecturer in English, University of Queensland

University of Oklahoma Press

NORMAN AND LONDON

Library of Congress Cataloging-in-Publication Data

Stratton, Jon.
  The virgin text.

  (Oklahoma project for discourse and theory;
  v. 1)
  Includes index.
  1. Fiction.   2. Feminist literary criticism.
3. English fiction—History and criticism.
I. Title.   II. Series.
PN3335.S77   1987   809.3   86-40530
ISBN 0-8061-2054-1

The Virgin Text is Volume 1 of the Oklahoma Project for Discourse and Theory.

Contents

Acknowledgements

I am grateful to Chris Austin, Yuki Asano and Jennie Davies
for so patiently listening to many of the arguments in this
book when I am sure they had much more important matters
of their own to talk about. I would particularly like to thank
Lyn Finch who not only was prepared to listen to me talking
about the material in this book but actually read and
commented on two drafts of it. Thanks are also due to Jock
MacLeod who read and commented on the Introduction and
Conclusion. Though I am sure he does not remember such a
chance encounter, I would like to thank Stephen Knight, who
in one of those late-night conference conversations,
encouraged me to write the book when my ideas were still at
an early stage of development.

I would like to thank my typist, Ira Gowlett, who did a
magnificent job and I would also like to thank the School of
Humanities, Griffith University for granting me the money to
pay for the typing. In addition, Caroline Lemaire-Jones has
my thanks for her impressive editorial work on the
manuscript and for compiling the index.

Series Editors' Foreword

This is the first book in the Oklahoma Project for Discourse and Theory, a series of interdisciplinary texts whose purpose is to explore the cultural institutions that constitute the human sciences, to see them in relation to one another, and, perhaps above all, to see them as products of particular discursive practices. We hope that the Oklahoma Project will promote dialogue within and across traditional disciplines— psychology philology, linguistics, history, art history, aesthetics, logic, political economy, religion, philosophy, anthropology, communications, and the like—in a series of texts that locate themselves theoretically between and across disciplines. Recently, in a host of new and traditional disciplines, there has been great interest in such discursive and theoretical frameworks. Yet we conceive of the Project as going beyond local inquiries, providing a larger forum for interdiscursive theoretical discourse and dialogue.

Our idea, in short, is to present through the University of Oklahoma Press a series of critical volumes that will stage a theoretical encounter among disciplines, an interchange not limited to literature but covering virtually the whole range of the human sciences. It will be a critical series with an important reference in 'literary' studies—thus mirroring the modern development of discourse theory—but including all approaches, other than quantitative studies, open to semiotic analysis. Regardless of its particular domain, each book in the series will investigate characteristically post-Freudian, post-Saussurean, and post-Marxist questions about culture and the discourses that constitute different cultural phenomena.

The Oklahoma Project will be a sustained dialogue intended to make a significant contribution to cultural theory and contemporary understanding of the human sciences.

The title of the series reflects, of course, its home base, the University of Oklahoma, but, more important, it also signals in a significant way the *interest*—what Kierkegaard calls the 'in-between' aspect—of the Project as we conceive it. Oklahoma is a haunting place-name in our culture, a Choctaw phrase that means 'red people' and goes back to the Treaty of Dancing Rabbit Creek in Mississippi in 1830. It conjures up America itself for Franz Kafka, both Indians and vast plains (the first place named Oklahoma subsequently became Whitefield), what Henry Nash Smith called 'the Virgin Land.' It is a name with which Wallace Stevens begins his *Collected Poems*. Historically it is a place in which American expansion was reenacted in a single day in a retracing (and rewriting) called the Oklahoma land run. Geographically, it is the heartland of the continent, a frontier between the cosmopolitan East and West from which the series editors came. It is a frontier between what J. Hillis Miller in a recent interview called 'California-Foucault, New Haven-Derrida,' a crossing, a place of encounter. And that is precisely what we hope the Oklahoma Project for Discourse and Theory will itself become: a place of encounter for the study of culture.

It is fitting, then, that the first volume of the Project is Jon Stratton's *The Virgin Text: Fiction, Sexuality, and Ideology*—a book, in Stratton's words, 'best ... understood as a rewriting of the history of the novel.' No modern discourse of Western literature has interacted more deeply and complexly with culture than the novel, and studies to account for the history of novelistic discourse have rarely *enacted* (as Stratton does) the place of encounter that is the novel by situating it heterogeneously within the cultural discourses of politics, psychology, anthropology, history, and the like—within the complex cultural discourses the Oklahoma Project is about. A critical series devoted to the study of discourse is well served by beginning with 'a rewriting of the history of the novel,' a rewriting in the sense that all the Project volumes will be rewritings and retracings of so-called humanistic concerns repositioned as theoretical concerns in the human sciences. It is our hope that in the books of the Oklahoma Project, individually and collectively, the monologues of traditional scholarly discourse will become heteroglosses, just as such place-names as Oklahoma and such commonplace words as 'new' and 'novel' can be opened as sites for the dialogue and discursive play of culture. We are pleased to inaugurate the Oklahoma Project with this volume, believing that it sets a standard of critical insight and boldness that will characterize the books to follow.

ROBERT CON DAVIS
RONALD SCHLEIFER

Norman, Oklahoma

Introduction

This book might best be understood as a rewriting of the history of the novel. It is an attempt to locate the elaboration of what we, retrospectively, identify as the development of the novel within a specific socio-historical context. That context is what I will call the sexualising of the world as a fundamental element in the elaboration of bourgeois society.

In this project I draw on many of the theoretical assumptions of psychoanalysis and of Marxism. I want to argue that the bourgeois—middle class—culture which is articulated in and through the capitalist economic structure is unique in its mobilisation of sexuality as the realising force of that social order. This is not to say that this society is founded on sexuality but rather that the society of capitalism articulates itself through a sexual reconstruction of the world which gives that world the only, the 'real', meaning for those who live within it. Others have put forward similar arguments about the significance of sexuality in bourgeois society.[1] The specific form of my argument in the context of sexuality is to suggest that at the basis of bourgeois society lies a disunity which can be reconstructed in such twinned formulations as expression/repression. The bourgeois experience of reality is founded on a fundamental fracture which reconstitutes sexuality as both non-existent and everywhere. The material site of this sexualised order is the body. The constructive fetishistic structure which articulates males and females not simply as gendered but as charged, and charging, elements in the production of the lived world is constituted in desire. And desire has its lived end (which in such a fetishistic order is no end at all) in sexual intercourse.

In this world the female is constituted fetishistically, and dichotomously, by the male. The female lives her life as asexual; that is to say, bourgeois society has historically denied women sexual desire. Simultaneously, however, and as an expression of the original generative fracture, women are considered to have a dark side, an unassuagable sexual appetite which, manifested in desire, could, if let loose, destroy the social world. The woman as fetish—and as asexual—forms the basis for the bourgeois reality. Constructed as she is from within the dynamics of a male desire, itself constituted as a part of the primal fracture, she is situated as asexual at the centre of the institutional *locus* of the bourgeois world. She is the centre of both the asexual family and, more generally, the asexual domestic domain.

In the same way that the bourgeois reality of women as asexual is called into existence by, and dependent upon, the repression of an overwhelming (excessive) sexuality which is itself a construct, so the same can be said for the family and the domestic domain in general. It is the fetishistic charging of woman, family and domestic domain which, in the lived world, gives them their claim to the site of the reality of the bourgeois social order. Correspondingly, the male is constructed as having a procreative, constituting desire which is articulated as sexual. If the female is constructed as asexual, then the male is constructed as pervasively sexual and, similarly, the masculine world outside the domestic domain is recognised as sexualised. As a part of this seamless structuring, the asexual domestic domain is also seemingly evacuated of all capitalist exchange, while the rest of the world, permeated by sexuality, is the world of the capitalist economy.

We must not forget the dynamics of power within this structuring system. In the lived world it is women who occupy the site of social order, the site of 'reality'—that is, the family. The illusion is that this is, let us say, a desirable site; that it is the site of power and that women occupy it voluntarily. This, however, is the reality as it is lived in bourgeois society. The repressed reality is that women are constructed into this position. Within the sexualised, fetishistic system males are constructed as the fixers and females as the fixed. Thus while both males and females are a part of a single system, it is in fact males who are the real realisers of society. It is males who embody the site of power.

Such a social order did not come into existence fully formed. In Chapter 1 I will discuss the sexualising of the world in detail. The production of a fetishistic system is not limited to human beings. From within this system all objects take on fetishistic qualities. As we shall see, such an effect is directly linked to the commodification of the world within a capitalist economic system based on money and exchange value. This is the moment of connection, in theory, between a Marxian notion of commodity fetishism which argues that in capitalist society value appears to inhere in the object itself and a psychoanalytic notion of fetishism as a function of desire. In an important sense much of this book is concerned with the processes which have called the lived bourgeois world into existence. This is because in much of this book I am concerned to argue that the development of the novel as a specific form of writing is intimately bound up with the deployment of the bourgeois world; hence my concern with the epistolary novel.

The epistolary novel is a stage in the development of the bourgeois novel. One way of thinking about the development of the novel is in terms of an ongoing movement towards objectness. The novel becomes a world in its own right experienced as alienated *ab origine* from the reader who is him/herself articulated as an isolated, individualised person. Epistolary fiction structures the reader into its complex of meaning by forcing upon him/her the effort of pulling all the letters together and constructing his/her own meaning by a revision of the disparate representations which she/he is given in the novel. Subsequent fiction styles are premised on the idea that the individual and the novel operate as entirely separate entities which must be united in the empathic act of reading. The fetishised novel is consumed by the fetishised individual in the sexually charged act of reading. The epistolary novel may be considered as one important moment in this development.

As bourgeois, capitalist society discovered and elaborated a discursive world founded on notions of sexuality,[2] so writing, as an aspect of that world, also took on a sexualised, fetishistic aspect. The history of the novel form may then be seen in the context of the historically specific development of a 'real' discourse of sexuality, one fundamental determinant of which was the repression of the sexuality so constituted. The climax of this development is, of course, the work of Freud, which reveals and articulates as absolute the sexuality which is called into being by its own fetishised repression.[3] The epistolary novel form occupies an important place in this particular history of the novel which links the fetishisation of the lived world with the deployment of the novel form, and in particular with that genre of the novel privileged by the label 'realist'.

Texts are always constructed, and constituted, within a framework of lived practices. These practices develop over time and have to be learnt by the members of the society as an aspect of their socialisation. From this point of view it is possible to understand the movement of literature under capitalism as a movement towards a particular formulation. I do not mean this in the classical and teleological bourgeois sense of the importance and value of the modern novel form, but rather that the modern novel form is acceptable to our society because it partakes of fundamental attributes of our society's ideology. Hence we are not talking about the inevitable elaboration of the 'correct' form of the novel but the gradual articulation of a form, and content, of writing which is determined by, and reinforces, the presuppositions of the evolving society.

What is taught as literacy is the most obvious way in which our society determines our understanding of what is a text, a 'work' or a book, and therefore our apprehension of that thing. In capitalist society in the movement from hand-writing to printing, writing is increasingly articulated as an object *sui generis*, as a construct finally constituted in the process of publication which then exists within the public domain as a fetishised commodity. The social production of textuality is inversely experienced in terms of an inevitable textual absolute, which is in turn related to apparently inevitable ways of writing and reading. The validity of this understanding lies in the lived experience of its correctness by writer and reader. The alienation of the text from the capitalist, bourgeois lived world—with appositeness this might be called its fictionalisation—may then be seen not only as producing the constituting practices of textual forms such as the novel but also as determining the articulation and reception of content. In the high capitalism of the late nineteenth century a triad of writerly forms would appear to be discursively separable as 'realism', 'Gothic' and 'pornography'. In this sense it is not only society which constructs the writer and reader but also the text. Baudrillard has argued for an understanding of commodity fetishism not as an individuated phenomenon but as a system-based one: 'It is not the passion (whether of objects or subjects) for substances that speaks in fetishism, it is the *passion for the code*, which by governing both objects and subjects, and by subordinating them to itself, delivers them up to abstract manipulation'.[4]

Capitalism by means of its production of the libidinised world generates a fetishised total system of objects energised through the individual's experience. In this system the text—and not just the written text but the film, radio and television text also—occupies a special place, for it is not just an object in its own right, it is capable of productively reproducing the system of which it is itself a product. However, the denomination of the text as fetish—that is, as energised and able to be utilised for cathexis (this is always present in the bourgeois experience of catharsis)—is a historical development. The lived double articulation of sex in bourgeois capitalist society—that is, *ex*pression and *re*pression—articulated in the commodity as fetish, structures all three levels of the bourgeois text, material form, formal structure and content. In this book I will mainly be concerned with formal structure and with content. However, it is salutory to remember that this classically bourgeois concern is founded on the equally classically bourgeois repression of the material, commodity status of the written work.

In bourgeois society it is the fetishisation of the material text which constructs it as female, as asexual and as a product of a male creative process. The historical shift in attitude towards the writer and the novel as a function of the fetishisation of the text has been well brought out by Showalter. Showalter[5] has discussed how male strategies in the literary tradition meant that through the nineteenth century works by women were criticised as products of a particular group, women, and how women to gain acceptance and publication in a masculine world would take on male pseudonyms. Thus Charlotte Brontë published under the name of Currer Bell, Harriet Parr used Holme Lee, Mary Kingsley used Lucas Malet and Mary Hawker used Lucas Falconer, to name but four. This, however, was not an eighteenth-century phenomenon. In the eighteenth century, women writers such as Mrs Manley and Mrs Haywood were able to work whilst acknowledging that they were female. As the novel moved from the epistolary form to the third person 'world in its own right', as it became increasingly both objectified and fetishised, so, simultaneously, women were increasingly forced out of the creative role of writer.

The novel is already a world of its own as the reader relates to it. To be a world of its own the novel must exist in another world, a world which is not its own. This is what the public domain of capitalism is. The world outside the domestic domain is experienced as alien. The individual's perception of the objects which constitute the world is precisely the perception of an estranged world. The strangeness can only be overcome by the appropriation of objects and their positioning within the domestic environment; but the world out there carries on existing as estranged. The fantasy of the novel is that, as a complete world, it can be familiarised. The reader does not exist in the world. The completeness of the estrangement produces the reciprocal possibility of complete familiarity. The fictional reality of the novel and the ideological fiction of the domestic domain both articulate a fantasy which, if successful, is lived as real.

We must identify two trajectories implicit in the history of the novel. On the one hand we have the trajectory of form which starts with the epistolary novel and moves towards the alienated unity of the third (or sometimes first) person novel. On the other hand we have the trajectory of genre in which the founding fracture of the bourgeois world is rearticulated in the parallel generic categories of realism and Gothic. Traditionally, the development of the novel has been seen in terms of the development of the realist novel. For example, neither Leavis in *The Great Tradition*[6] nor Watt in *The Rise of the Novel*[7] concerned themselves with the limits of the realist novel and questions about alternative novel genres. Only relatively recently has the Gothic (or fantasy, as the genre is sometimes known albeit with rather different defining criteria)[8] become an acceptable literary area for study. In Chapter 2, I want to suggest that, simultaneously with the trajectory of form, there can be found in the novel a trajectory of genre in which, as the novel comes to occupy its estranged, objectified and sexualised position in the bourgeois world, so in terms of content it again replicates the foundational fracture appearing in the dual guise of repressive (realist) and expressive (Gothic).

The realist novel, which critics have traditionally defined in terms of a realistic portrayal of the world, in fact replicates the repressed, apparent, asexual reality of the bourgeois existence. The Gothic novel, on the other hand, expresses the other side of the constituting fracture, the strange, the hints of Otherness, the potential for disorder, the sexualisation of the world. Both these genres come into existence at the same historical moment. In this book I will be pairing two novels by Richardson: *Pamela*, as a proto-realist novel, and *Clarissa*, as a proto-Gothic novel.

There is one other genre with which I am concerned in this book, and that is pornography. The extent to which pornography may be said to be a genre in the same sense as realism and the Gothic is, of course, problematical in the sense that wider societal concerns about what may be said to be obscene bear on the issue of pornography. Nevertheless, as we shall see in Chapter 2 pornography does seem to constitute a very specific form of writing, and it arose, in no way coincidentally, during the period of the sexualising of the world. Pornography is a complex phenomenon in that it straddles both the realist genre, with novels such as *Fanny Hill*, and also the Gothic genre, with novels such as *The 120 Days of Sodom*. Pornography asserts what both the other generic formulations repress, that reading is a sexualised practice in bourgeois society and that the text is a fetishised object. In addition, the construction of the genre of pornography recognises what literary criticism tends to repress—that the construction of genres is, in part, a function of the reading process. It is the acknowledgement of these elements in the context of sexually explicit writing that makes pornography a different kind of genre.

The realist novel, conventionally the only novel genre, is in fact, like 'woman', an unstable fetish. It is produced as asexual but exists only in the denial of, on the one hand, its Gothic Other and, on the other hand, its existence as the site of displaced libidinous desire. The realist novel, indeed, might be said to be the site of virtue. Virtue quite literally constitutes the problematic of *Pamela*. To simplify my argument it would be possible to draw an equation between the realist novel and the ideal, asexual, passive bourgeois woman; the Gothic novel and the sexualised, active woman of bourgeois fantasy; the pornographic novel and the prostitute. Such is the seamless nature of the desiring structure of the bourgeois world as it is constituted on the fundamental fracture articulated in repression/expression.

In bourgeois society marriage holds a central position. It is the nexus of the signifying system which underpins the reality of that society. The fetishisation of the (female) body constructs the female as a commodity. As a commodity she may become property. In this context one interpretation of the bourgeois obsession with virginity, and defloweration, may be understood as a concern with new, not secondhand, goods. In the importance of intercourse here we can see the literal operation of bourgeois sexuality. It is the act of intercourse which consummates the marriage. It is, then, also the act of intercourse which irrevocably constitutes the woman as property. She becomes the object owned. We may say that the operation of the cash nexus is a form of cathexis, the desire which overflows the bourgeois marriage is used up in realising the bourgeois world. In marriage, intercourse in a world constructed by the male is not only the moment of fixing property by use but also the moment when the world of fetishised objects is fixed and reaffirmed by the thrust which teleologically legitimates the fetishism of the woman as body. In the same act the whole reality founded on the repression of sexuality in the domestic domain is asserted. The married woman is not only an object; she is an asexual individual who lies at the centre of the domain which is experienced as giving meaning to the bourgeois capitalist world. It is by this means that the world of fetishised appearance is validated as the real world.

I have noted that the fetishisation of women is constituted in the structural organisation of desire. I might add that, dialectically, the Other of desire is love and that it is love which constitutes the male as fetish. In the context of writing this is well demonstrated by the importance of love as the basis of the Romance fiction so often categorised as women's fiction. Desire/love move towards the fetishistic fixation of intercourse/marriage; however, desire/love are themselves constituted in the act of sight. In bourgeois society it is sight which calls desire/love into being—the currency of the phrase 'love at first sight' illustrates this point well. In terms of the realising of the bourgeois world, then, sight is the most important of the senses. It produces the gendered person as Other and incorporates them into the structural web of desire. It is a primary fixing which constructs the person as fetish. Given that sexuality and its determining power are male qualities in bourgeois society, the power of sight gains its significance as a masculine quality.

Later, in Chapter 7 particularly, I will have more to say about sight. However, it may be useful to give an example here of the literary preoccupation with this sense. In the novel by Laclos *Les Liaisons dangereuses*, which I shall discuss in more detail in Chapter 4, the Marquise de Meurteuil (the translation 'death-eye' echoes the importance of sight) has the fundamental structuring màle attribute of her world; that is to say, she has desire. She successfully hides her desire from the world so she also has social acceptance.[9] However, she does not have the power, potency, the phallus as the signifier of the male, to consummate her desire. In the lived world her metaphorical lack is supplied by her lack of a penis and, in the end, her power of penetration, by sight and by penis, is found wanting when she does not anticipate Valmont's final move in their fight and is exposed and fixed by a man. In Freud's formulation of fetishism it is a function of sight and it is located in the male as a consequence of seeing the female's 'lack' of a penis. Miller sums up well the difference between the Marquise and Valmont when she writes, 'His victories derive tautologically from the fact of his maleness, hers from the subversion of phallocentric truth.'[10] Finally, Laclos, subscribing to the values of his society, inscribes Valmont in the place of worldly production, reproducing his own position as creator of the world of the novel. Freud's theory enables us to generalise this patriarchal inscription for bourgeois society as a totalising system. The Marquise de Meurteuil tries to usurp the gendered male role of producer of her society. Her name, 'death-eye', has a dual connotation. Insofar as she uses sight in a male way in the service of desire, she fixes, and therefore metaphorically kills, the men she desires. By the end of the novel, however, the power of sight 'kills' her. Her beauty is disfigured by smallpox, an outward and visible sign of her internal immorality, and she has been forced to leave her social world. Her loss of the world in which her sight had meaning is another 'death'. The extreme punishments which Laclos exacts on the Marquise signal the conservative closure of a novel in which a woman attempts to usurp the male role.

Intercourse is fundamental to bourgeois reality because of its axial position linking sexuality and marriage. However, where the stability of that reality is guaranteed by other means, intercourse may take second place to the fetishisation of the body. In pre-Revolution France, as I shall discuss in Chapter 4, this stability was ensured by the entrenched and ossified framework of the feudal hierarchy. The elaboration of the absolutist state provided a fixed non-capitalistic structure within which the bourgeois system of signs could be brought to fruition. The stability thus engendered allowed for the development of a reality of appearance which required no point of contact with the discourse of sexuality, only its existence. Hence we have the paramount importance of desire in France structured, in the sexualised writing of the novels, by letters.[11] In this sense the French *monde*, the society based on the court, was coterminous with what was called, by Bayle originally, the Republic of Letters.[12]

In the society of *ancien régime* France, it was desire/love rather than intercourse/marriage which was crucial to the sexualised social order. The practical reality of such a system was to be found in the sexual/asexual pursuit rather than the fixity of intercourse/marriage. With *le monde* structured in this way, the letters of such novels as *Les Liaisons dangereuses* are, one might say, only signifiers to the one of the liaison who still feels love/desire.[13] They assert his/her individuality because they assert his/her reality. In France the letters of epistolary novels become more than a signification of the structural ordering of a fetishistic reality; they become the articulation of reality. As Laclos demonstrates at the end of *Les Liaisons dangereuses* (note the pun in the title) they represent power in their ability to reveal a further, more real reality beyond, but determined by, the reality of appearances created in *le monde*.[14]

We can compare the conventional bourgeois preoccupation with the fixing of reality in the (female) body in the twinned practices of marriage and intercourse with the French idea of *l'honnête femme*. This starts from a similar position where marriage and honesty are linked to reality and moves in the peculiar structuration of *ancien régime* France to a position exemplified in *Les Liaisons dangereuses*, where honesty and virtue are allied to the dissimulated reality of appearance. In this world, where bourgeois desire does not need to be harnessed and limited to marriage in order to secure the permanence of reality, honesty and virtue consist in being successfully dishonest and unvirtuous. In classical bourgeois society, which includes post-Revolution France, the significance of the importance of the marriage/body/intercourse/love combination[15] lies in the attempt to unify the repressed reality of desire with the lived reality of social life. The importance of honesty (truthfulness), as a bourgeois concept, is a reflection of the need to give depth to the social reality founded in marriage. It is in relation to marriage that those other concepts—virtue, chastity and virginity—have their reality and their meaning. Fundamental to Clarissa's tragedy in Richardson's novel of the same name is her desire to resolve these two realities, something which is impossible for a female in a fetishised world who does not wish to be 'already' constructed by bourgeois ideology. *Ancien régime* France represents a special case of the sexualisation of the world, and its novels need to be understood within this context. Post-Revolution France reconstructed its sexualised social order along the lines I have outlined for Britain.

This manuscript was written during late 1981 and in 1982. Since its writing, a number of books have been published which, had I written the book now, would have gained a place in my discussion. There are only two which I would like to mention here. One is Terry Castle's book on *Clarissa*, entitled *Clarissa's Ciphers*.[16] Castle's book is an extremely interesting analysis of the significations of *Clarissa* and the way in which Richardson implicates the reader in the shifting 'meanings' of the text. In many places my reading of *Clarissa* will be seen to correspond with Castle's much more detailed analysis. The other book I must mention is Terry Eagleton's *The Rape of Clarissa*.[17] Eagleton's book stands as a Marxist and feminist recuperation of *Clarissa*. These ideological perspectives similarly signal a correspondence with my enterprise. My project is broader than that of Eagleton, however. Eagleton, and Castle for that matter, continue to priorise the text. Eagleton views the 'content' of *Clarissa* as a function of Richardson's class location. My argument is more structuralist that this. I have tried to produce an argument which does not priorise the text in any conventional sense but which rather locates the text, its production and consumption, within the context of the underlying determinations on which bourgeois society is constituted. It is from within this larger, contextual perspective that the novel becomes sexualised, becomes, in fact, a virgin text awaiting the reader.

CHAPTER 1

Sexuality and Confinement

In bourgeois capitalist society everyday life is experienced as being pervaded by the sexual, and simultaneously, as being asexual since sex is repressed not only out of 'polite', social conversation but also out of the discourses and practices which make up our world. This is true at the empirically real level where public caressing, let alone public sexual intercourse, is considered by the dominant culture to be shocking, and where the public 'display' (the very word is an illustration of the bourgeois ideology in practice in its suggestion of something usually kept concealed being revealed) of male and female genitalia, including female breasts, is a cause for moral outrage. It is also true at the level of conversation where discussion of intercourse is socially proscribed so that even partners in the act often have difficulty communicating their sexual needs and where discussion of the body is never far removed from the awareness of the body as the site of eroticism. At the same time, intercourse within marriage is considered to be of paramount importance, so much so that the very marriage itself is called into question if it has not been consummated.

Arguments about whether or not women should, or do, wear sexually stimulating clothes are irrelevant in a society where it is impossible to wear clothes which are not sexually stimulating precisely because they are already perceived as things which conceal. This argument can be extended to the body itself, which is perceived as not simply naked—it is the concealed revealed.

What this book will argue is that these are not chance

1

occurrences, but that the play of concealment and revelation articulates a displacement which is at the foundation of the bourgeois lived reality. This displacement is manifested in eroticisation. Intercourse is no longer concerned with the fulfilment of sexual needs or with reproduction, its achievement no longer simply the exercise of an assumed patriarchal right; the body is no longer something which is only stimulating under certain circumstances. Intercourse and the body become the *loci* of the set of lived practices which manifest the bourgeois sexualisation of the world.

Foucault[1] has written about the bourgeois production of the body as the site of sexuality; what he has not talked about is the instability of the body thus produced. The bourgeois sexualised body is unstable precisely because it exists, in its very production, as a fetish, a site of unstable reconciliation. It exists as an aspect of a strategy to penetrate, and in doing so fix, the structured sign-system of the bourgeois world and enable it to be experienced as the permanence of an absolute reality.

The individual person's experience of sexuality is of a condition essentially articulated in the body. It is this condition which subsequently requires control—a control often articulated as confinement. The connections between sexuality and capitalism that are made on the 'body' are well brought out in Deleuze and Guattari's *Anti-Oedipus*, where the human being is described as a desiring-machine.[2] The idea of the body as a machine which sexually desires is a motif which goes back to la Mettrie in *l'Homme machine*, which was first published in 1747. If we use desire in a more general sense, we find the first well-known example in Hobbes's description of the individual in *Leviathan*. It would be neat to be able to suggest that the notion of the body as a machine which requires regulation is a metaphorical elaboration of the concern with machinery during the Industrial Revolution. However, it seems much more likely that the concern with the regulation of machinery in such ideas as the 'discovery' of the division of labour, the relating of machines to 'efficiency', and the perception of the machine itself as an object in an equilibrium where the requirement of its operators is to keep it in equilibrium, is dependent on the capitalist understanding of the world as a place of dynamic equilibrium kept as such by regulation.

We might, with justification, talk about a sexual economy of the body in which the body is not only equated with a bourgeois invented machine but is perceived as being constructed with the same capitalist requirements for regulation. William Acton's preoccupation with regulating male seminal emission is a case in point. Acton considered 'excessive' seminal emission so dangerous that, having created the problem, he turned it into an illness called spermatorrhoea. This is all the more significant when we place it alongside the use by the anonymous author of the Victorian *My Secret Life* of the term 'spend' for ejaculation.[3] Truly, we are in the presence of a sexual economy.

Economic thinking from Adam Smith and Ricardo perceived the capitalist economy as a natural economy based on seventeenth-century notions of individual acquisitiveness, property and value, while Marx argued that society was always a product of the economic formation. What Freud and Marx have in common is that they took the two constituting aspects of bourgeois society and elaborated them into theories of the origin of all society. Capitalist economic organisation requires a fundamental unit of conversion which we understand by the term 'money'. In the sexual organisation of bourgeois society the universal solvent is 'desire'. It is the deployment of money which enables the market economy to exist and the deployment of desire which brings into being the fetishism which gives bourgeois society its reality.

The result of sexualisation is the libidinous charging of the objects which to go make up the world of bourgeois experience. This world becomes a charged system. Baudrillard suggests that:

> What is fascinating about money is ... its *systematic nature*, the potential enclosed in the material for total commutability of all values, thanks to their definitive abstraction ... What is fetishised [in money] is the closed perfection of a system, not the 'golden calf', or the treasure.[4]

The ability of capitalist society to use money as a 'universal solvent' may be understood as founded on the bourgeois fetishisation of the lived world. The foundation of that world, that which enables the participants to make sense of their world, is the potential of money to resolve the individuated fetishises into a systematised world of fetishised commodities. The bourgeois world is articulated as a system of signs which are experienced as being the real world. The success of this systematisation depends upon the closedness, the confinement, of the system. The place occupied by sexual intercourse as the nexus of human reproduction is occupied by the cash nexus in terms of capitalist social reproduction. Both these forms of reproduction have been drawn together in bourgeois society in the priorisation and valorisation of marriage as a societal practice.

Marriage operates to demarcate the capitalist, sexualised world from the affective, apparently non-sexual, world. The status given to marriage in bourgeois society is a reflection of the importance given to the family and the domestic sphere in which it exists. Bourgeois thought perceives it as fundamental to the ordering of that society. It is a place of stability and the real, a base from which the capitalist world may be encountered. It is Coventry Patmore's 'tent pitch'd in a world not right' (a quotation from his poem 'Angel in the House'). Its significance derives from the bourgeois perception of the domestic family as both non-sexual and non-economic.[5]

Primary displacement occurs in the individual's experience where the all-pervading sexuality is counterbalanced by the all-pervading proscription of sexuality. If, as I will go on to argue, the one socially sanctioning act of intercourse, marital consummation, places the woman as the repository of bourgeois patriarchal reality, then she is also the ultimate *locus* of that confinement. In her creation as the place of confinement, the woman is produced as an unstable fetish vacillating between Truth and Dissimulation, sexuality and lack of sexuality, reason and unreason, and above all, reality and 'Reality'.

In suggesting that the Reality of bourgeois society is founded upon a displacement which in practice is the productive double articulation of expression and repression, certain points need to be made concerning the sexualisation thus generated. The most important moment in the structuration of societal sexuality is the experience of the empirical and discursive praxis of heterosexual intercourse. The understanding of sexual difference in our society is conceptually based upon the criterion of the physical activity of intercourse. Freud's work represents the most obvious example of this phenomenon. He compartmentalises the human being into the only two categories which he, and our society, allows. Quite simply, persons are to be defined as 'male' if they possess a penis and as 'female' if they possess a vagina. The point may be given more authority by quoting Garfinkel who, in his study of gender ascription in American society, writes, 'for normals the possession of a penis by a male and a vagina by a female are essential insignia. Appropriate feelings, activities, membership obligations, and the like are attributed to persons who possess penises and vaginas.'[6]

The Oedipus complex which Freud considered to form the basis of the domestic crisis of reproduction is structured around this conceptual organisation by way of its emphasis on intercourse. The Lacanian elevation of the notion of Penis Envy into the Phallus as the primary signifier which in turn enables us to consider absence not only as a theoretical concept of production but as a real articulation of the patriarchal determination of female-ness also reflects the taken-for-granted bourgeois concerns of capitalist society. The importance of heterosexual intercourse—that is, intercourse involving penis (Presence) and vagina (Absence)—determines, and is determined by, the sexuality of the person. This forms the basis of the person's pretence to realness and, subsequently, to individuality. The woman as Absence may also be interpreted as the manifestation of the primary displacement. From within bourgeois society, woman as Absence is used as a metaphor for Absence as woman.

Freud considered the sexual to constitute the foundation of all societies—not just the one founded on the capitalist mode of production. Since the Freudian revolution, it has become acceptable to discuss the sexual nature of our world. However, such discussion does not erase the repression which constructs the world; indeed, the twentieth-century preoccupation with such discussion and with sexual behaviour itself is actually a function of that repression and is determined by it. The mistake is to assume, as did Freud, that individuals have a libidinal drive which is not affected in its degree by the society in which they live. The supplementary mistake is to assume that all societies are equally constituted within a sexual problematic. The object of this chapter is to demonstrate the historical construction of our experience of sexuality in order that I can then examine how that has affected the construction of the domain of literature and the products therein.

Bullough, in his discussion of Christian attitudes towards sex, has called Christianity a sex-negative religion.[7] By this he means that Christian theorists were antipathetic towards sexual activities. St Augustine in *De bono coniugali* states that while marriage is a good thing, continence within marriage makes it better:

> But, in a good marriage, although one of many years, even if the ardour of youth has cooled between man and woman, the order of charity still flourishes between husband and wife. They are better in proportion as they begin the earlier to refrain by mutual consent from sexual intercourse, not that it would happen of necessity that they would not be able to do as they wished, but that it would be a matter of praise that they had refused beforehand what they were able to do.[8]

Sexual intercourse for St Augustine is a product of Adam and Eve's original sin. Intercourse can only exist between mortal bodies because, like death, their knowledge of it is dependent on eating of the Tree of Knowledge. As a result of eating the apple, Adam and Eve and Man, their progeny, come for St Augustine into a closer relationship with the lower world of animals. What saves intercourse from being inherently bad for St Augustine, as it was later to become for Cathars, was its necessity for procreation. Intercourse was considered a step leading to the good which is the propagation of the human race in fulfilment of God's command to 'Be fruitful and multiply: fill the earth'.[9] All forms of intercourse then become measured against the possibility inherent within them for conception and procreation:

6

> In marriage, intercourse for the purpose of generation has no fault
> attached to it, but for the purpose of satisfying concupiscence, provided
> it is with a spouse, because of the marriage fidelity, it is a venial sin;
> adultery or fornication, however, is a mortal sin.[10]

St Augustine does not go on to speak of other forms of
intercourse such as oral or anal which do not allow even the
possibility of procreation to exist. His concern seems to have
been simply to justify the practice of an act otherwise to be
associated with animals.

St Thomas Aquinas, writing in the early thirteenth
century, re-emphasised St Augustine's ideas and considered
that intercourse for the purpose of procreation was a
fundamental part of the natural, reasonable order:

> A sin, in human acts, is that which is against the order of reason. Now
> the order of reason consists in its ordering everything to its end in a
> filling manner ... Now just as the preservation of the bodily nature of
> one individual is a true good, so, too, is the preservation of the nature of
> the human species a very great good ... [Thus] the use of venereal acts
> can be without sin, provided they be performed in due manner and
> order, in keeping with the end of human procreation.[11]

For the medieval Christian sexual intercourse was
inseparably connected with procreation; it did not exist as a
thing in its own right. All other acts which used the same
human parts were, therefore, to be condemned, as were those
coitions which did not have as their intention the conceiving
of children. Lustful intercourse, for Aquinas, is a sin because
it 'exceeds the order and mode of reason in the matter of
venereal acts'.[12] Here we find a link between reason and
sexual intercourse. Intercourse is reasonable when in the
service of procreation because then it is a part of the natural
order. Lustful intercourse is not reasonable. The individual
has selfishly disturbed God's reason-based order for his/her
own enjoyment. The extent of that enjoyment demonstrates
the extent to which God's order has been disturbed:

> Now the end of lust is venereal pleasure which is very great. Wherefore
> this pleasure is very desirable as regards the sensitive appetite, both on
> account of the intensity of the pleasure, and because such like
> concupiscence is connatural to man. Therefore it is evident that lust is a
> capital vice.[13]

7

For Aquinas the significance of sexual sin comes from the manner in which it fits in with other offences against reason. It is the individual as a part of the natural, God-given order which is important. Within bourgeois ideology it is the individual as the foundation of the social order who is important. The importance of the fear that reason may be lost in intercourse may be illustrated by another example. For Aquinas there is only one acceptable position in which intercourse may take place. He does not describe it but evidence would suggest that it necessitates the female being on her back with the male on top of her. Aquinas writes that it is a species of lust when a couple do not observe 'the natural manner of copulation, whether as to undue means, or as to other monstrous and bestial manners of copulation.'[14] The effort is being made to keep Man separate from animals. It is for this reason that Aquinas makes bestiality the gravest sexual deviation because, as he writes, 'use of the due species is not observed'.[15] Other positions for intercourse such as rear entry literally make Man like the beast because they are so commonly used by animals, added to which the missionary position, because of the placing of the clitoris, is notoriously unsuccessful in stimulating female enjoyment. As a result, intercourse in this position is not only least similar to animal intercourse but enables lustful indulgence—particularly of the female—to be kept at bay.

The publication in Italy of Romano's *Positzione* in 1524 with descriptive sonnets (known as *Sonnetti lussuriori*) by Aretino marked a stage in the new significance of sexual intercourse as something in its own right. They reflect the development of the bourgeoisie's reification of the activity. This transition is coupled with the new positioning of intercourse at the centre of male/female power relationships. It is unfortunate that, on the whole, we are only able to glean evidence about attitudes to sexual intercourse from the writings of Christian theologians rather than from evidence from the people themselves. What little evidence we have suggests that in day-to-day life sexual activity was not perceived as being of inherent significance. As a consequence, we may surmise that coital positioning did not greatly bother the average individual who was not subject to a great deal of Christian control.

In the 1960s in America, however, Beigel found in a short survey of attitudes towards coital positions that:

> Wives who objected to being on top said it was undignified, animalistic, cold, greedy, unfeminine. Men who objected to it called it unnatural and felt that they were relinquishing their initiative and aggressiveness. To both sexes it represented a violation of their sex roles.[16]

Here we can see very clearly how, in the first place, intercourse is experienced in bourgeois society as fundamental to the individual's articulation of his/her sex role and, second, how the position for intercourse carries a set of evaluations associated with the bourgeois division of attributes between male and female. This new attitude has assimilated much of the classical Christian ideology. For example, non-missionary-position intercourse is perceived both as unnatural and associated with animals. This, Beigel found, is particularly true of coitus where the male enters from behind. The old Christian system has now been re-evaluated as a set of justifications for the coital replication of male/female power relations. It is this which the missionary position now exemplifies. The work of Romano and Aretino signals a stage in this shift.

As this new attitude towards heterosexual, 'normal', intercourse evolved, so, concurrently, there evolved new attitudes towards homosexual activity. In the views of Augustine, Aquinas and other theologians, homosexual activity represented an offence against nature. It is instructive to turn once again to Aquinas, who places homosexual activity as next to bestiality. If bestiality is the most heinous sexual sin because order of species is not observed: 'After this comes the sin of sodomy, because use of the right sex is not observed.'[17] Aquinas's gradation is in terms of distance from the natural order. Hence he makes no distinction between male homosexuality and female homosexuality. Just to demonstrate that Aquinas's view was common to the Church, we might quote a summary of Thomas of Chobham (c. 1160 to c. 1240) on the subject: 'Thomas rates unnatural sex between men and women as least sinful, auto-sex as more sinful, sex between members of the same sex even more so, and sex with animals the most sinful of all.'[18] The only difference between Thomas of Chobham's schema and that of Aquinas lies in the positioning of masturbation. Aquinas rates it as less sinful than any form of deviant copulation between male and female.

The Church's attitude towards homosexuality was based on two overlapping concerns. One was the degree of deviation from the possibility of procreation, the other was the degree of non-observance of the natural order. Goodich, summing up his analysis of the *Decretum* of Burchard of Worms (a compilation of canon law made in the eleventh century) suggests that on the whole the penalties for lesbian acts were lower than for male homosexual acts.[19] However, the problem is not this simple as the penitentials in patriarchal society would be more likely to discriminate between types of act and performers of those acts with reference to the dominant male group. The *Libri duo de synodalibus causis et disciplinis* of Regino of Prum, written about 906, bears this out. In this work the range of penances for female homosexual acts goes from three to seven years; for a male, however, the range of possible penalties for anal intercourse varies between three years and thirty years, showing a greater concern with male 'deviance'.

As the Church tightened its grip on European society, so the penalties increased. The Council of Orleans in 1260 enacted, for the first sodomitical offence, mutilation, for the second castration or clitorectomy, and for the third burning. For the Church, then, there was little difference between male and female homosexuality—both were equally sinful. By way of contrast, Goodich's discussion of Germanic tribal law suggests that, except where the Church had already made inroads such as Visigothic Spain, homosexuality is rarely, if ever, mentioned as a crime. Boswell, in a more detailed examination of the attitude towards homosexuality in Visigothic Spain, suggests a rather different reason. He sees the strict laws relating to Jews and homosexuals as a scapegoating device utilised by the Arian Visigoths to deflect conflict with their Catholic subject population.[20] The choice of scapegoats would still have been determined by the underlying Christian principles of both groups. This outline would suggest that the more removed from Christian influence the people were, the more they adhered to a very different understanding of sexual behaviour.

As society became more bourgeois and secular, a shift occurred in attitudes to homosexuality. First, there appears to have been an increase in male homosexuality. We would expect our examples to come from Italy because it was the first bourgeois society and this is indeed what we find. In Florence in the late twelfth century, for example, the extent of pederasty lead the Germans to call pederasts 'Florenzer'.[21] In 1432 Florence went so far as to create the Ufficiali de Notte, whose job was to eradicate sodomy from Florence and the surrounding district.[22] Similarly in Bologna an order of the Dominicans known as the Societa Beate Maria was set up c. 1265 specifically to hunt out heretics and sodomites.[23] At Ascoli Piceno a bounty was paid to anybody who denounced a heretic or sodomite.[24] The question is the extent to which all this activity reflects either a change in attitude towards homosexuality and the creation of a moral panic, or an actual increase in homosexual activity or a combination of these things. In answering this, we may note the development in Italy in the fourteenth century of a neoplatonic attitude towards love. The most obvious example of this is the work of Marsilio Ficino, who suggested that non-sexual male/male love was of a higher order than male/female love. At the same time that Ficino was writing, several hundred accusations per year were being made to the Ufficiali de Notte.

Gradually, the Church laws which took equal cognisance of male and female homosexuality were replaced by civil laws which punished only male homosexuality. In Britain, for example, an attempt was made to pass a bill making female homosexuality a punishable offence as late as 1911. It was thrown out by the House of Lords because proper females, as opposed to prostitutes, were believed to lack a sex drive; therefore, they could not be homosexual. As society became more sexually orientated, so homosexuality came to be perceived not as a sin against the natural order but as an offence which deviated from the normal form of intercourse, heterosexual intercourse. Homosexuality came to be perceived as a physical activity not primarily as a category disturbance.

As sexuality came to be placed at the foundation of the developing structure of power relations, we might hypothesise that this would lead to a new concern with sexuality and sexual practice, coupled with a 'real' series of prohibitions concerning the overt articulation of sexuality. This would apply in particular to male sexual practices and, in particular, to the penis as it becomes the physical manifestation of power and reality in the new fetishised order. The significance of the basis of social, bourgeois reality lay in the denial of the new discursively real order. The eroticisation of the developing bourgeois world was part and parcel of that development. In this context we can see why male homosexuality should (seem to) be so common and yet so proscribed. In England in 1790, for example, Mrs Thrale wrote that 'there is a strange propensity for these unspeakable crimes.'[25] It would seem that by this time male homosexuality was both prevalent and determinedly punished well outside the English Court circle where, as with the French, it had for a long time been tolerated. It is significant in the light of what I have said about Italy that the English tended to lay the blame for what was perceived as an increase in homosexuality on the Italians. Defoe wrote in 1701:

> Lust chose the torrid zone of Italy
> Where blood ferments in rapes and sodomy.[26]

As bourgeois society spread from Italy across Europe, so also did a concern with sex and with the practice (and proscription) of male homosexuality.

One example of the shift in the conception of homosexuality may be found in the upsurge in discussion about what constitutes female homosexuality. This was discussed from a male genital viewpoint. Freud's understanding of the clitoris as a diminutive penis has an echo as far back as Lodovico Sinistrari, who in a book called *Peccatum Mutum*, published in 1700, suggested that in some women the clitoris was so large that it could penetrate another woman's vagina—or even sodomise a man.[27] In 1745 Robert James in his *Medicinal Dictionary* says the same thing. In some women the clitoris 'becomes so far prominent [that] they make attempts to converse in criminal manner with other women.'[28] Thus the 'normal' woman would be incapable of a satisfactory homosexual relationship, and a penis is so necessary to the practice of sexual activity that female/female sex becomes inconceivable. Intercourse, not procreation, now becomes the determinant feature of sexual activity. As a consequence, 'misuse' of the penis calls for strict laws because the power/reality associated in bourgeois society with the penis should not be diverted from its proper place— vaginal intercourse.

Women become desexualised, like the domestic sphere, except for any 'male' attributes. This includes the selling of their labour power, most obviously in prostitution, but 'real' women look after the home—they do not go out to work. The result is that female/female homosexual relationships tend not to be articulated in sexual terms: 'Even in our own sex-conscious age, women who identify themselves as lesbian are, according to numerous studies, less interested in sex with other women than in a life commitment with them.'[29] I might add that the phallic determination of female homosexuality is present in the iconic, fetishing power attributed to the penis in the male folklore of bourgeois society which suggests that 'All a lesbian needs is a really good poke' to enable her to recognise the happiness in being a heterosexual female in bourgeois society. Perhaps the most well-known acting out of this fantasy in modern popular literature is in Ian Fleming's *Goldfinger*. The female homosexual in question is called Pussy Galore, already the male fantasy overdetermines her sexuality, and James Bond, the hero as bourgeois prick, succeeds both in seducing her, and as a result, reorientating her sexuality.

It is the male who constructs the female as fetish, but it is as a result of this construction that the male is able to take on the role of the dominant power of reality in the fetishised social reality of bourgeois capitalism. The positioning of the woman as sexualised (repressed) fetish provides the key for a generalised sexualisation and commoditisation of the world.

In this way fetishism/commoditisation operates as a dual system based on the universalising capacities of desire and money. Baudrillard expresses this last point like this:

> fetishism is not the sanctification of a certain object, or value ... It is the sanctification of the system as such, of the commodity as system: it is thus contemporaneous with the generalization of exchange value and is propagated with it. The more the system is systematized, the more the fetishist fascination is reinforced.[30]

The upsurge in concern with the physical activity of sex may be demonstrated in other ways. There was, for example, the development in Restoration London of those 'clubs' described by Ned Ward in *The Secret History of Clubs* (1709). These clubs were composed of youthful members of the artistocracy and could be seen as having some limited continuity with the medieval groups of male youths who tended to exercise patriarchal norms over the single or newly married women in the villages. It was these groups who might exercise sanctions against a girl who wished to marry outside the village or against a newly married couple in whose relationship the woman appeared dominant. The new aristocratic clubs, however, far from enforcing norms, concerned themselves in the main with ribald and sometimes lawless sexual activity. This new understanding of sexual behaviour is reflected in the usage of the terms 'libertine' and 'libertinism'. One club, called The Beau's Club, was given to having lectures 'on the finer points of strumpets', while one of the favourite activities of the Mohocks (occasionally spelt Mohawcks) was up-ending women and girls, placing them in barrels and rolling them down hills. Another group, calling themselves the Bold Bucks, went in for rape; it is said that if a victim was not available on the street, they would go into a home and get one.[31] This is the kind of activity which shows the possible continuity between these groups and earlier groups. However, these rapes would have been experienced as an assertion of male power and sexuality and, correspondingly, as a violation of the individual, rather than being associated with the norm insisting on marriage. While the act is similar, the import is radically transformed by the new attitude towards sex.

At the same time that sexual concern was focused on the body, such concern was heavily socially proscribed. Hence not only did social violation of restrictive norms become common but the punishment for such violation was also correspondingly heavy both legally and morally. This is most obvious in the case of male homosexuality where the Church's strict sanctions were carried over into secular law. In England as late as 1772 a Captain Robert James was executed for sodomy. The normal punishment was the pillory, where the luckless person would often be killed by an enraged mob, comprised, it would appear, mostly of women.³² These women constructed and positioned by bourgeois patriarchy became, in practice, the upholders of the new bourgeois morality.

The new concern with sex had one additional feature which is common to bourgeois sexual life. This is the male concern with his prowess and the comparative size of his penis. This is a good illustration of the male's understanding of the iconic power of the penis; the bigger the penis, the better it is for constructing the world. This male fantasy may be found explicitly articulated in the first fully realised English pornographic work, John Cleland's *Fanny Hill*. Louisa, Fanny's friend, ascertains that Dick [*sic*], the half-witted delivery boy, has been compensated by nature with a larger than normal penis. Louisa makes use of it and is more satisfied than she ever has been before. It should be added that Louisa, and Fanny, are allowed to have sexual natures because they are prostitutes. Later, during the Victorian period, Pearsall notes that 'The pornographic prints give great play to the penis of great length, as do the stories.'³³ The most extreme and well-known example of this concern is the white Anglo-American myth of the size of black male penises.³⁴ Here, as has been repeated so often that it needs no reference, the white fear of the socially inferior black is translated into a 'Freudian' fear of black male sexuality. Just as 'pornography' as a particular genre originates in Italy about the time of Aretino and in England a bit earlier than John Cleland, about the time of Rochester, so, certainly in literature, at this time there arises this new concern with male sexual prowess evidenced in a concern with penis size and also with potency measured by the frequency of male orgasm.[35] Here, again, we can relate the sexual economy with the capitalist economy by remembering the overlapping usages of 'spend' for both sperm and money.

Reiche has suggested that this new concern with male sexuality reflects a new appreciation of sexuality in which it is measured quantitatively, as an exchange value dependent on male potency. He goes on to write that, analogously, it is measured for a woman by 'how many offers of marriage she has refused, how often men turn in the street to look at her, how frequently she is accosted.' And adds, 'In being endowed with exchange value, however, sexuality is deprived of all value of its own.'[36] That women in patriarchal bourgeois society do view sexuality in the way Reiche suggests is not, however, a function of the new attitude to sex itself but a function of the bourgeois structure in which the 'male' creates the 'female' as already constructed. This slippage towards a bourgeois understanding of male/female sexual relationships is unfortunately continued in Reiche's idea that sexuality could lose its value. Since value can never be intrinsic *per se* but is only comprehensible in terms of something else in the system of fetishes, sexuality has lost no value. It has, in fact, gained a value. One empirical piece of evidence of this is the rise in prostitution during the bourgeois period. Henriques suggests that in the eighteenth century, Paris had approximately one prostitute for every ten men, and estimates a ratio of 1 to 5 for a bourgeois London not under the cultural and political sway of the *ancien régime*.[37] Even if we accept the suggestion that, as a result of war and emigration, England had a sexual imbalance in favour of women,[38] and the assumption that the figures Henriques has culled are gross overestimates, we still have to account for city populations which, by modern standards, were extraordinarily high in the percentage of prostitutes. The reasons may well have to do with a lag in the development of bourgeois sexual repressive morality; the hold of the new obsession with sex is proved by the figures themselves.

One more piece of evidence for the new commercial attitude to sexual intercourse is the eighteenth-century introduction of the Parisian-style brothel into London—

although I would hypothesise that its origin was Italian:

> Profiting by several extended visits to Paris, where she was a close observer of the current system, Mrs. Goadby rented an attractive house in Berwick Street in the West End. The main principle imported from France was the rigid control exercised by the Madame. The Parisian brothels appeared to have been somewhat single-minded, not to say utilitarian in their approach.[39]

The brothel has become a factory with Mrs Goadby the entrepreneur, the owner/manager using her supply of labour to 'manufacture' sexual fulfilment for her male clientele.

The change in attitude to sexual intercourse brings us to the problem of virtue. Virtue in bourgeois society refers in the first place to the preservation of one's (particularly a woman's) virginity—a virginity to be given up after marriage when virtue consists in having sexual intercourse only with her husband. Virtue is, in this sense, the reification of a social practice. The focus on virginity as it is embodied in the physical, and particularly female, body is a shift from Aquinas's and the Church's position that 'the integrity of a bodily organ is accidental to virginity, in so far as a person, through purposely abstaining from venereal pleasure, retains the integrity of a bodily organ'.[40] Here the principal concern is an abstention from unreasonable acts. It is in this context that Aquinas, following Augustine, justifies intercourse solely for the purpose of procreation. The condition of virginity is here simply a condition of not giving in to temptation. Its relation to marriage is that marriage is the socially and religiously sanctioned situation in which procreation may take place. In this formulation virginity is not linked to marriage as a necessary condition containing connotations of innocence and experience, new and used goods. Rather, the virtue of virginity lies in the complete denial of venereal pleasure as defined in the activity of intercourse: 'virginity denotes that the person possessed thereof is unseated by the heat of concupiscence which is experienced in achieving the greatest bodily pleasure which is that of sexual intercourse.'[41]

In bourgeois ideology loss of virginity is understood as the acknowledgement of the person as sexual. In this context it is

interesting to note Gerson writing of masturbation in the
fifteenth century that it: 'has taken away the child's virginity
even more than if the child, at the same age, had gone with a
woman.'[42] Gerson was a forerunner of the new movement
which associated childhood with (sexual) innocence. From
this point of view, masturbation becomes as much a
recognition of sexuality as the physical act of intercourse.
Hence loss of virginity here does not require penile
penetration. Although Gerson is here talking of the male, it is
an argument which would equally apply to the female.

Marriage is fundamental to the bourgeois system of signs
because it is the social sanctioning of sexual intercourse. Thus
it is only the (social) *appearance* of virginity which is
important—provided the male believes this appearance to be
real. Virtue then is also a part of the bourgeois reality of
appearance. Another way of discussing virginity to make the
same point is to describe it as an ideological construct. Berger
and Wenger in their research on modern American attitudes
towards virginity found that loss of virginity in a woman is
determined in the majority of cases (81.3 per cent) by penile
penetration of the vagina and not by the rupturing of the
hymen by other means.[43] Virginity in the woman, then, is
determined not by the *having* of something, as demonstrated
by the unruptured hymen, but by the act of a male. The
problem arises of demonstrating not that something has
happened but that it has not. It is this aspect of the ideology of
virginity which has appeared to lend itself to anatomical
demonstration. As Peters has pointed out,[44] seventeenth-
century midwifery manuals—and this, of course, is a
continuing bourgeois preoccupation—have much discussion
of the questionable possibility of anatomical proof of female
virginity. It is worth adding that the kind of proof demanded
of the female, such as the rupturing of the hymen, would be of
no use at all in determining male virginity. The cultural
specificity of spousal defloweration is something important to
remember. In many societies such as that of the Todas of
Southern India and the Kamchadal it is regarded as
important that the female should already have been
deflowered before she is married. In these cases the rupturing
of the hymen may have entirely different significations such

as a coming of age initiation signifying entrance into the adult world. Often the act is performed by the girl's mother or other older women.[45] In the eighteenth century in Britain defloweration became a male obsession. In London a book published in 1760 stated that a virgin cost fifty pounds.[46] In the nineteenth century we find the author of *My Secret Life* spending much time and money procuring young virgins. The procurement of virgins for brothels became a highly organised activity. John Cleland reflects this new attitude in *Fanny Hill* when Fanny's virginity, now defined as lack of previous experience of sexual intercourse, is sold to the highest bidder—her first placement in the cash/sexual structure of society.

The structure of the ideology of virginity thus centres upon the first act of intercourse which, in the bourgeois world, consummates the public rite of marriage. The French novel of worldliness emphasises this by setting up a problem on these terms. Sassus has noted that:

> The most popular form of the [renunciation] motif during the last decade of the [seventeenth] century is expressed through the character of the *honnête femme*, who, though married, is in love with another man and must therefore struggle to reject this new love to remain faithful to her husband.[47]

This development is to be expected as a counterpart of the bourgeois development of the marriage/intercourse/body combination. However, as the French *monde* has an alternative form of structuration, the importance of the appearance of virtue over the reality of virtue can be stressed. This is exemplified well in *Les Liaisons dangereuses* by the episode between Prévan and the Marquise de Meurteuil in which Prévan, having called the Marquise de Meurteuil's virtue into question, claims he will prove his assertion by having intercourse with her. The Marquise de Meurteuil turns the tables by constructing a situation in which she does willingly have intercourse with him. Subsequently, she has him caught in her boudoir fully clothed as an attempted rapist so that it appears to *le monde* that she has not had intercourse. Her virtuous reputation has been preserved. In this way she beats Prévan at his own worldly and male-determined game,[48] but she, in turn, is beaten by the bourgeois reader, who is able to see into the objectified and real world of the book. As Laclos demonstrates so well in *Les Liaisons dangereuses*, virtue, like marriage, exists in bourgeois society as a manifest function of a hidden sexualiy.

The increasing significance of virtue is simultaneous with the development of bourgeois preoccupations with chastity. The Oxford English Dictionary notes the use of virtue in a specifically sexual context no earlier than Shakespeare in 1599. The physical state of virginity and the social state of virtue are both defined in bourgeois society with relation to the fetished and fetishising act of intercourse. The loss of (female) virginity acknowledges the positioning of a person within the bourgeois social structure and as a part of bourgeois reality.

For the bourgeoisie, intercourse always takes place at night. It is in the dark that the unseen penis penetrates the unseen vagina. The absolute fetishisation of the bodies and the act is completed by the absolute repression of the sense which generates that fetishism—sight. Thus bourgeois sexuality, and its repression, moves outward from the act itself to the site of that act, the bed, to the bedroom and, finally, to the house, the limits of which are generally understood to be the limits of the domestic domain. We are back with Coventry Patmore's tent.

In the pre-bourgeois period, living space was undifferentiated—even in those homes which were large enough to allow for such differentiation. Historically, we may see the development of the bed as a privatised area overlapping with the development of a private sleeping room (also, of course, a room allowing privacy for intercourse)—a bedroom. The end result in the classic bourgeois house is the placing of the bedroom upstairs, hidden well away from the parts of the house most likely to be seen by visitors.

Origo, in her outline of the day-by-day life of the Datinis in Prato at the turn of the fourteenth century, writes:

> It will be observed that, though there were many servants, there were no servants' rooms—the explanation being that they slept wherever was most convenient—in the kitchen, on the landing, or on truckle beds in the room of their master or mistress.[49]

Not only does this imply a certain lack of privacy for master and/or mistress but the lack of a room of their own would suggest a complete lack of privacy for the servants. The idea of privacy among the bourgeoisie gradually developed and filtered downwards through the social structure. The Italians, however, were once again ahead of northern Europe. (In France specialisation of function in the bourgeois and aristrocratic household developed through the seventeenth century.) Alberti had noted that in his fifteenth century Florence:

> I remember ... seeing our most notable citizens, when they went off to the country, taking their beds and kitchen utensils with them, and bringing them back on their return. Now the furniture of a single room is bigger and more expensive than that of a whole house on a wedding day.[50]

Here we can see Alberti himself linking the new concern with objects to value in the new money-based capitalism. Previously, household goods had been mobile and utilitarian; now they have become objects of worth and therefore objects with a significance which may be measured by comparing them with other objects. These objects are now specifically placed in the new evaluative reality; that is, a reality founded in a systematised fetishism. Moreover, they are now not mobile, although evidence suggests that the bed was reified and fetishised even earlier than the fifteenth century. The development of the 'tester', a canopy which encloses the bed, seems to have been a fourteenth-century occurrence, but the final elaboration of this phenomenon in the four-poster seems to have reached England some time in the sixteenth century. So important was the bed regarded as being at this time that a particularly favourite bed might even be given a name. The Earl of Arundel called his favourite bed 'Clovis'.[51] What better confirmation of the individualisation and fetishisation of the bed could we ask for? Also at this time, the practice, which was appropriated by the bourgeoisie from a much older fertility rite, of carrying a bride over the threshold entailed carrying her over the threshold of the bed. It is only as the domestic domain is consolidated and as the rite is appropriated fully within the bourgeois sexual system that the bride comes to be carried over the threshold of the house.

One other way of approaching the privatisation and sexualisation of the bed is through the sleeping habits of its occupants. Sharing one's bed with a member of the opposite sex with whom one was not engaging in sexual activity was a practice (it is impossible to say how common) during the medieval period. Its proscription seems to have occurred early and been strongly enforced—as one would expect from my argument. However, certainly in France, members of the same sex were allowed to sleep together—although it was not regarded as acceptable—until into the eighteenth century. For this we may take the evidence of an etiquette book:

> You ought ... neither to undress nor go to bed in the presence of any other person. Above all, unless you are married, you should not go to bed in the presence of anyone of the other sex.
>
> It is still less permissible for people of different sexes to sleep in the same bed unless they are very young children ...
>
> If you are forced by unavoidable necessity to share a bed with another person of the same sex on a journey, it is not proper to lie with him so as to touch him.[52]

We may judge from this that first sexualisation then privatisation encroach on sleeping habits. As the function of the room itself becomes established as differentiated and specialised, so the curtain disappears. Hence privatisation and specialisation of purpose spread out from the bed which, in bourgeois ideology, is the only place acceptable for that most intimate of (married) activities. As the rooms become differentiated and specialised in their function, so architecture alters to make greater use of corridors so that rooms need not be used as thoroughfares. In Gothic horror, where the 'non-sexual' domestic arena is permeated by illicit sexuality, corridors take on an obvious 'Freudian' significance. In *Jane Eyre* it is in a long, dark passage that Jane hears the moans of Bertha Rochester confined in her attic. Perhaps the best use of this motif is in Roman Polanski's film *Repulsion*, in which a woman walks down a corridor (vaginal/womb suggestion) which itself becomes threatening as she thinks hands reach out to grab and sexually molest her.

At the same time as house contents are becoming fetishised

objects, the house itself is becoming an object separate from, but containing, the family. It is not without cause that being sent to one's bedroom is a common bourgeois punishment for children. In the punishment scene in *Jane Eyre* the bedroom becomes literally, a place of confinement but also metaphorically, a womb from which Jane emerges to a new life. The house is the site of repression. The acceptance of that repression turns it into a place of apparent freedom. In Richardson's account of the bourgeois idyll, Pamela clearly articulates the effect that marriage should have. Immediately after the ceremony she writes that 'my prison has become my palace.'[53] Marriage 'liberates' the woman while confining the sexuality of the male. There is no more sexual discussion in the book after Pamela's marriage. The rejection of this ideology of unbounded freedom in confinement is a hall-mark both of the Gothic and of the female critique of bourgeois patriarchy.

Showalter has argued that 'In their rejection of male society and masculine culture, feminist writers had retreated [in the Victorian period] more and more towards a separatist literature of inner space.'[54] This retreat matches the consolidation of the domestic domain. As early as 1792 in *The Vindication of the Rights of Women*, Mary Wollstonecraft was using what subsequently became, particularly in the writings of Poe, a Gothic image of immense strength: 'Do you [this is part of a prefatory address to M. Talleyrand–Perigord] not act a similar part to male tyrants when you *force* all women, by denying them civil and political rights, to remain immured in their families groping in the dark.'[55] The repression which defined the domestic domain also enabled Gothic literature to exist. The image of the female struggling to escape a dark entombment is common to both feminist critique and Gothic writing.

One example of the bourgeois experience of the objectness of the house may be defined as the Gothic motif of the house as threat. This is an idea usually embodied in a theme which we might call that of the 'living house'. There is, perhaps, here an echo of the pre-bourgeois notion of the *domus*, where family and house were assimilated into one unit. For bourgeois society, however, the idea of a live house is one of horror. The object which contains the domestic and private, and provides the venue for socially sanctioned but discursively displaced coitus, alters from being the passive container which the married couple may fill to becoming an active container threatening the sanctuary which—previously—it had provided.

The archetype for this development may be found in Poe's story *The Fall of the House of Usher*. In this story the destiny of the Ushers and of their mansion is shown to be inextricably linked. While in an earlier period this would have been regarded as quite normal, Poe is able to use this idea to create a sense of fear and horror in his readers. Roderick Usher himself seems to stand astride aristocratic and bourgeois heritages. Poe gives him 'a very ancient family' which used to be noted for the creation of great works of art but which, in recent times, had gone in more for that much more bourgeois activity of 'deeds of munificent yet unobtrusive charity'. Roderick, however, is quite unambiguously linked to the House:

> it was this deficiency, perhaps, of collateral issue, and the consequent undeviating transmission, from sire to son, of the patrimony with the name, which had, at length, so identified the two as to merge the original title of the estate in the quaint and equivocal appellation of the 'House of Usher'[56]

Also the house is described as having 'vacant eye-like windows'. In bourgeois society, sight validates the commodity as object placing it as fetish in relation to the person, who will, in turn, be perceived as fetish. The house's life is found in its windows/eyes, those things which in the first place enable the occupants to look out and give light to the inside now become things which themselves view.

Showalter[57] has commented on the nineteenth-century fashion among women novelists for blinding their heroes. The most well-known example must be Rochester in *Jane Eyre*. Showalter suggests that the reason for this is to make the male inadequate so that the heroine may be given a role. This does not, however, exhaust the imagery. If it is sight which materialises the object as fetish, then the denial of sight to the male denies his ability to position the female. It also entombs him in the darkness of his body. It is interesting in this context that, having married Jane to Rochester and given them an idyllic existence, Charlotte Brontë gives Rochester some of his sight back. In the end Brontë affirms bourgeois society. This implication of sight as the constructor of fetishism is reaffirmed in a much more Gothic text. In *Dracula*, Dracula's eyes glowed as he was about to bite a victim. (I will discuss *Dracula* in more detail in Chapter 7.)

At this point we must turn to Roderick's painting in which a windowless vault is, nevertheless, brightly illuminated. The painting may be read as a metaphor for those inside the house who are contained in an object which looks out onto the world. Usher, the narrator tells us, paints an idea. The abstractions which he places on canvas give off 'an intensity of intolerable awe'. The painting which the narrator goes on to describe articulates the image of confinement:

> A small picture presented the interior of an immensely long and rectangular vault or tunnel, with low walls, smooth, white and without interruption or device. Certain accessory points of the design served well to convey the idea that this excavation lay at an exceeding depth below the surface of the earth. No outlet was observed in any position of its vast extent, and no torch or other artificial source of light was discernible; yet a flood of intense rays rolled throughout, and bathed the whole in a ghastly and inappropriate splendour.[58]

There are two modes of confinement here. The first operates as an aspect of the narrative structure of the text. The written description claims to be a 'feeble' reproduction of a painting. The painting, the narrator maintains, represents an idea. The second operates as a result of the line of narrational form. The passage is itself experienced as embedded in the narration, the story, which in its turn was first embedded in Burton's *Gentleman's Magazine* and subsequently in book-length collections of Poe's work and in anthologies of horror stories. In this case the confinement of the story is expressed both as a function of its internal continuity *vis-à-vis* the material surrounding it and of the practice of the case nexus to which Poe subscribed. The story, as experienced by the bourgeois reader, is confined by, but read as separate from, the cash nexus. On one side the story exists to be 'lived' by the reader, on the other side the text exists as a material product, itself a part of the market economy. The physical manifestation of the text marks two symmetrical and opposed closures. In this there is nothing remarkable about *The Fall of the House of Usher* as an example of bourgeois literature.

The painting replicates the embedded confinement which is a part of the existence of the text. The painting is of a long vault or tunnel, illuminated from no discernible source, which exists beneath the earth. It is, then, a painting of confinement, of a space—an absence—which is present because of the earth which confines it. It is, the narrator has told us, a painting of an idea; not a particular confinement. It is a painting of the story's motif which is also the 'real' experience which enables the story to exist. This quality of reflexive commentary in the story calls to mind the theme of double articulation which has been interestingly discussed elsewhere.[59] This aside, both Madeleine and Roderick are confined. Most obviously Madeleine is placed in a vault under the earth. Roderick feels himself not just a part of the house but confined by it. He tells the narrator, 'I shall perish in this deplorable folly. Thus, thus and not otherwise, shall I be lost'.[60] Although he feels himself linked with it, Roderick will not necessarily die at the same time as the House (although he does) but inside it confined by the physical perimeter of the bourgeois domestic environment. It might be argued that, in this, Roderick represents a failure of bourgeois male sexuality.

Roderick's painting of a vault or tunnel may be analysed by the critic favourably disposed to Freud as a repressed description of a womb or vagina. The vault, and the house, may be similarly described. In bourgeois, sexualised society such a description cannot be incorrect for either writer or reader. In our sexualised world the *locus* of confinement is female (the car, the boat are both referred to conversationally as female) and the domestic environment is the responsibility of the woman. It becomes an extension of her, and her of it. It is the 'asexuality' of the domestic place which generates the power of sexuality. In *The Fall of the House of Usher* it is the confined absence which Roderick attempts to paint which preserves the House. As soon as sexuality is acknowledged in the domestic space, all is destroyed. Not until Madeleine is presumed dead do the narrator, and the reader, discover the bonds which unite brother and sister closer than bourgeois morality would allow. At the narrational level Madeleine's death makes the revelation safe. At a metaphorical level[61] not until this 'death' does Roderick acknowledge his link with his sister to the narrator:

> A striking similitude between brother and sister now first arrested my attention; and Usher, divining, perhaps, my thoughts, murmured out some few words from which I learnt that the deceased and himself had been twins, and that sympathies of a scarcely intelligible nature had always existed between them.[62]

The implicit suggestion of incest here counterpoints the problematic end of the story. At the end Madeleine breaks out of her man-made confinement and goes to her brother:

> There was blood on her white robes, and the evidence of some bitter struggle upon every portion of her emaciated frame. For a moment she stood trembling and reeling to and fro upon the threshold—then, with a low moaning cry, fell heavily inward upon the person of her brother, and in her violent and now final death-agonies, bore him to the floor a corpse and a victim to the terrors he had anticipated.[63]

The sexuality of the end is as questionable as the sexuality of Roderick's painting. It is, after all, a story which itself exists in repression. Brother and sister die on top of one another with Madeleine on top. The position, we may note, is the reverse of the accepted bourgeois coital position. The patriarchal power reaffirmed in the position in a society where the act of intercourse is a *locus* of power (and reality) is reversed just as Roderick is portrayed as passively sexual and Madeleine as actively sexual. Madeleine has escaped her confinement and Roderick dies a victim of his fears, fears which he/Poe had attempted to express in the painting. The release of Madeleine's sexuality destroys the house. The feminine structuring of the space of the domestic domain which is the product of repression disappears, and the house which images the space collapses in on itself. Madeleine has escaped her fate but, in doing so, she has completed the destruction of the constructed, confined world of her brother and herself. The space produced by confinement is the space occupied by the text of *The Fall of the House of Usher*. It is also the space which calls the story as narration into meaning. The collapse of one space gives us the climax which ends the other. Madeleine has remarkable similarities to Richardson's Clarissa, who is also trapped and realised by a male, but she only enables her reality to be reconstructed after her death, whereas the Gothicness of Poe's story lies in Madeleine's destruction of the live house and the real domestic domain it contains. It should be remembered that Clarissa asserts—in the hearing of Solmes, the suitor forced on her by her family—her willingness to be walled up in the family vault rather than marry him. Of course, had she married him, the literal walling-up would become the metaphorical walling-up of Mary Wollstonecraft's image.

What we find developing during the bourgeois period is a pattern of sexuality in which all objects which enter the system of capitalism are 'feminised' as commodities. This refers in the first place to those whom bourgeois society constructs as female. These people are positioned as desired but in themselves asexual beings, lifting off from a libidinous foundation in biological reproduction which spills over the residue of constructed desire into a fetishised—and feminised—world. The construction of a domestic domain which is constituted in a repression of those forces of sexuality and capitalism upon which that domain is founded, and which are most powerful in that place, enables the capitalistically acceptable use of money to replace the unacceptable operation of desire in the world at large. The system is articulated through the production and repression of desire. Money, then, is the fetishised material form of desire. It is, as Baudrillard has pointed out, money which structures the reality of commodity fetishism. It is the effect of fetishism to give objects an (illusory) essentialism. This essentialism, which, as a product of fetishism, is of a feminine quality, is most interesting when the object contains a message, a text. This is exactly what bourgeois literature is and, in the rest of the book, it is the construction and constitution of this asexual, feminine, discourse which I shall examine.

CHAPTER 2

Fetishism and Marriage

Epistolary fiction illustrates the lack of permanence in the newly developing world of fetishism. In the British letter novel, as in the bourgeois world in general, the relation of the sign of marriage to the sexualised act of intercourse comes to be articulated in a fetishisation of the (individual) body.[1] Epistolary fiction represents one moment in the historical development of the realist novel and the completion of the capitalist systematisation of the world as sign. It is in the realist novel that the omniscient, individualised author confronts the mental *tabula rasa* of the reader and offers him/her an alienated, fetishised world of commodities, a world which structures the distance between the sexualised individualism of author and that of the reader through the libidinisation of the writing itself.[2] Writing, in other words, takes on a sexuality which it did not previously possess, while it is the sexualising of the world which gives it its specifically capitalist reality, known as realism in literary circles. I should add that my choice of letter novels is limited and those chosen are used for exemplification.

The reality of the letters lies in the Real which they articulate through the social interaction which they mediate. The key to this reality lies in the elaboration of what Day has aptly called subjective narrative.[3] The reader is structured into a reality which appears to be on-going as the reading proceeds and the events which occur are experienced as being immediate. This development is only partly achieved in the epistolary novel but, again, it represents one stage in that process. The importance of this shift is that the 'world' of the novel is lived as a linear flow, the readers experiencing the 'world' as they do their own world. Fixity of the social real is achieved through the repetition of writing.

The logorrhoea of characters in epistolary novels may be viewed as the necessary consequence of attempting to construct the reader within an as yet incomplete, and therefore not fully systematised, world of signs. In the context of the novels, writing generates not only the social real (note *not* the signification of the social real) but also, in the participatory demands made on the letter writer and reader, it becomes an extension (and in this case *is* a signification) of the site of libidinous individuality which is in the process of formation. With this in mind, we can understand why so many letter novels are concerned with love and intercourse. Miller has remarked, in the context of the letter novel, that 'One could ... say that all is lost once a chaste girl reads a letter; but once she does, and because she answers, her loss *becomes* the novel as the novel records the traces of her passage into desire and death.'⁴

In reading an epistolary novel, the reader is forced to occupy the position of the character to whom the letter is sent. The letter in the novel manifests the fetishistic desire which underpins the new bourgeois world. The reader is placed in a double articulation of fetishism: in the first place within the web of desire which is the novel, and in the second place in the sexualised experience of the novel itself as fetish. The chaste girl in the novel and the reader of the novel enter the sexualised world of commodities at the same time. In bourgeois society love and intercourse express the individual as the site of individuality. They also manifest the new eroticisation of personal experience. We can now suggest why so many love-affairs in these novels are terminated with the request that the letters sent be returned. This is true as far back as the nun in Guilleragues' *Lettres d'une religieuse portugaise*, published in 1669 to instant popularity. The letters, being the realiser of reality, no longer structure and fix an appropriate reality once the love-affair is over—and in these novels it is over only after intercourse has taken place, or when intercourse has been placed outside the bounds of possibility. The structuration of society is still dependent upon the individual effort of structuring. The letters of epistolary fiction may be read as commentaries on this process. They are commodities which being the novel they constitute into being.

A number of other experiential categories related to the bourgeois world were also still in the process of formation. The one which is most obviously demonstrated in the novels under discussion is the lack of certainty regarding the limits of the polarity of real/fictive. This reflection of the as yet uncertain bourgeois real-ism is not confined to the works themselves where descriptions of acts are always repetitions. Just as the reader has no clear view of the actions in the works, so she/he is often told of the real nature of the letters which compose the work. Thus Richardson's *Pamela* (1740) contains even in the title the implication of the real-ness of the enclosed letters: *Pamela: or Virtue Rewarded. In a Series of Familiar Letters from a Beautiful Young Damsel to her Parents. Now first published in order to cultivate the Principles of Religion in the Minds of Youth of Both Sexes.*[5] Fielding plays on this implication of the real-ness of the letters, when in the title of his satire on *Pamela*—*An Apology for the Life of Mrs. Shamela Andrews: in which the many notorious Falsehoods and Misrepresentations of a Book called Pamela, are exposed and refuted*—he ends an equally long title by writing: *The whole being exact copies of authentic Papers delivered to the Editor.* He thus spoofs not only Richardson's novel but also its reality both in its claim to be factual and its claim to a bourgeois truthfulness of appearances. We discover, for example, that the *locus* of reality is really named Shamela. The only person in the book to call her Pamela is the Squire, the representative of the newly developing bourgeois reality of appearance; though, we are told at the end of the book, when Bobby asked for the letters to be collected the writer who reconstructed them decided that Shamela was too comical a name and changed it to Pamela. The real dissimulation of Shamela's name is then replaced by the dissimulated apparent reality of Pamela not only for the Squire but for the readers of Richardson's fictive reality. Hence Fielding is suggesting that the readers of Richardson's *Pamela* have been tacitly interpolated into the same bourgeois reality as that articulated by the text's realism. The book *Pamela*, as both Richardson and Fielding agree, is about appearance, the only question concerns the status of the reality to give that appearance.

The expression of repression in the terms of bourgeois reality is confinement. In works read by the bourgeois reader the assumption is always that the text is enclosed. It is the premise of confinement which enables the reader to experience the text as an object containing meaning. In *Pamela*, as we have seen, the status to be given the letters has been laid out for us by Richardson in both the title and the introduction. They are real; the book, then, is real. However, although the letters are not real in the sense that they were written by the characters involved, in another sense Richardson may be absolved, for his claim actually tells us something about how the work fitted into the bourgeois social reality of his time. Richardson intended the story to serve both as a model for letter-writing and as a model for social behaviour on the part of lower-middle-class girls. *Pamela* is a real work in the degree to which it successfully reproduces the constrictions of bourgeois life. The same claim might also be made for other fictional works of the period which claim to be real, such as *Robinson Crusoe*. The need to claim the reality of texts was involved in an understanding that certain works could be perceived as invalid, unreal—not because they were fictional but because they did not replicate the repression of the new society.

It may be said, then, that it is the very realness of *Pamela* which assures it of its status as a fiction in bourgeois literature. Its realness is a function of its successful replication of confinement. For the bourgeois reader this confinement begins with the work itself. The book as an entity is bought—or borrowed—in a cover which announces what the book is. The book is confined by its cover and confined by its title. The material limits of the book are its limits as object for its commoditisation in the capitalist cash nexus.

The title is a bourgeois invention, and once again its earliest use seems to be in Italy by the bookseller Vespasiano da Bisticci in the early fifteenth century. Titles announce texts but, in doing so, they distance the reader from the work and confine the text in the reader's expectations. Within the book the confined text is read by the bourgeois reader as free of all constraint. It becomes, in the realist novel, the world in its final bourgeois production as an object which bourgeois readers—and critics—can enter and observe, extrapolating situations and characterisations from the words on the page.

Pamela forms the basis for the elaboration of the repressed, apparently asexual work *Pamela*. She is the *locus* of a duplication of repression and confinement, for her successful domestication and repression replicates the repression inherent in the fetishised commoditisation of the text. The bourgeois reader's experience of the text and his/her experience of the contents reinforces the repressive confinement of each and positions the repressed reader in relation to an unbounded text articulating a story of female success and happiness. Fielding touches well on the already existent sexuality of *Pamela* in his critique *Shamela* when he makes Parson Oliver write to Parson Tickletext, who, ironically but significantly, given his name, has been taken in by *Pamela*:

> And notwithstanding our Author's Professions of Modesty, which in my Youth I have heard at the Beginning of an Epilogue, I cannot agree that my Daughter should entertain herself with some of his Pictures; which I do not expect to be contemplated by one of my Age and Temper, who can see the Girl lie on her Back, with one arm around Mrs. *Jewkes* and the other around the Squire, naked in Bed, with his Head on her Breasts, with as much Indifference as I read any other Page in the Novel.[6]

What Fielding is commenting on is the voyeuristic nature of the exercise of reading in bourgeois society. The writing is sexualised in the act of reading whether or not the reader subsequently represses that sexuality.

In *Pamela*, then, there is present only one reality built on one morality which is a function of sexualisation and its repression. This reality is assumed by all the characters and its unproblematised formulation is replicated in the uncritical bourgeois reader who him/herself is also subject to the same realising morality. Many writers recognised this either consciously or unconsciously, and *Shamela* was just one of a large number of works which utilised *Pamela* either to reveal, pornographically, the 'truth' about her supposed virtue or to comment on the prudery of the period or to cash in on the success of the book by writing sequels—something which Richardson himself did.[7]

When reading *Pamela*, the reader is placed in an uncritical position in respect of the new bourgeois morality. This lack of critical purchase enables the morality to be (mis)taken for the only morality and the novel is constructed—realised— around this morality. Pamela is positioned as the main narrator, and it is around her that the novel's action occurs. The female text is reduplicated in the heroine. It is around her letters that the epistolary (re)construction of reality takes place. Pamela's, and her parents', morality is contrasted with that of B., her employer, potential seducer and attempted rapist and, finally, her husband. When considering Pamela's bourgeois attitudes, it should be remembered that her parents have come down in the world. In their very first letter to Pamela this is made clear: 'We are, it is true, very poor, and find it hard enough to live; though once, as you know, it was better with us.'[8] In the deployment of B. the reader is confronted with a character who begins as an aristocratic wencher whose likely attempts to have sexual relations with lower-class women is accepted, if not condoned, by his sister. The idea that servant girls were always open to propositions from their male employers was pervasive and persisted until well into the nineteenth century. When B. does not allow Pamela to enter the household of his sister, Lady Davers, the implication of this is obvious to Lady Davers: 'Mrs. Jervis tells me, the lady shook her head, and said, "Ah! Brother!" and that was all.'[9] However, by the time of B.'s and Pamela's marriage, it becomes evident that B. and Pamela are operating within the same moral criteria. The conversion of B. from aristocratic rake to a repressed bourgeois is pivoted on their marriage. The strength of the signification of marriage in bourgeois society enables a reinterpretation to take place of B.'s attempt on Pamela's virginity as well as shedding a new light on his earlier concern with the importance of inheritance. Pamela writes that, when asked why he did not go through with a mock marriage ceremony, B. replied:

for when I considered that it would make *you* miserable and me not happy; that if you should have a dear little one, it would be out of my own power to legitimate it, if I wished it to inherit my estate; ... when I further considered your untainted virtue, what danger, trials, and troubles, I had involved you in, only because you were beautiful and virtuous, which had excited all my passion for you; and reflected also on your prudence and truth![10]

B.'s designs on Pamela are here being rewritten as occasions on which Pamela's virtue was tested. Her refusal to succumb is now understood by both B. and Pamela—and the uncritical bourgeois reader—as a sign of her moral strength. Bourgeois morality underpins all the actions of the novel. It is, then, not simply being advocated; it is being utilised as the foundation on which all social reality is built.

In terms of the novel's development, Pamela's morality assimilates B. and he is then able to realise Pamela by marrying her. This double movement is acknowledged by B. himself. In talking of what he read in the journal Pamela kept, after B. had by ruse abducted her and kept her prisoner, he says (or rather Pamela writes that he says), ' "during her confinement (that is, ... when she was taken prisoner, in order to make me one; for that is the upshot of the matter), in the journal she kept. ..." '[11] Pamela's confinement by B. is here being reinterpreted *post facto* as a stratagem which led to the marriage in which B. claims to be the one confined. However, that, in the context of the social reality, it is not B. who is confined is clear by the fact that he is in the process of revealing something Pamela wrote in the journal intended only for perusal by her parents. The bourgeois illusion is that Pamela has captured B. by means of her virtue. This is the reality portrayed in the writing of the journal, which is replicated in the writing of the letter, which constitutes a part of the book. The bourgeois reality is that in the context of the patriarchal ordering of society, Pamela's marriage articulates her as the realiser of her and B.'s morality, upon which their world is built. Madeleine in *The Fall of the House of Usher* is placed as socially 'dead' but in reality 'alive' in the foundations of the House. Pamela's confinement is perceived by her in true bourgeois fashion as a liberation.

In *Shamela* there are two realities interacting. The first is the socially constructed one of Squire Booby, who, frustrated in his lust for Shamela, transforms his lust into a proposal of marriage and claims to be (and indeed is in his world) her lover.[12] It is now that the relation of love to lust is transformed by the new understanding of the person as being essentially sexual. In the new bourgeois discourse, love becomes a function of the repressed erotic. In England the first known written use of the term 'make love' to mean the activity of copulation dates from Lyly in 1586.[13] In France *faire l'amour* meant to court[14] before it acquired its modern meaning of having intercourse. Given the direct translation, we may presume that the English, complete with meaning, derived from the French since the English term does not seem to have previously existed. The conflation of 'love' as a discursive term with the physical activity of sexual intercourse marks an important development in the bourgeois construction of intercourse. Intercourse becomes the moment not when love/desire is fulfilled but when love in the sense given by bourgeois Romanticism is created by the body as fetish.[15]

The second reality of *Shamela* is that of Shamela herself, her mother and Mrs Jervis, all of whom obviously, but importantly, are women. They are not sexualised and repressed into domestic asexuality like Pamela, but are people for whom sexual activity is itself a thing to enjoy. For this reason they become, for the bourgeois reader, wanton women. What is noteworthy here is that Fielding is not giving a portrayal of a genuine alternative society, a lower-class or peasant society where sexual activity is merely one activity among many. Instead he is describing a sexualised but unrepressed society—in fact, a bourgeois male-orientated fantasy which, in eighteenth-century England, would have been read in the main by women. Aiming for, and achieving, bourgeois readers, Fielding got a readership which would inevitably apprehend his alternative society as sexualised and who would engage voyeuristically with his text.

The voraciousness of the female sexual appetite was a myth prevalent in medieval patriarchy:

Every woman is ... wanton, because no woman, no matter how famous and honoured she is, will refuse her embraces to any man even the most

vile and abject, if she knows that he is good at the work of Venus; yet
there is no man so good at that work that he can satisfy the desires of any
woman you please in any way at all.[16]

In bourgeois reality this myth has been assimilated, centred
by the centring of sex within the structuration of society, and
subsequently 'repressed' as the sexuality attached to the
female was itself repressed. In Shamela and her associates the
myth is reactivated in its bourgeois formulation. It is Shamela
who holds the power in her book and the Squire who is
confined.

The humour in *Shamela* comes from the position which the
reader occupies. She/he does not enter a single reality as in
Pamela—co-opted into the process of creating meaning. In
Shamela the reader slides between two realities—that of
Squire Booby based on bourgeois sexualised morality and
that of Shamela. Unlike Pamela, Shamela has not been
already assimilated by bourgeois ideology. The more
powerful reality in the text is that of Shamela if only because it
is from her position that the reader is able to view Squire
Booby's reality as a social construction. It is precisely the
revelation of that construction which produces Squire Booby
as a comic figure. However, as the prefacing letters make
clear, Fielding's intended audience for *Shamela* was precisely
that audience which had given *Pamela* such a favourable
reaction, namely the bourgeoisie. For this bourgeois
readership Fielding stripped away the repression on which
their sexualised reality was constructed. In doing so he
produced a 'pornographic' work. The reader brings an
already articulated sexuality and is confronted by a work in
which sexual activity is openly discussed—at least by those
people who are not in Squire Booby's reality. But this critique
of *Pamela*'s repression in the last resort becomes an assertion
of the reality on which it is founded as the text is repositioned
by its already bourgeois constituted readership. We might say
that Squire Booby is blinded and confined within his reality
of appearances; so too are the bourgeois readers of *Shamela*.
The humour for the bourgeois reader comes from the reader's
textual reality being produced through Shamela's letters.
This betrayal of bourgeois allegiance, founded on the

bourgeois displacement of sexuality, enables the reader to find Booby's deception funny.

In *Pamela*, where the overt power is held by B., his power is manifested in his desire. However, Pamela, in taking for granted and asserting the bourgeois reality, does not wish for its consummation in illicit sexual activity. The libidinal drive and its overflow is a prerogative of the male. For Pamela there will be no sex before marriage because that sex would challenge the cornerstone of the social order. Thus Pamela, having repulsed the first of B.'s lustful advances, ends the letter to her parents containing her descriptive repetition of the event: 'I will soon write again, but must end with saying that I am, and always shall be, *your honest daughter*.'[17] Pamela's claim to honesty revolves around the understanding of intercourse and marriage as being the only possible point at which the fetishised reality of appearance and the reality of desire may meet. Her honesty, and her virtue, depend on her preserving her virginity until desire may be satisfied in marriage. When B. says, after his marriage to Pamela, 'my wife *is* my wife'[18] he is referring to an ideal where the fetishised object becomes the legally sanctioned object of desire, where the sexualising of the patriarchal bourgeois world is completed because the object of desire and the object of possession are one, united in the married fetish. It is this which *Shamela* tries to show up as dissimulation; that *Pamela* is the myth of the new bourgeois worldliness.

In desire the bourgeois world is kept permanently structured by a fetishism of the female which places her both as sexual object and as the embodiment and foundation of social reality. In this way woman comes to image the absence which is the space of the sexualising displacement. This history is the history of the fetishisation of the female body. The *locus classicus* for this production may be found in the work of de Sade.[19] Here, in a violence which reflects the ideological repression of its production by the *ancien régime*, the body is asserted as both the site of sexuality (indeed, of desire) and of the bourgeois object of worldly meaning—the individual.

The second reality of *Shamela*, then, is the reality of sexual interaction. However, the matter-of-factness with which

Shamela and her mother discuss sexual activity is a far cry from the determined monomania, and seriousness, of bourgeois pornography. It would appear that Fielding's aim was to portray a genuinely non-repressed society. This would be a pre-bourgeois society. Fielding's problem would seem to have been twofold. In the first place, he equated the obsessive repression of *Pamela* with an opposite which was an obsessive sexual liberation. This sexual liberation he seems to have considered 'natural' rather than another function of bourgeois sexuality. In this sense a tradition may be mapped out from Fielding to the sexual liberationists of the 1970s. Fielding then linked this understanding of unrepressed sexuality to the taken-for-granted unenhanced sexuality of the ideologically non-reconstructed peasants of his own day. Fielding wanted to win a bourgeois readership. He succeeded. However, constructed into a sexualised society this readership inevitably related to Fielding's text voyeuristically.

The attitude which Fielding wished to express is similar to the one put forward by Quaife in his work on Somerset peasants in the early seventeenth century when he writes:

> The large number of peasants who accepted the sexual act as amoral behaved with a considerable degree of sexual freedom, men and women alike, but in an environment in which a woman was seen as sexually voracious and the man by the rapid thrust of his own lust capable of readily and quickly satisfying her.[20]

Fielding's sexually unrepressed characters are precisely that; however, they are also characters already positioned by the bourgeois, sexualised reader who then perceives their reality as unrepressed. In *Shamela* this is how Fielding has produced these characters, feeding off the lower-class and peasant acceptance of sex as a day-to-day concern among many. The attitude towards sex which Quaife is here describing does not imply equality in matters sexual; the importance of patriarchal domination in peasants' sexual lives is obvious from the quotation. The point, however, is that sex occurs as a function of an inevitably socialised but, in this case, not fetishistically enhanced libido.

Quaife documents well the Church's lack of success amongst the lower strata of seventeenth-century society. The success of subsequent Puritan attitudes towards the body and intercourse was dependent on the radical structural shifts engendered by capitalism. Cloaked by religious ideology, we can see evolving in Puritanism a new attitude towards sexual intercourse, the body and marriage. Intercourse demonstrated the God-made difference between the two sexes but was not something which, of itself, could—or should—be given any significance. Indeed, as we find even in Milton's *Paradise Lost*, it is the 'knowledge' given by the apple of sensuality and its pleasurableness which is frowned upon by God. The 'knowledge' which eroticises Adam and Eve's world is also the cause of their fall from grace. It is illuminating that Milton's distinction is between unsexualised love and eroticised intercourse; from this perspective the poem becomes a commentary on the embourgeoisification of the world. Having eaten of the apple, Adam says:

> But come, so well refresh't, now let us play,
> As meet is, after such delicious Fare:
> For never did thy Beauty since the day
> I saw thee first and wedded thee, adorn'd
> With all perfections, so inflame my sense
> With ardor to enjoy thee, fairer now
> Than ever, bounty of this virtuous Tree.[21]

Genesis 3:7 says nothing about intercourse or sensuality. It simply states that, having eaten the apple, Adam and Eve realised that they were naked, and covered themselves: 'And the eyes of them both were opened, they knew that they were naked, and they sewed fegge leaves together, and made themselves aprons.' The assumption that the shame they feel is a shame associated with nakedness is a function of bourgeois concepts of the body. It is much more likely that the shame was originally allied to the transgression of God's wishes, which was manifested in their recognition of the fact of their nakedness. The questionableness of the text as being intended to have a sexual meaning is highlighted by the fact that when Adam was forbidden to eat from the Tree of

Knowledge, Eve had not yet been created.[22] For Milton the 'knowledge' which Adam and Eve gain not only produces desire but also, as a consequence, ensures that they must leave the garden, where everything they require is simply available, and forces them to experience work as labour in commodity production. *Paradise Lost*, however, as has often been remarked,[23] is a work ambiguous not only in its Puritanism but also for its problematic relationship to bourgeois ideals.

The twin effects of Puritanism were to raise the importance of marriage within Christian ideology and to make acceptable the sexual act within Christian marriage. Milton's Adam and Eve, we may remember, were at least married when they experienced lust. Daniel Rogers whose *Matrimonial Honour* was published in 1642 wrote:

> Marriage is the Preservative of Chastity, the Seminary of the Commonwealth, seed-plot of the Church, pillar [under God] of the world, right-hand of providence, supporter of Lawes, states, orders, offices, gifts and services: the glory of peace, the sinewes of warre, the maintenance of policy, the life of the dead, the solace of the living, the ambition of virginity, the foundation of Countries, Cities, Universities, succession of families, Crownes and Kingdomes.[24]

Leaving aside the hyperbole, it is quite clear that, for Rogers, marriage occupies a place of importance in both Christian theory and social practice quite unlike that given to it by a medieval Church which for a long time did not even view it as a sacrament. Marriage is seen here as a fundamental to the familiar ordering of society. As Hill notes, 'For Puritans the lowest unit in the hierarchy of discipline was not the parish but the household.'[25] Puritanism, unlike Catholicism, tended not to see itself as a religion of example but as a religion to be lived by the faithful. The living of Puritanism meant the absolute identification of individual behaviour with Puritan ideals. Church discipline and community order became the same thing, and the household, the smallest unit of social order,[26] became also the unit of religious order. The household was legitimated for both religion and state by the Christian rite of marriage. In the Rogers quotation we saw how intercourse is legitimated within the Christian married unit. Marriage is the 'ambition of virginity' and also the preserver of chastity for, as with virtue, coitus within marriage does not make one unchaste.

The illusion here is that chastity is an attribute which one, particularly a woman, *has* rather than a socially constructed attribute into which a person is socialised. Its ideology is a constraint imposed on the woman and legitimated by her subordinate position in relation to her husband. Vives in *The Instruction of a Christian Woman* (trans. R. Hyrde, 1541) wrote, 'A woman hath no power of her own body, but her husband, ... thou dost the more wrong to give away that thing which is another body's without the owner's licence.'[27] The preservation of chastity within marriage is based on the relation of sexual partners to the constraints of marriage and the placing of the female by the male within marriage in the sexual act. For the Puritans chastity was a function of marriage itself and the significance of marriage as a demarcation of sexual and social arenas is illustrated by the 1640 Parliamentary Act which made adultery a felony, the penalty on the second conviction being death.

All intercourse (including rape) with anyone other than one's husband was unchaste. The most important aspect of it, apart from such intercourse being morally wrong, was that it was generally considered to liberate that female desire and lasciviousness which bourgeois morality had worked so hard to repress. Richetti writes that, for the eighteenth century, 'Once a woman has been ruined, her appetite for vice (which may have been virtually non-existent before the act) is automatic and insatiable.'[28] The sexual needs credited to prostitutes throughout this period have the same origin. It is marriage which makes intercourse safe for women. In the structure of chastity the myth of female wantonness is used against women to ensure their submission to the constrictions of marriage. Within marriage, within the 'asexual' domestic domain, intercourse itself loses its libidinous properties.

There were attempts to apply this understanding of chastity to men, but the attempt only highlights a contradiction in bourgeois ideology. The success in applying it to men would have provided the ultimate valorisation to marriage. However, to succeed would have entailed decreasing the always necessary overdetermining capacity of bourgeois male sexuality. Perhaps the literary work most wellknown for its epousal of male chastity is Richardson's *Sir Charles Grandison*. It is significant that this extraordinarily long book (the libido of the author compensating that of his creation?) is usually considered to be somewhat colourless. Grandison's chastity is simply not as interesting to the bourgeois reader as the complications attendant on a female chastity constructed around repression and subject to the depredations of the (over)productive male. Pamela and Clarissa reduplicate the femininity of their texts, the former reinforcing it and the latter problematising it. Grandison simply denatures his text constructing, both literally and metaphorically, a happy marriage.

Mandeville in *A Modest Defence of Publick Stews* (1724) took for granted the notion that there should be a differentiation between male and female sexual behaviour in marriage. The pamphlet is based on the assumption that males have a sexual desire which must be satisfied. This, of course, is the reverse of the medieval voracious female. Mandeville was not alone in this. Among others, Martin Madan wrote three volumes urging polygamy rather than prostitution. Mandeville sees male satisfaction occurring by means of state-run brothels.[29] Here we find a good illustration of the translation of libido into a structuring foundation for the social order. The need for state-run brothels was to protect the institution of marriage. The wife could exist in the home with her sexualisation repressed while her husband found a cash-nexus-based outlet for the male sexual drive. This is a good illustration of the new sexualised world.

One of Mandeville's more important reasons for the legislation of prostitution, one to which he returned in *The Fable of the Bees*, was that it would protect married women from being debauched. The woman was positioned in reality by marriage, forming, herself, the articulation of the displacement which was sexuality. Hence we find the horror of female adultery where the woman as property and fetish has described herself as sexual and, indeed, active. This is well demonstrated in divorce legislation, where it was not until 1923 in Britain that equality in grounds of divorce was given to both sexes. Previously, while a woman could be divorced for simple adultery, a man could only be divorced if that adultery was compounded by some other crime such as incest or rape; a ruling was continued when divorce was transferred from canon law to civil law in 1857. In the House of Lords debate on this bill, the then Lord Chamberlain said:

> It had ever been the feeling of that House, indeed it was a feeling common to mankind in general that, although the sin in both cases was the same, the effect of adultery on the part of the husband was very different from that on the part of the wife. It was possible for a wife to pardon a husband who had committed adultery; but it was hardly possible for a husband ever really to pardon the adultery of a wife.[30]

Wives, in forming the basis of bourgeois reality, contain (indeed, confine) asexuality, property and fetish while husbands construct the world through an elaborated sexualised power structure founded in a sexual drive which continually bursts the bounds of its bourgeois monogamous restrictions and is forced to slake its lust in the eroticised market-place where sexuality and capitalism overlap. From this perspective Mandeville's state-run brothels could be seen as an early argument for nationalisation, and the argument against it would be the same—it inhibits enterprise by bounding it. The essence of bourgeois male sexuality and of capitalism lies in the same overdetermination present in the joint myth of unboundedness. In this sense the ideology of growth and the fantasy of Casanova are the same. Montesquieu came close to the recognition of the importance of the married woman as the foundation of bourgeois society when he wrote:

> So many are the imperfections that attend the loss of virtue in women, and so greatly are their minds depraved when this principal guard is removed, that in a popular state public incontinency may be considered as the last of miseries, and as a certain forerunner of a change in the constitution.[31]

This argument Montesquieu puts forward as the reason why legislators in republican states have 'ever required of women a particular gravity of manners'. In this argument we can see again the centrality of sex. Montesquieu's position is founded on a comparison of hierarchically ordered states and republican states. In states where the people form the basis of government, order is founded on the proscription of female sexual activity. Montesquieu's argument is, in effect, remarkably similar to Mandeville's, both place sex(uality) as central and both wish to see women placed as asexual. In Montesquieu, living under the *ancien régime*, however, women are still viewed as possible corrupters of the male while in the more bourgeois Mandeville it is the protection of the domesticated female from male lust which is important.

The effect of Puritan thought was to give women a conceptual importance equal to that of men while preserving the patriarchal ordering by emphasising the social inferiority of women: 'The new ethic was reflected in Puritan doctrines of the help-meet, insistence on the wife's rights (in subordination) in the family partnership, on marriage for love and on freedom of choice for children (though not disregarding the parents' views).'[32] The delineation of women as having an equally important, if subordinate, role to that of men is based on the Christian significance of the humaneness of both sexes, which is now priorised as a result of the priorisation of marriage. This opens the way for the domestic sphere to become the domain of the wife in a subordinate but structural opposition to the public and capitalist sphere of the husband.

The newly developing bourgeois reality is ontologically founded on the assumption that male and female sexual natures are compatible, in order that they may be codetermining. The raising of marriage to its new importance is completed by the addition of God's help in the sphere of domestic affection:

> He [Rogers] admits ['a secret sympathie of hearts'] is not at work in every coupling of man and woman, but, even when some other cause has brought the two together, God's hand intervenes to eke out the love which might otherwise prove insufficient. Conjugal love is thus more than the spiritual affection common to Christians, more than mere carnal attraction, 'rather brutish than humane'. It is 'a sweet compounde of both religion and nature'.[33]

It is this which, for Rogers, is 'properly called Marriage love'. The ontological component in conjugal love reappears in secular form in the ideology of Romantic love. In both cases the ontology helps raise the importance of marriage in bourgeois society to a transcendental level. Sexuality is thus acknowledged as an aspect of marriage, contained *within* it. The struggle to articulate and repress sexuality in this way is reflected in the sexual hedonism of many Christian sects in the 1640s, such as the Ranters.[34]

There is a remarkable homology between woman and realist novel where the realist novel is both commodity and the container of a commoditised world. In *Clarissa*, Hill has argued, Richardson's '*conscious* desire in writing the novel was to assert the bourgeois and Puritan conception of marriage against the feudal cavalier standards of Lovelace and the Harlowe emphasis on concentration of property.'[35] However, this is really to postulate a false trichotomy. The incompatibility of the bourgeois and Puritan individualist ideology of Romantic love and free choice of marriage partner, with the bourgeois emphasis on marriage as a means of accumulating property, can only be sustained when the 'woman' is not, herself, experienced as an object. Once the woman is secured as a fetishised property object in her own right, the ideology of individualistic love becomes the expression of the experiential displacement. The articulation in *Clarissa* of the three positions reflects the uncertainty of the new bourgeois reality. The predicament that Clarissa's father places her in by trying to force her to marry Solmes exists because he discriminates between woman-as-object and woman as transmitter of property. In fact, the property-alliance marriage was a debased form of the aristocratic lineage marriage. It may be viewed as the capitalistic counterpoint to the uncontrolled increase in licentiousness during the same period.

It is only rarely that the limitations on marriage partner are today overtly discussed in terms of property ownership. Where these cases do exist and where they are allied to the person's wish to marry someone beyond these limitations, the conflict is articulated in terms which compare marriage for love with marriage for money. Fielding, in *Shamela*, once again demonstrating the repression inherent in *Pamela*, this time in terms of the love/money distinction, has Parson

Williams telling Shamela that she should have two husbands, one 'the object of your love and to satisfy your Desire'; the other 'the object of your Necessity, and to furnish you with those other conveniences'[36]—by which he means material goods. The success of bourgeois ideology is that these two are so often experienced as being united in one person—the loved one—though often it is recognised that either more love or more money might be desirable. The woman, then, is the sexualised embodiment of both property and the transmission of property. As was written in *The Whole Duty of Man* in 1804, 'The corrupting of a man's wife is by all acknowledgement to be the worst sort of theft, infinitely beyond that of goods.'[37] The same argument has been put forward about writing and the potential of the media of communication as a whole which, as property, also have the capacity to transmit, if not property, then information.

One aspect of the medieval patriarchal attitude towards women was, as I have mentioned, a view of them as insatiable, their sexual drive unable to be satisfied by the activity of any one man and they themselves unwilling to curb that drive. The new acceptability of intercourse within marriage coupled with the raising of chastity/virtue to a supreme good, determined in their demarcation again by marriage, enabled the ideology of women's sexual drive to be contained by marriage also. In addition, as the woman's position as property is confirmed by the consummation of marriage, the male is placed in the position of guardian of the chastity of the female. Chastity is no longer demonstrated by her 'virginity' but by her faithfulness to one man. Squire B. becomes just such a 'generous Protector and Rewarder of [her innocence]' for Pamela (Book II, p. 145). Women's sexual drive becomes not only contained but repressed and rearticulated as desire. The virtuous woman becomes a person who is not only dominated and, in the process, determined by bourgeois patriarchy but who legitimates the bourgeois order by articulating the structure of repression on which it is founded through her acceptance and upholding of the social order which contains and represses her sexual drive, now, of course, given a sexualised significance. In the context of my later discussion of rape, I should add that the male retort of 'all

48

women really want it' is a reaffirmation of this attitude concerning women's sexual needs. Much of the strength of Pamela's virtuous image comes from the bourgeois reader's awareness of a tension between women's 'natural' drive and Pamela's ability to control it and live within the flowering bourgeois social fabric which allows for its repression and consequent sexualisation.

The repression of the legitimacy of sexual activity may be illustrated again by examining the shifting mythological significance of Venus from her use in *The Art of Courtly Love* by Capellanus to her bourgeois usages. For Capellanus the 'work of Venus' is intercourse; for bourgeois writers Venus is associated with beauty and Romantic love, as in the Botticelli painting, and with unrepressed sexual activity— 'pornography'—as in the poem 'It Was on the Good Ship Venus'. Here, then, we find another example of the dualism of repression and expression which structures bourgeois sexuality.

It was Puritanism which gave ideological covering to the bourgeois sexualising of 'reality' in Britain. The joke of *Shamela* is the ability of the lower-class women to understand the importance of desire in the bourgeois world while manipulating it to gain material, bourgeois advantage. The irony is that it is the desire of the bourgeois readership which positions the work as pornographic. The joke has its fundamental expression in Shamela's sexual experience. Unlike Pamela, whose real virginity is the real power (or, should I say, the power of reality) of that novel, Shamela only pretends to virginity. Indeed, she only pretends in the bourgeois world of pretence of Squire Booby. Her power in his world rests in Squire Booby's belief that she is a virgin, that his act of penetration fixes her as uniquely structured in relation to him as desirable and as bourgeois individual. Her power is consolidated in her ability to dissimulate the act which he considers to have proved the real:

> Well, at last I went to bed, and my husband soon leap'd in after me: where I shall only assure you, that I played my Part in such a manner, that no bridegroom was ever better satisfied with his Bride's Virginity. And to confess the Truth, I might have been well enough satisfied too, if I had never been acquainted with Parson Williams.[38]

In bourgeois society the person who recognises that reality resides in appearance and who is able to dissimulate the best is the person who holds the power. However, the ability to control appearance is, in the end, always the prerogative of the male because it is the male who libidinously produces that reality through his production of woman as fetish. This structure of male production is reflected in the bourgeois ideological concern with male potency. Indeed, in the first place it is reflected in what would seem to be a nineteenth-century sexualising of the word 'potency' which made it applicable to the male capacity to ejaculate fertile sperm. The usage is a recognition of the final appropriation of the potential for creation (economic production) by the male and of the power which appropriation betokens in bourgeois society. I have already discussed the male concern with penis size. Now we must look briefly at the male appropriation of the power to conceive.

The medical ideology of conception which dominated through the medieval period had its origins in Aristotle: 'If, then, the male stands for the effective and active, and the female for the passive, it follows that what the female would contribute to the semen of the male would not be semen but material for the semen to work upon.'[39] Aristotle, using incidentally the same understandings of the male as active and the female as passive which were to be used by Freud, differentiates the roles of male and female but leaves the female with a specific passive yet creative role. It was a common medieval idea that women also ejaculated semen and the proper mixture of the two semens was necessary for conception to occur.[40] In the medical world the belief in female semen seems to have died out about the seventeenth century, leaving the bourgeois woman with no creative role at all. Simultaneously, the development of a new scientific medicine dominated by men began to encroach into the area of conception and birth which, previously, had been the province of the midwife.[41] Thus the female was removed both ideologically and institutionally from participation in conception and birth. The lay belief in female semen did not die out. Rather, it was appropriated into the male concern with ejaculation. Ejaculation is the physical representation of male sexuality. To say that a female in bourgeois society ejaculates, then, is to pass a comment on her femaleness. It suggests, in the first place, that she enjoys intercourse rather than passively accepting it. Such enjoyment places her amongst that category of female already discussed whose repressed desires have been unfortunately activated. This is the moral subtext which we must bring to, for example, *My Secret Life*'s reiteration of female ejaculation.[42]

If we return to literature we can see how this process has been replicated in the ideology which surrounds and constructs the text. The exclusion of women from writing—or, at least, from 'good' writing—is an obvious replication of the appropriation of conception by males. This appropriation occurs simultaneously with the consolidation of the text as female. Thus we find Rochester's Timon in the seventeenth century remarking that:

> A Song to Phillis, I perhaps might make,
> But never Rhym'd, but for my Pintles sake.[43]

Here, writing is understood as the manifestation of male desire. Writing links Timon with Phillis in just the same way as eighteenth-century letters in epistolary novels articulate the desires of the participants. Already, writing itself has become a masculine institution. In the late seventeenth century, for example, we find Anne Finch, Countess of Winchilsea, writing:

> Alas! A woman that attempts the pen
> Such an intruder on the rights of men![44]

Desire, and its fertile possibilities, is a male prerogative. Thus, not only is woman appropriated, sexualised and fetishised but the text also goes through an analogous reconstruction. In the process the creative power of writing is reconstituted as a male prerogative. The institution of writing becomes masculinised and women who persist in the occupation are either forced to 'hide' their sex by special devices such as pseudonyms[45] or are placed in that special category of the 'female writer'—a category which often carried overtones of Bohemianism and sexual deviation.

Moers notes: 'The domination of the English novel by
women at the turn of the eighteenth century came to an end
for a while at least when Walter Scott, rather late in life, put
aside poetry for fiction.'[46] What is actually being lost is the
possibility of a woman writing a realist novel which is not
always overdetermined by a male fetishising ideology. Miller
in *The Heroine's Text* puts an argument similar to my own.
She writes of a 'feminocentric' eighteenth-century novel by
which she seems to mean the inscription of a lived and, in
terms of the plot, non-male determined female destiny. The
end of this period of writing she places with de Sade in France
and Jane Austen in England. However, for Miller the
eighteenth-century novel is a novel in which men attempt to
achieve written control of women. She writes, in the context
of Lovelace's need for written proof of Clarissa's love, 'It
seems to me, however, that the text of feminine surrender
must be seen as at least a double fiction: a masculine
representation of female desire produced ultimately for an
audience not of women readers but of men.'[47] Where Miller
goes wrong is to confuse the ideological male with the real
male. The readers need not necessarily be male because the
bourgeois social order constructs the position of reader as
male. It is this positioning of the reader which is important,
the learning to occupy a male position as constructed by male
ideology regardless of one's gendered sex. De Sade and
Austen are, indeed, key points in the tradition, but while de
Sade celebrates the success of male sexualised, ideological
hegemony, Austen articulates the female defeat (and the
success of the bourgeois sign system) by reproducing
confinement as freedom. To quote Miller again:

> With Austen feminocentrism is no longer a pretext, but the text itself.
> The center of her universe is a crowded and a full space. The vicissitudes
> of the quotidian, courtship, the desire for the happy end, the fate, in
> particular, of the marriageable daughter become not opportunities for
> playing with the anxieties of a *male* self ... but the occasion for exploring,
> with wit and irony, the possibilities of feminine mastery in a world
> circumscribed by income and the intersubjective.[48]

The female writer and reader, then, accepts her ideological
determination and in the process of being reconstituted

within this ideological overdetermination she comes to perceive the repression and confinement of the realist novel as freedom.

By the nineteenth century the ideological conflation of sexual conception and writing is complete. In 1886 we find Gerard Manley Hopkins writing to a friend that 'The male quality is the creative gift.'[49] He is concerned with writing but he might have been writing about biological conception. What the male creates is the female text, the fetish. This creation is homologous to the production of the female as fetish constructed in the act of intercourse. The gradual decrease in the importance of consummatory intercourse may be compared with the decrease in the importance of letters and epistolary novels. Both devices lose their paramount importance once the system of commodity fetishism is complete.

CHAPTER 3

Repression and Pornography

The realist novel forms a continuum with the genre of pornography. Historically where one ends and the other begins has itself been problematic. Partly this is because pornography is a socially defined genre. However I want to argue that such definition is only partial; pornography is the product of the sexualising of the world and, specifically, of the practice of reading. In the realist genre the sexualisation of reading is repressed, as is the sexualisation of the world. In pornography the sexualised world becomes, itself, the only world, and this world exists for the purpose of sexualised reading.

Within the sexualised text the female characters are doubly constructed. In the first place, they are the creation/production of the author. Thus they are completely constructed by a male—or a person positioned as male. The late-eighteenth-century development of the domestic novel and the novel of society allowed women to produce/create themselves—but in a special case. Here women were working to replicate their own repression and confinement. The femaleness of author, text and character constituted an acceptance of their position as male products. In the second place, the female character is finally constructed by the hero. The story of the text becomes the question of whether the already constructed female will be constructed again and by whom. It is possible to see Jane Austen's work, at the turn of the nineteenth century, as a key moment in the consolidation of this development. It is not coincidental that Austen is conventionally regarded by critics as the first realist novelist.

Pamela is an extremely good example of this double construction. The consummation of the text, Pamela and B.'s marriage with its hidden consummatory intercourse, occurs almost three-quarters of the way through. The last part consists, in the main, of domestic arrangements of an interpersonal and material nature. The interpersonal matters amount to the problems encountered by Pamela in gaining acceptance in her new world. The climax here is her acceptance by B.'s sister, Lady Davers. The material matters climax in the making by B. of his will and his subsequent discussion of the disposition of his goods with Pamela. Pamela, constructed by B., will be well provided for by him in case of his early death. We are returned to B.'s male preoccupation with inheritance and material possessions, which now include Pamela. The narrative of *Pamela* is conservative in that it replicates the valorised social order. Pamela, fixed by marriage, is confined as another commodity—albeit as the generative source of meaning within the domestic domain. At the beginning of the novel Pamela arrives at the house to work. The drama of desire/love which is articulated in the central section of the book is thus itself confined by a concern with the economic at both ends of the book.

The acknowledgement of desire as the conferrer of reality, and the utilisation of it to produce/create that reality, is the preserve of bourgeois patriarchy. The males in the texts replicate the 'males' who produce those texts. The double construction of Pamela lies in her construction by Richardson and by B. The potency of the author is assimilated into that of 'his' hero B., Booby or Lovelace. It is worth speculating whether Charlotte Brontë aimed to increase the potency of her hero to compensate for her own femaleness and to match the independence of action she gives her heroine when in *Jane Eyre* she calls him Rochester, echoing the name of Lord Rochester, whose poetry was regarded as so pornographic it was unavailable in unexpurgated form during the nineteenth century. Desire is also the attribute of Werther in *The Sorrows of Young Werther*, which I will discuss in more detail in Chapter 7.

The myth of *Pamela*, which, in its lack of reality, is a part also of the tragedy of *Clarissa*, is that the unique moment of defloweration, the moment of penetration, will literally/metaphorically fix the structure of marriage and desire in a permanent and unique and real structure.[1] The bourgeois reality of *Pamela* is that sex disappears at the *rite de passage* of marriage, the moment it becomes socially acceptable. Defoe, the Dissenter, makes this point explicitly in his book on marriage:

> Yet let J. A. take a modest Hint upon the grossest Indecency of that kind (conjugal crime), which this part of town has ever shown; when with the grossest Immodesty he gave the detail of his Marriage Night's Performances to a grave and eminent Magistrate of the City upon the open Exchange, and was handsomely reproved and exposed for it, as he deserved.[2]

J. A. is exposed for revealing what, by this period, should be hidden, repressed and confined. For Pamela, herself, marriage is not only the operator which realises the social world, it is also her entry into that social world. While we are told in some considerable detail of B.'s attempt to rape Pamela before they are married, intercourse after their marriage is never mentioned. Shamela's wedding night description has no counterpart in bourgeois discourse because it is only by the repression of sex that the fetishised world may be realised.

The successful fetishisation of the text in the early nineteenth century occurred concurrently with the establishment of the 'third person' novel form and the discursive triad of novel types: 'realism', 'Gothic' and 'pornography'. It was also concurrent with the development of publishing as an identifiable capitalist institution which bought texts from writers and sold them to readers, in the process operating as a gatekeeping institution which placed texts as objects in the capitalist market-place.

The types referred to are actually points on the continuum of the bourgeois reader's experience of the 'text'. None is any more 'real' than any other because all are products of (and may be read as commentaries on) the productive capacity inherent in the readerly apprehension of the fetishised text. Indeed, as I shall discuss, pornography is a socially defined category which actually mobilises realist techniques. Just as the writer of the bourgeois text is positioned both socially and libidinally as male, so the reader is structured into his/her relationship with the text—also as male. This structuring cannot be altered by adjusting the content of the text because the position (experience) of the content is always already determined by the capitalist placing of the text as fetish.

Barthes in *The Pleasure of the Text* has discussed the text as sexualised. His notion of pleasure, which he describes as 'contentment', is that it extends into bliss, which he describes as 'rapture',[3] and the both are underpinned by an idea of all-pervading sensuality.[4]

The process of reading in our society places the text as object and assumes it to be appropriated by the reader in a more or less disguised cathexis. Fiction is not only by definition 'escapist' (the apparent tautologous use of this term by popular fiction blurb writers is intended to denote a pleasurable experience), it is inevitably so—something determined by the objectness of the text. The reader reads as voyeur. This is important because of the historical links between a rising female readership and the development of 'fiction' and of the novel form as a practice.

Watt has commented that in the eighteenth century, 'Women of the upper and middle classes could partake in few of the activities of their menfolk, whether of business or pleasure ... Such women, therefore, had a great deal of leisure, and this leisure was often occupied by omniverous reading.'[5] Accurate figures for female literacy during this period are harder to find than figures for male literacy. It is not just modern prejudice which converts Lawrence Stone's article 'Literacy in Britain during the Industrial Revolution'[6] into an investigation of male literacy. It is also a historical problem of patriarchy. For example, Hardwicke's Marriage Act, and the demands of the Church of England, required that only bridegrooms had to sign the register and, in doing so, they revealed a limited knowledge of their writing ability. In general we can say that middle-class women were less educated than middle-class men. They were less likely to be sent to school, and when they were, were given a domestic education, Latin, Greek and classical literature being a male prerogative. This was certainly the case in the nineteenth century, and Showalter cites many cases of women writers worried about demonstrating their academic inferiority. Nevertheless, female literacy among the bourgeoisie and the upper classes as well as the petit bourgeois servant class, had a background which lay well back in the seventeenth century.

Female literacy in England would seem to have its ideological origin in Puritanism.[7] The same Puritanism which provided the repression for the new sexual preoccupations also promoted the idea of the wife as help-meet and the importance of individual reading of religious works. Louis Wright comments that:

> The mother was expected to read the Bible to her children and, in the absence of her husband, to conduct family worship, which the whole household, children, servants and apprentices, were expected to attend. Hence, it was a godly duty—indeed, a necessity—for mothers to know how to read.[8]

The valorisation of the role of women in the domestic sphere occurred at the same time as the legitimation of their access to literacy. Simultaneously, the woman as sexualised object— distantiated and fetishised in the same manner as the text—is denied her integral sexuality. This was a necessary process in the male construction of woman as fetish. It would be expected, then, that the newly developing literary area of fiction would appeal predominantly to 'women', a group in this sexualised sense called into being by their own repression. The consuming of the content of the object, the text, became a strategy for escaping and articulating the repression of the bourgeois experience. Dreams, as Freud recognised, are important in the bourgeois world for the same reason—they express repression. The difference is that the reader of fiction is always determined as male, and usually as passive, in relation to the female, fetishised text. The passivity of the reading process in our society ensures both relief from repression and further repression as the female reader constitutes herself as male as she voyeuristically consumes the text. Anna O.'s rebellion against Freud's recuperation of her dreams into male bourgeois ideology may be equated with the action which occurs when a person 'reads critically', that is to say, preserves the distance between him/herself and the text, which is exactly *not* what is expected of the bourgeois reader. The assumption that the reader should be involved with the text underpins the bourgeois literary criticism of such groups as the Leavisites and the New Critics, whose purpose is always to disinter the 'real' meaning of a text by demonstrating how it should be read.

Hard as it is to ascertain the extent of female literacy in the eighteenth and nineteenth centuries, it is even harder to reach any general conclusions about what women read. Ian Watt[9] notes that both Lady Mary Wortley Montague and Mrs Thrale (upper and middle class, respectively) were great readers of literature. These, however, might simply be two idiosyncratic examples. Day, in his book on epistolary fiction before Richardson, writes that Addison's *Spectator* 'pointed out that brisk young men-about-town ... read [epistolary] novels, either to ingratiate themselves with the "fair sex" or for frothy amusement of an amatory nature'.[10] He goes on to write, 'It was clearly for women, however, that many of these early examples of letter fiction were intended. References to such books are found in the diaries and letters of women of the upper classes, as well as in satirical comments on the tastes of feminine readers.'[11] The suggestion that the early part of the eighteenth century identified women as being the target audience for epistolary fiction is important when placed side by side with Richetti's conclusion concerning the other major form of popular fiction during this period. He writes, 'It is probably no accident that the most considerable writers of scandalous memoirs during the early eighteenth century were women, and it is certainly likely that their most eager readers were women as well.'[12]

We may note, parenthetically, that these eighteenth-century writers, the most famous of whom were Mrs Manley and Mrs Haywood, saw no need to change their authorial sex. While the epistolary novel was fictional but denied its fictional status, the scandal novel was truly only semi-fictional. These novels, English equivalents of the French *chroniques scandaleuses*, which we shall come across in Chapter 4, were fictionalised and lubricious accounts of the political and mostly licentious goings-on of the upper classes.

The scandal novel died out, as did the epistolary novel, to be replaced by the completely fictional and objectified third-person novel. I think it may be claimed with justification that the epistolary novel was more the forerunner of the novel as it later became because it was more essentially fictional. The scandal novel had its basis in the real world. It is in the context of successfully figuring the age and, with our hindsight, successfully prefiguring the future that we must take cognisance of Richardson's *Pamela* and *Clarissa*. Richardson combined an epistolary style with a sexual/amatory content to produce works of objectness, thereby satisfying the need for involvement while articulating the ideological concerns of the (female) readers within a male-determined ideological structure.

As the category of pornography developed to express what had become socially unexpressible, so realism developed as the expression of a society founded on repression. By the early nineteenth century, development of what has been called the 'domestic novel' and the elaboration of realism as a genre was the end of a movement which started in the seventeenth century. As Wright says: 'Despite Puritan objections to idle reading—perhaps in part as a result of it—the Renaissance woman, like her modern sister, found in fiction the literature of escape which the strenuousness of her life demanded.'[13] Watt's suggestion that reading was less objectionable to Puritans than other entertainments,[14] and this apparent disagreement with Wright, is founded on the problem of what should be read: 'To woman's reading of voluptuous love stories was attributed much of her moral depravity, so lamented by Puritan writers.'[15] Puritan sexual repression cannot be separated from the repression of women and their bourgeois production as sexualised objects—as fetishes. Having sexualized them as objects, they must, subjectively, be lacking in sexuality and hence 'escape' must be to an equally asexual (repressed) fantasy, that which came to be called realism. In this way, also, Richardson was the model of his time. Day, in *Told in Letters* remarks that 'not until the time of Richardson did most of the neo-Puritan "middle-class" find novels of which they could approve'[16]— that is to say, novels of sufficient repression. Richardson's espousal of the new realism and of repression is most obvious in his rewritten, bowdlerisation of L'Estrange's translation of Aesop's fables. Thus the round is completed, the reality of bourgeois society is validated by its mirroring in fiction within asexual texts which, like asexual women, are nevertheless created by men. This represents the completion of the bourgeois literary sign system in correlation with the final commodification of the bourgeois world.

In this context we might understand the bourgeois experience of reading the bourgeois novel as a form of intercourse culminating in the desired orgasm. The passive, feminine text does not conclude itself; it is worked on by the reader who completes it himself, the female reader here established within a male ideological position. It is no wonder that the novel of suspense and the detective novel are both inventions of the nineteenth century. We might, with justification, describe the mystery thriller as the most thoroughly bourgeois of the realist novel genres. With this perception it is understandable why novels climax with sexual activity, or with its signifier—marriage. Barthes describes the elaboration of narrative suspense as an unveiling, as in a corporeal striptease: 'the entire excitation takes refuge in the *hope* of seeing the sexual organ (schoolboy's dream) or in knowing the end of the story (novelistic satisfaction).'[17] This, however, is a description just as the revelation of the sexual organ is itself the description of another event removed from actuality by desire. It is only once writing has become sexualised that 'pornography' can exist. Its existence is dependent on the repression/revelation dichotomy which forms the displacement experienced as bourgeois sexuality.

This dichotomy places *Pamela* as repressed and *Shamela* as unrepressed and both as equally 'truthful'. To explain this dichotomy more clearly, we can compare *Pamela* to John Cleland's *Fanny Hill*,[18] first published in 1749, whose pornographic nature was reaffirmed in Britain in the 1964 trial. Epstein, in his book on Cleland, notes that 'Books which seem to devote most of their energy to sexual arousal did not appear regularly in Europe until the middle of the seventeenth century.'[19] *Fanny Hill* was the first 'classic'

English work to fill this description. It is in pornography that the repressed is revealed in a world where meaning is not simply derived from, but exists in, sexuality. Pornotopia is the word Marcus uses to describe the world within which the activities which constitute pornography exist.[20] It is a fantasy world in which sexuality and meaning are conflated and, for the bourgeois reader, it is a forbidden fantasy. Above I have compared the act of reading to the act of intercourse, suggesting that it is the sexualisation of the text which energises reading for the bourgeois reader. On this parallel the experience of the climax of the text becomes equivalent to orgasm. But orgasm, manifested in ejaculation, has, as I have explained, historically been appropriated by the male in bourgeois society. The female, positioned as male when reading a text, assumes a forbidden sexuality and resolves the paradox by a repression which leaves her passive, ideologically uncritical in her enjoyment of the writing. For the male, reading simply reinforces his own understanding of the world, including his own sexuality.

The feminisation of the text is manifested in what the text is allowed to say. It is not merely the descriptions of certain things and activities which become forbidden but words themselves. Written (and spoken) language becomes sexually charged. The new domain of pornography brings one other practice into being—expurgation. The assumption of the link between expurgation and sexual matters may be traced to the use of 'castrate' as a metaphor for the activity. The *Oxford English Dictionary* traces its first use to 1623; certainly in the eighteenth century Samuel Johnson wrote that he castrated Rochester's poems for publication. It seems to be taken for granted that text and contents are one and the same. The castration of the contents gives us a legitimate text. In a society determined by the phallus and the male-appropriated power of ejaculation, the removal of the testicles denatures the male. He who becomes a non-male—in a society where only two sexes exist and where the male determines that existence—must therefore become in some senses female. We may argue, then, that expurgation gives us a feminine text. From the turn of the nineteenth century onward expurgation reached a peak in Dr Bowdler and his sister Harriet Bowdler's notorious version of Shakespeare's works. They, however, were not alone. There were about six expurgated versions of Shakespeare made during the nineteenth century and at least three expurgated versions of the Bible.[21] Uncastrated texts are not male, however. What they are is bourgeois society's next best thing—a sexually active female. What content is considered to be sexually excessive and therefore should be regarded as pornographic is both relative to the individual and also, and more importantly, historically determined.

Interestingly, the publication of *Fanny Hill* came after the development in Britain of an obscenity law which extended state censorship from merely political matters to include matters of morality. The rapid deployment of censorship as an aspect of state control in the seventeenth century is first of all a reflection of the increasing coherence of the state as an institutional entity, a *locus* of power implicit in the ideology and practice of government. Such a development of state control entailed the possibility of conflicting views between individuals and the state, in doing so acknowledging and creating a division between individuals and state. It is the recognition and horror of this division which concerned Hobbes in *Leviathan* and *Behemoth*. It is the recognition and acceptance of it—indeed, the attempt to justify it as beneficial—which we find a century later in the work of Mandeville. Obviously, the extension of the censorship laws to cover obscenity would only have occurred when it was considered that certain printed works could be obscene. This, in turn, demands a view of sex, as an area of praxis, in which certain forms of writing could be considered by the state as injurious to the morality of the Commonwealth. In the development of the British Obscenity Law, we find this taking place.

Foxon[22] has traced for us those cases which might be considered to antecede that of Curll in 1727 in which the King's Bench finally gave reality to the new law. One of the most interesting is that of John Wickins who was fined forty shillings in 1683 for publishing a translation of Pallavicino's *Rectorica delle puttane* called *The Whore's Rhetorick*. Unfortunately, we do not know what the grounds were for this conviction. Whatever the nature of the case, the transgression was obviously considered of much less significance than that of Francis Smith Jnr, who in the same year was fined ten pounds for publishing a libel entitled *The Irregular Account of Swearing the Two Pretended Sheriffs.* That a number of individuals were moving to a position from which they considered that printed works could have an undesirable sexual content is demonstrated by the story (again told by Foxon) of Wells, a bookseller, who in 1677 had his shop closed down by Mr L'Estrange because he was selling, among other books, copies of *Escole des filles* and *Aloyisae Zigaea amores* (this latter would seem to be the book by Nicholas Choriet, first published about 1660). Wells's brother-in-law complained to Sir Joseph Williamson, who considered the complaint justified, that 'this manner of proceeding of Mr. L'Estrange was both illegal, unjustifiable and uncivil, for 'tis of ill consequence to cause a young man's shop to be shut up.'[23] Earlier, in 1600, we find John Donne writing to Sir Henry Wotton: 'I am sorry you should (with any great earnestness), desire anything of P. Aretinus, not that he could infect',[24] the implication being that certain works could 'infect'—although how, he unfortunately omits to explain.

When in 1707 James Read was unambiguously brought to court for the publication of *The Fifteen Plagues of a Maidenhead* it was in the context of a libel case. Read won because the court ruled that a general offence against morals could not be seen as a personal libel. Morality was still in the ecclesiastical and personal domain not yet that of the state. In the development of the discourse of obscenity Read's case is important because it demonstrates the fundamental importance of virginity to bourgeois morality. This poem described fifteen reasons why women should wish to lose their virginity in terms such as:

> Alas! I care not, Sir, what Force you'd use
> So I my Maiden-head could quickly lose:
> Oft do I wish one skill'd in Cupid's Arts,
> Would quickly dive into my secret parts:
> For as I am, at Home all sorts of weather,
> I skit—as Heaven and Earth would come together,
> Twirling a Wheel, I sit at home, hum drum,
> And spit away my Nature on my thumb.[25]

It was one of a number which Read published with titles like *The Fifteen Comforts of Whoring* and *The Fifteen Comforts of a Wanton Wife*, but only *The Fifteen Plagues of a Maidenhead* seems to have been considered worthy of prosecution. What we have here, then, is confirmation of the importance of virginity in the bourgeois world. By the time of Read's trial the first Society for the Reformation of Manners, against which Mandeville wrote, was eight years old.[26]

What is interesting about defining a law of obscenity is that the precedent on which it was founded did not come from laws on printing at all, but from a case involving Sir Charles Sedley, who in 1663 was sent to prison for a week and fined 2,000 marks when he behaved in a way considered so outrageous that it provoked a riot. Having imbibed alcohol at a public house in Bow Street called (ironically enough) the Cock, he appears to have gone up onto the balcony (I should say that defence and prosecution differed in their accounts) and, after dropping his trousers and exposing himself, either defecated or urinated, or both, on the people beneath. In this case we can see clearly that the body—and particularly the genitals—were becoming fetishised.

In 1619, forty-four years earlier, an English etiquette book was placing emphasis on just these features:

> let not thy privy members be
> lay'd open to be view'd,
> it is most shameful and abhord,
> detestable and rude.
> Retaine not urine nor the winde
> which doth thy body vex
> so it be done with secresie
> let that not thee perplex.[27]

Here we can see the concealment of nakedness becoming a social concern. Elias has demonstrated how nakedness and its covering went through a transitional stage where shame was associated with differentiation of rank: 'First it became a distasteful offence to show oneself exposed in any way before those of higher or equal rank; with inferiors it can even be a sign of benevolence. Then, as all become socially equal, it slowly becomes a general offence.'[28] The first stage here is a hangover from the ideology of the feudal hierarchy with its integrated system of reciprocity. The evolution of social equality is, in fact, the development of a new social order based on a differentiation between private and public. Nakedness is not accepted in the new public domain. Mention or performance of those excretory functions associated with the areas most obsessively concealed was also prohibited. All Freud's stages in a child's development, therefore, are associated with those areas most highly fetishised in bourgeois society. Yet this confinement/revelation of the body and its functions and the results of those functions *is* a bourgeois phenomenon. As late as 1558 *Galateo* by Della Casa was stating:

> it is not a refined habit, when coming across something disgusting in the street, as sometimes happens, to turn at once to one's companion and point it out to him.
> It is far less proper to hold out the stinking thing for the other to smell[29]

What occurred between the cases of Sedley and Curll is a shift in attitude whereby writing could now carry the obscene, sexual overtones previously only attributable to the body. Moreover, the reason why this idea was so believable to the court was that a body of literature originating in Italy was evolving which demonstrated the new sexual nature of writing and which, from its popularity, satisfied a new need. The first well-known work to be labelled as 'pornographic' was the *Ragionamente* of Aretino, published in two parts in 1534 and 1536. It was, doubtless, to this work that Donne was referring in the passage quoted earlier.

The debate over Aretino's *Dialogues* as either pornographic or satirical is as much of a non-debate as—and indeed is commensurate with—modern debates over fiction/reality retrospectively applied to eighteenth-century novels. Aretino's work stands at the boundary between bawdiness and pornography, the moment when sexual repression creates a voyeuristic, descriptive writing sexualised by displacement. Rochester's work stands at the same boundary in the development of English bourgeois society.

Some years earlier Aretino had written a series of sixteen
sonnets to go with a set of engravings made by Marcantonio
Raimondi from drawings by Guilo Romano which showed a
variety of positions for sexual intercourse. This work, known
by the name *Positzione*, was in print by 1527. In his
dedication to this work Aretino wrote: '[The sonnets']
wanton memory I dedicate to you [Battista Zatti of Brescia]
(*pace* all hypocrites), for I renounce the bad judgement and
dirty habit which forbid the eyes to see what pleases them
most. What harm is there in seeing a man on top of a
woman?'[30] Here we can see clearly expressed the voyeuristic
articulation of the fetishised body. Aretino's query indicates
that this act, which previously had gone unnoticed, was now
something fascinating and repressed. Naked bodies having
sexual relations has become the subject for a genre of
literature and drawing—and later photography and film—
justified as a liberating force making unrepressed what
uptight society expresses. However, in the bourgeois
experience the body as sexualised fetish is already inscribed
as repressed.

In Aretino's work we can see this repression coming into
existence. One example of this in the *Dialogues* is the
recurring interchange between the two prostitutes, Nanna
and Antonia, as to what kind of language should be used when
talking of sexual organs and activity:

Antonia: Oh, I meant to tell you and then I forgot: Speak plainly
and say 'fuck', 'prick', 'cunt', and 'ass' if you want
anyone except scholars at the University of Rome to
understand you. You with your 'rope in the ring', your
'obelisk in the Colosseum', your 'leek in the garden' ...
why don't you say it straight out and stop going about
on tiptoes? Why don't you say yes when you mean yes
and no when you mean no ...

Nanna: Don't you known that respectability looks all the more
beautiful in a whorehouse?[31]

The language is itself becoming energised, and Antonia,
interestingly the younger and less experienced prostitute, is
advocating the repressed language of direct sexual
expression. Nanna justifies her use of circumlocution by

claiming respectability for her disquisition precisely because of the language she is using. In effect, however, her language itself becomes another form of voyeurism as the reader has to consider the meaning and appropriateness of each metaphor. The respectability for which she is arguing has become yet another example of repressed sexuality. The debate itself may be seen as a microcosm of the elaboration of the bourgeois displacement. It is as if Aretino is reflexively commenting on the emergence of the bourgeois sexualised world.

In England Lord Rochester's bawdy/pornographic poems occupy a similarly ambiguous position about 150 years later. Here again we can see the time difference between Italy and England in the consolidation of bourgeois society. It is fifty years after Rochester that we get in England the dichotomous commentaries on bourgeois sexuality implicit in *Pamela* and *Shamela*. It is in the gap between the experience of the two language usages that the displacement resides, and it is this gap which is yet narrow enough for Aretino's *Dialogues* and Rochester's poetry to straddle uneasily.

In Aretino's *Dialogues* intercourse is much discussed, but it is argued by those who would consider the work a bawdy satire, it is not intercourse or parallel activities such a sodomy or flagellation which are the *locus* of representation in the work; it is, rather, a jaundiced analysis of society. However, in a bourgeois, voyeuristic world it will be the sexual preoccupation which is emphasised.

Fanny Hill, the first English pornographic novel, written, like *Pamela*, in the form of letters, has many descriptions not only of sexual intercourse but also of bodies engaging in this activity. The erotic nature of *Fanny Hill* lies in its voyeuristic possibilities for those who live in a sexualised society. It is only as writing became sexualised and capable of being used for erotic stimulation, thus placing the reader in the role of voyeur, that writing came to focus on the act which lies at the heart of the expressive repression of sexuality.

In the context of the revelatory repression that constitutes pornography, it is inevitably patriarchy which is the voyeur. For pornography is the validation of the construction of the female as fetish. It might be hypothesised, although impossible to prove, that the bourgeois period has seen a meaning given to voyeurism. However, one piece of evidence suggests itself and that is the English voyeur *topos* found in the Lady Godiva story. The story as originally told by Roger of Wendover in the thirteenth century does not appear to have included Peeping Tom, who seems to have entered the story in the seventeenth century—a hundred years after Richard Grafton had introduced a new element into the story. This was Godiva's summoning of all the magistrates and officials from Coventry to order them to ensure that during her ride all the inhabitants of the city stayed indoors with their windows shuttered. Here we can see clearly the first, Puritan stage of the fetishisation of the body. Godiva's body must not be seen; she must become invisible. The acknowledgement of the successful establishment of the fetish comes with the invention of Peeping Tom. He is a replication of the reader or auditor of the story. Tom establishes the existence of the repressed, the invisible, and becomes a commentary on the reader or listener's own voyeuristic engagement with this story of a woman displaying her nakedness in the public domain. One is left wondering what the original meaning of the story was; why it was so significant that she should be naked. If we remember Elias's point about class restrictions on which groups were allowed to see which other groups naked, I would hazard that it was a sign that Godiva, for whom the Virgin Mother was especially important, was prepared to lower herself to the level of the people she cared about. It was this proof of her care which changed her husband Leofric's mind and persuaded him to free Coventry from the burdensome toll which he had imposed upon it. It would seem, then, that it was only at the time when nakedness was becoming sexualised that the voyeur was introduced into the story. Kinsey *et al.* in their study of American sexual attitudes in the 1940s found that 77 per cent of males who had seen portrayals of sexual activity found that they had been aroused erotically; by contrast, only 32 per cent of females had found such scenes erotic.[32] These figures would suggest the success of the bourgeois differentiation between the male as sexual and the female as asexual but fetishised. The 32 per cent of women erotically stimulated by such voyeurism might then be argued to have been improperly socialised from a bourgeois point of view. They are women with some degree of (masculine) placing. The ideologically male reader of the (asexual) novel also is not overtly a voyeur. Nevertheless, the ultimately charged nature of the bourgeois reading process makes him/her so.

The internal development of Aretino's *Dialogues* is interesting from the point of view of the voyeuristic placing of the reader. Nanna's story begins with descriptions of paintings of sexual activities which were in her nunnery. Here we can see the importance of pictorial reproduction in fetishistic sexuality. It is the same importance which led to the earlier *Positzione* and to the permanent importance of visual pornography. Nanna is led to a cell by the Bachelor, with whom she will have her first sexual experience. From chinks in the cell's plasterwork Nanna was able to view the sexual activities in each nun's cell. Finally, after these descriptions, Nanna starts to tell Antonia of her own sexual experiences. The reader is in the position of overhearing their conversation and is moved through a series of decreasingly displaced, and decreasingly remote, voyeuristic experiences. However, just as the reader cannot enter a completed bourgeois reality in the letter novel, so she/he does not reach the moment of absolute displacement/involvement in the dialogue and letter based pornographic works. In both cases, and for the same reason, the reader still has to contribute to the fabrication of the reality, in the process of which she/he is finally positioned.

La Puttane errante, still a dialogue, has, however, a less equivocal standing than the *Dialogues*. This work, published about 1600, was 'the first imaginative prose work which deals directly and exclusively with sexual satisfaction ... It ends with a named catalogue of thirty-five postures'[33] *La Puttane errante* was not rendered into English until very late, 1827, but its importance coming so soon after Aretino's work lies in the focusing in it on sexual intercourse—a focusing which gains in subtlety as the genre of pornography develops. In these early works whores predominate. The inversion of capitalist cultural values necessitated in the acknowledgement of prostitution is analogous to, and serves as a useful justification for, the inversion recognised by the new genre of pornography. The increase in the number of novels concerned with sexual arousal through (re)-presentation of bodies and intercourse is correlative with the development of bourgeois society as a social reality based on sex translated into marriage, where the body has become the site of contradiction. It is this which *Shamela* is a commentary on. However, both *Pamela* and *Shamela* are products of bourgeois society, and while *Pamela*'s realism is based in the creation and repression of sexuality, so *Shamela*, in revealing the repression, places itself (and is placed by its bourgeois readers) as bawdy—only a step away from pornographic. It is within this context that we must place the oft-repeated claim that *Pamela* is the first English novel.

CHAPTER 4

Desire and Worldliness

For a brief period in *ancien régime* France it is not intercourse and the body which are important but the desire for intercourse. In the society of worldliness, sex is no longer tied to noble feudal notions of blood and kinship and lineage, in which virginity and marriage become a real part of the mythology of descent. Nor is it, as it becomes in the truly bourgeois world, the moment which fixes the world of signs to the world of desire. The peculiar combination of feudal and capitalist social structural and economic forms in France enabled displacement to realise and (re)-present itself in the structuring of desire.

Throughout the period of Absolutism the bourgeoisie, and bourgeois ideology, were making inroads into the cultural practice of worldliness. The king positioned himself at the apex of a system which deprived the old feudal nobility of their power based in rights and obligations but which also stabilised and checked the new commercial capitalism. The king achieved this through securing taxation and balancing power between the classes. Goldmann, following Maugis, sums up this climactic stage of absolutism like this:

> In [this] stage the king becomes independent not only of the rest of the nobility but also of the Third Estate and of the *Cours souveraines*. He governs through his *corps de commissaires* by maintaining a balance of power between the different classes, especially between the nobility and the Third Estate, while at the same time justifying his power in the eyes of both classes by arguing the need for a central authority strong enough to put down popular revolts.[1]

What I am suggesting is that the public domain exists as a determining experience of capitalism. It is founded on the individual's understanding of the world as estranged. In England the terms 'public' and 'private' began to take on their modern meanings in the seventeenth and eighteenth centuries, the same period that the novel began to come into existence as a fictional world in its own right. In France absolutism not only held the development of capitalism in check but also emphasised the unity of lived society. As *le monde* was undifferentiated, women were not perceived as objects to be appropriated for the domestic domain but as locations in the structuration of desire. Sexual intercourse was valued as a consummation in its own right. The fixity of the system was not guaranteed through fetishism but by the neo-feudal control centralised in the king.

One consequence of this special development of capitalism lay in the type of literature which was produced. Watt sensed this when he contrasted the history of the novel in France with its history in England:

> In France, the classical critical outlook, with its emphasis on elegance and concision, was not fully challenged until the coming of Romanticism. It is perhaps partly for this reason that French fiction from *La Princesse de Clèves* to *Les Liaisons Dangereuses* stands outside the main tradition of the novel.[2]

Romantic love articulates the problem of bourgeois desire. Romanticism is a celebration of the essentialism of the individual, and is an effect of the success of the construction and systematising of fetishism. The English novel moves steadily towards Romanticism and assertion of essentialism, while the French novel of the eighteenth century tends to deny its own essentialism, its status as a world in its own right, reflecting the denial of essentialism in the culture which produced it. The English novel of the eighteenth century is working towards an essentialism of difference. The concept of fiction is an articulation of that difference. The French novel is grounded in the unity of the culture, of *le monde*. It operates within it as yet another aspect of a seamless unity. This is the reality of La Bruyère's *Les Caractères ou les moeurs de ce siècle*, which was first published in 1688. This book is not a novel; it most certainly would not have been considered as fiction by La Bruyère. It is an attempt to portray the characters and customs of his time. Barthes has written that this 'book corresponds to a kind of initiatory experience, it seeks to reach that supreme point of existence where knowledge and conduct, science and consciousness meet under the ambiguous name of wisdom'.[3] The book is written from within the world and is part of it as opposed to the bourgeois 'sociological' ideal of a book written from outside the world delineating the parameters of its existence. Brooks suggests that La Bruyère's book is able to operate in this way because it was written within a culture and for a readership which was so small that everybody knew everybody else. As a consequence it is able to capitalise on the depth of common experience.[4] I am sure that there is truth in this, but it is limited. The common experience reinforced the overriding unity of Parisian culture. London society of the period was not much bigger—the respective city populations were, very approximately, Paris 450,000 and London 700,000—and yet seventeenth-century English writers were preoccupied with constructing classificatory systems. Bacon's *Novum Organum* is an example. The crucial difference lay in the estrangement of the world.

One example of the constitution of the novel as Other is in the development of plot. Both *Pamela* and *Clarissa* have obvious central plots. By contrast *Les Liaisons dangereuses* is, as its title suggests, a novel of structures. The structures relate different realities, all products of desire. *Pamela* and *Clarissa* use the epistolary form for a purpose, to attempt to construct an alternative but real world. Watt has remarked that French fiction of this period is too stylish to be authentic.[5] *Les Liaisons dangereuses* does not set out to be realistic in this sense; it is a novel of style, of appearance, in a world where appearance not essence is the reality. In this sense it revels in the epistolary style rather than using it to attain another end.

At the end of *Les Liaisons dangereuses* Madame de Volanges writes that the Marquis de ----, commenting on the Marquise de Meurteuil's disfigurement by smallpox, remarked that 'the disease has turned her inside out, and that her soul is now visible on her face.'[6] This last phrase, which has the ring of an aphorism, is exactly that. Two hundred years earlier Erasmus wrote, 'Ce n'est pas au hasard, en effet, qu'il a été dit par les anciens sages: *L'âme a son siège dans le regard.*'[7] Erasmus's work is one of that great flowering of etiquette books which started, inevitably, in Italy with the publication of Castiglione's *Il cortegiano* in 1528. While explicitly Erasmus is denying any gap between public and private—ostensibly the purpose of his book is to put the soul in the face thus ensuring that a gap does not exist—implicitly he must be assuming that such a gap does exist. If it did not, his book would not be necessary. The origins of bourgeois etiquette lay in the Renaissance Courts' preoccupation with the visible.[8] However, the essentialism of bourgeois fetishism and the split into public and private domains turned etiquette into a series of rules governing social, public interaction. Erasmus's concern with keeping individual and social, private and public, behaviour united marks a stage in their separation.

Brooks has noted that 'Worldliness emanates from a nucleus of courtliness'.[9] *Le monde* was constructed in an on-going attempt to keep reconciled the undifferentiation of courtliness and the differentiation of bourgeois public and private behaviour. By the time of *Les Liaisons dangereuses*, published in 1779, the attempt might be summed up as producing a lived hypocrisy. The retention of the old, undifferentiated modes of behaving had, as we shall see, become the necessary practice of ritual.

Louis XIII and XIV redefined power in the new centralised state so that the old feudal nobles of the *noblesse d'épée* retained their position within the system while their actual power was minimalised. The Bourbons were able to achieve this because of the gradual deployment of a money economy. While the *noblesse d'épée* paid a comparatively insignificant amount to the royal revenue by way of direct taxation, they were not absolved from their feudal rights and obligations. Meanwhile under the Contrôleur Général and the *secrétaires d'état*, the *ancien régime* saw the deployment of an entirely new bureaucracy, the purpose of which was to design and collect the taxes which underpinned the new order. One result of this was that the peasants, whose feudal obligations sustained the wealth of the *noblesse d'épée*, were taxed again by the new order. This structure of double taxation was not finally abolished until 1793 at the height of the Revolution. The *noblesse d'épée* found themselves in a new economic structure where their feudal rights no longer gave them access to political power. Instead that power came to reside in the hands of the new *noblesse de robe*, in those of the more blatantly bourgeois *fermiers* who sometimes made fortunes out of collecting the taxes, and in the hands of the *financiers* who advanced money to the Crown to cover gaps between income and expenditure.

However, the social entrenchment of the *noblesse d'épée* provided a kind of anchor which stabilised the old feudal structure in a new economic order. Hence the *noblesse de robe*, most of whom had acquired their nobility through occupancy of governmental positions which entitled them to noble status or through the practice of buying such posts in the judiciary or civil service, regularly married into the *noblesse d'épée*, the former bringing their money and the latter their ancestry. As a consequence the new order was culturally measured by a group who had no economic function in the new system. The development of *mondanité*—worldliness—reflects this. It would be easy to describe *le monde* as a world under siege from the flowering capitalist economy and culture, and while this was in effect what became of it, its original purpose was as a synthesis of the two distinct cultures of the feudal court and the bourgeoisie. Brooks has written that:

> The idea of worldliness emerges from a systematic, closed, self-conscious society, a milieu whose closure to the outside world and internal publicity makes it a theater, a stage for the individual's representations of his social life, and elicits a conception of man as a voluntary artistic self-creation whose social life is the most important fact about him.[10]

The enclosure of the society within a stabilised, monarchical, neo-feudal structure was one key to its success. The other was its ability to persuade itself, and those outside it, that it was the only society. The reality that was appearance in *le monde* could not be counterpointed by a reality of essence. The shifting structuration of desire only served to enhance the reality of appearance. When all of reality is a mirror the concept of distantiation and, therefore, also of confinement, cannot exist. *Le monde* experienced itself as whole, not as confined but as complete. The estrangement inherent in a money-free market economy was not allowed to enter.

Louis XIV had confined the old nobility's public roles to either soldier or courtier, and at the root of the evolving cultural order was the old nobility's antipathy to trade. They defined their culture and the limits of their cultural hegemony in opposition to the new bourgeois concern with work. The contrast shows even in the development of economics. In Britain the movement is to view wealth as a product of industrial labour in a market economy. In France the Physiocrats evolved a theory based on the importance of agriculture, a theory which has haunted French economic policy well into the twentieth century. The culture of the *noblesse d'épée* was a culture which only spent money. The earning of money was not a recognised activity which could be assimilated into the cultural discourse. It would have drawn the nobility out of their neo-feudal existence and placed them in the new capitalist society founded on labour and the burgeoning state's market economy, destroying the oppositional basis on which the culture of worldliness was based. At this point the concerns of the monarchy and of the nobles merged. The Bourbons wished to confine the political power of the nobles. This they did by not allowing the nobility a place in the new politico-economic structure; the nobility on the other hand wished to preserve their cultural identity and hegemony. This they did by founding their culture on the rejection of the very activity which provided the basis for the new system. The effect was that the *noblesse d'épée* made themselves ever more dependent on the largesse of the monarchy, in so doing reinforcing the hierarchical ossification necessary to the functioning of absolutism.

The discursive structuration of the culture of worldliness was not as a rejection of another cultural order but as the articulation of the *only* cultural order. This point is forcibly illustrated in a review by the critic Grimm in 1753 of a novel which is about the love affairs of a young provincial studying law in Paris.[11] Not only do the characters of the novel have no existence in society but, if they do exist in real life, their customs are not those of the nation. The assumption is one which underpins wordly literature: that situations and people outside worldly society are not fit subjects for good art. Art may be tainted by its subject matter, as also it may be by its language—hence the development of the *style noble* and the rulings of the Académie Française. This does not reflect an energising of language but rather an awareness of how language may be utilised to reinforce group solidarity. However, Grimm's problem—and that of the culture of which he was a part—is rather more complicated than this; he has both to acknowledge the existence of the culture which he is rejecting and deny that it can be accorded any claim to legitimacy. This he succeeds in doing by appropriating both the terms *société* and *nation* and claiming for the nation only those customs which come from his culture, *le monde*. Worldliness here is not based on an opposition to bourgeois society but on a claim to be the only culture in the society. The claim of worldly society is that it is of a different epistemological status to other cultural groups. It is a claim not just to a greater degree of reality and truth, but to be the foundation of the only Reality and Truth. It is the customs of the cultural world founded on the assumptions of the *noblesse d'épée* which are the customs of the nation, not those of the majority—the taxpaying population.

Culture and Reality meet, then, in the one legitimate world, that of the Court and its ancillary institutions. The monarchy realises itself as the moment of connection between two otherwise irreconcilable discursive 'realities'. All this, of course, is in marked contrast to the bourgeois literary culture of England, so much so that when Mme Riccoboni translated Henry Fielding's *Amelia* she reclassed the two leading men in order to make them acceptable (understandable?) to worldly society.

The suppression of the capitalist functioning of money and wealth may be traced through the history of worldly society. As Clark has noticed, in early works such as *La Princesse de Clèves*, wealth is assumed.[12] Even when, as in *Manon Lescaut*, wealth is problematised through the ability in capitalist society of losing it, Prevost's aristocratic hero does not consider earning money. It is the *active* aspect of a capitalist market economy from which the worldly culture most wished to disengage itself. It is not work as such which is exorcised from worldly culture as it is in the mythology of bourgeois culture, but the translative power of money as it determines an individual's place in the total system of a capitalist market economy. The reality of appearance of the *ancien régime* was based on the belief that the regime's culture was not based in a capitalist economic order but owed its reality to the monarchy. As a consequence, the fetishisation and the fracturing which are fundamental to the operation of money-based free-market capitalism, were suppressed.

One way of looking at the cultural changes in worldliness during the *ancien régime* is to examine the gradual embourgoisification of its culture while it struggled to retain its fundamental character as a non-bourgeois society. There developed a gradual ritualisation of day-to-day behaviour. In the time of Louis XIV the Court lived an essentially public life; access to the palace and to the king was open to all. This was because, as I have explained, there was no differentiation between 'private' and 'public'. The Bolognese priest Locatelli wrote in 1665:

> I went to the Louvre, where I walked about at full liberty, and, passing through diverse posts of various guards I finally arrived at that door which is opened as soon as one touches it, more often than not by the King himself ... It is the King's wish that all his subjects should freely enter.[13]

The accessibility of king and Court could only be possible in a society where there was a lack of distantiation, an uncritical belief in the social structure and its cultural practices. Locatelli, from Italy, was obviously surprised enough at the French Court's behaviour to comment on it. This is understandable as a century earlier the Florentine Francesco da Barbarino made a similar observation contrasting the 'good-natured friendliness of [Phillipe de Bel's] royal manners to the haughty pride of the Florentine nobles.'[14] Social bourgeois developments during this period, move into northern Europe from Italy. In a Paris where bourgeois development of public and private domains had been checked, Locatelli must have felt he was stepping into the past. In *ancien régime* France, etiquette does not mark the acceptance of a new moral order, and a new reality, but the attempt to preserve the form of the older, undifferentiated order. Thus there is a continuity between Locatelli's ability to watch the public *toilette* of Louis XIV's queen and Marie Antoinette's performance of her *toilette* in public. The difference is that while Louis XIV's queen must have regarded the nature of her *toilette* as quite natural, Marie Antoinette obviously did not. For example, having been forced to stand in complete nakedness one winter's day while the complicated rules of etiquette were observed so that she might receive her chemise, the queen 'bursts into a laugh to conceal her impatience, but not till after saying several times between her teeth: "It is odious! What a tiresome fuss!"'[15]

This world, increasingly penetrated by the practicalities, and practices, of the new market economy, which was, in its turn, increasingly permeated by its ennobled practitioners, nonetheless perceived itself as tied by the monarchy to a different realm. On the one hand we find the emergence of the *philosophes* and the *Encyclopédie*, on the other the desire to preserve an etiquette as real which at one time had had the power of an unreflexive reality. We may note the key moments of that etiquette for they tell us a good deal about the arrival of the private domain: the public *toilette* which was to become a fundamental feature of the life of all courtly ladies must have had little meaning in an earlier time when the body was not fetishised. Locatelli, for example, was able to watch the complete process. By the time of Marie Antoinette, tiered benches had been installed and the whole performance could only be viewed by women, men having to leave after the queen had washed and put on her rouge but before she started dressing.

Brooks described worldly society as a theatre and this it was in the sense that appearance was reality. Questions such as whether somebody was actually dead or merely playing dead were not important. What was important was the effect, the reality produced. It comes as no surprise, then, to know that until 1759 patrons at the Opéra were allowed to sit on the stage and, as a matter of course, interrupted performances. The ritualisation of the *toilette* and the reconstruction of the play as the performance of an illusory reality were part of the same phenomenon. It is possible to find the construction of the play as a mirroring of reality in the historical development of the proscenium stage. This enabled the audience to become the so-called fourth wall. The use of this stage design began in the seventeenth century when it still included a portion of thrust staging and finally achieved full separation from the audience in the nineteenth century. It was this same phenomenon of alienation and reconstituted reality which produced the novel as a work of fiction.

There were three other events which bourgeois society considers fundamentally private, indeed as essential to the maintenance of a legitimised private domain, which the monarchy had to 'perform' in public. These were birth, death and sexual intercourse. To these we must add eating; eating may not be as hidden as the other activities but it is nevertheless viewed as private. The assumption in restaurants that each group would like their own table illustrates this well. The more informal the restaurant, the more likely it is to be prepared to break this taboo. All these activities, together with others such as spitting, defecating and blowing one's nose are subject to strong public taboos. This is because all call the solidity of the body into question. The bourgeois concealed/revealed, fetishised body exists as an object apart from and a part of the world. All the activities listed demonstrate the permeability of the body. It is, merely, a body. But, if this is so, it cannot be fascinating. Then it is not merely a body and these activities must be hidden away, including in the female one I haven't mentioned, menstruation. Its occurrence was often greeted with shock and alarm, and in eighteenth century it was considered so disgusting it was given the euphemistic appellation of 'flowers'. We might say that the fetishistic valorisation of the naked (female) body depends on the suppression of these essential activities.

Birth is not only a 'violation' of the body but is located in its most forbidden part, linking it to that other hidden activity, sexual intercourse, a physical linkage reinforced by medical knowledge. When Marie Antoinette went into labour the cry rang out: 'La Reine va accoucher!' and all in the palace, not just the Court, rushed to be present and witness the birth. This was in all likelihood the last French example of what was originally a feudal authenticating device. Death, too, was a public affair. Aries comments: 'The dying man's bedchamber became a public place to be entered freely. At the end of the eighteenth century, doctors who were discovering the first principles of hygiene complained about the overcrowded bedrooms of the dying.'[16] Aries here is talking of France; in Britain the bourgeois privatisation of death occurs earlier, uninhibited by the *ancien régime*. We need only turn to Clarissa's death for exemplification. Perhaps, however, the event which came to cause most embarrassment as a violation, and therefore assertion, of the private domain and bourgeois morality was the nuptial bedding of the heir to the throne. Padover, for example, recounts how impressed Louis XV was with the young (sixteen) Maria Josepha because when, on her wedding night, Louis XV 'and his court burst into the bridal chamber to bear witness to the consummation, the terrified young dauphin hid his naked body under the blanket while the bride calmly sat up and engaged His Majesty in conversation.'[17] The first act of intercourse becomes a performance, the very celebration of which assures the continuity of a culture in reality denied legitimacy by the ritualisation of the activity.

Only because intercourse, birth, death and eating have become private, domestic affairs is their public performance by the monarchy necessary for the maintenance of the culture of worldliness. After the Revolution, Napoleon, with his bourgeois awareness of the importance of etiquette, considered reviving the practice of *le grand couvert* when the reigning family dined in public.[18] Bourgeois etiquette separates the domains—it does not overturn them. Napoleon could not bring himself to reinstate it. We may agree with Funck-Brentano that, under the *ancien régime*, 'Court life became bourgeois, a kind of family life embellished with sociable friends who amused themselves and each other.'[19] However, at key moments bourgeois family life was discarded in order to affirm the absolute reality of an appearance based not on any contradiction or repression but on an absolute unity of life validated by the actions of the monarchy.

Within this culture the purpose of women was not to define and guarantee the real, as it is in classical bourgeois culture, but to operate as determinates of the desire which came to predominate in the demi-bourgeois culture. Intercourse was not required to perform the same function in worldly society as in English bourgeois society because the determination and fixing of the real was a task performed by the culture's link with the monarchy. As a consequence, desire was not restricted by the bonds of marriage with the attendant importance of virtue and chastity. William Alexander in *The History of Women* (1779) writes about French women:

> As chastity is a virtue which does not seem to flourish in a soil where too much or too little culture is bestowed upon it, we must not expect to find it remarkably vigorous among the French, where politeness is the first of all the virtues, and where chastity would hardly be entitled to a place as the second. ... [There is] general desire of intrigue among the women, and ... little notice taken of it by the men; both of which have established it as a fashion; and in France, not to be fashionable, is a condition much more dreaded than not to be virtuous.[20]

What he is describing to us is the French lack of concern with intercourse, which reflects a male lack of concern with the female as an object (property) as well as fetish. As *Les Liaisons dangereuses* demonstrates, the embourgeoisification, and sexualisation, of *ancien régime* worldliness was experienced simply as a repression whose only link with an otherwise determined reality was in the existential living of that reality of etiquette and ritual (appearance).

The increasing reliance of worldliness on etiquette and ritual coupled with the covert play of sexual desire for its preservation opened the way for a critique of that society in bourgeois terms, in spite of the fact that the society did not view itself in such terms. Thus, for example, even de Sade could not understand the significance of virginity/adultery for the bourgeois mind: 'J'avais quelquefois compris le chagrin d'être cocu après le mariage, mais je n'entendais pas qu'il fut possible de la devenir avant.'[21] Since marriage represented the woman's moment of entry into worldly society, what happened before was not in itself of great importance. Even after entry, deceived and dishonoured husbands in worldly society were rarely given the epithet *cocu*; this term was reserved for the bourgeoisie.[22] All this notwithstanding, by the latter days of Louis XV worldly society appeared close enough in structure for it to be understood and attacked on bourgeois grounds. Thus Darnton suggests, basing his suggestion on extensive reading in the Bibliothèque Nationale and the British Museum, that towards the end of the regime there was an increase in the number and importance of *libelle* literature. Darnton takes as the archetype of this literature of sexual scandal Charles Thévaneau de Morande's *Le Gazetier cuirassé* (1771), a work he sums up as being concerned with 'cuckoldry, buggery, incest and impotence in high places' and which Darnton considers, correctly, may be read 'as an indictment of the social order'.[23]

The other side of this literature of sexual scandal, that which gives it its meaning as literary text, is the gradual sexual charging of the text itself. I have already commented that Mrs Manley and Mrs Haywood in England published works similar in style to the *chroniques scandaleuses* of France. In both cases the works present a heightened voyeurism. The text still refers, transparently, to the real world, but it includes an increased amount of sexual depiction. The world of the text starts to become the eroticised world which is completed in the pornotopias of pornography. In France, as in England, the novel is claimed as women's reading.[24] However, we find two types of reader, or more exactly, two types of work aimed at two different audiences, emerging in the seventeenth century. La Bruyère writes critically of the vogue for works which deal with 'questions d'amour' among the bourgeoisie; in general, works destined for *le monde* would seem to have required a concern with *la politesse* and *la galanterie*.[25] Lough, in attempting to elucidate this distinction, finds it much easier to describe bourgeois reading than *le monde* reading. The reason for this is not hard to find. If the novel form is a bourgeois form, then a worldly novel is pretty much a contradiction in terms. The worldly novel must utilise strategies which are capable of denying the novel's separation from the world such as the epistolary form. Equally it must deny the sexuality which it replicates. Thus the worldly novel may be about affairs of the heart, but it cannot be about love, which was considered a bourgeois phenomenon. Moreover, the worldly novel must not have— or be able to have attributed to it—just that attribute most prized in the bourgeois novel, depth. Depth is a product of the perceived essentialism of the novel as object, fetish. It is a function of its 'world-of-its-owness'. We may now understand why La Bruyère's *Les Caractères ou les moeurs de ce siècle* is the archetypal worldly piece. In the reality of appearance which constituted worldly society the female-controlled *salon* was of major importance. The loss of power by women corresponded to the encroachment of bourgeois society and, in turn, the development of the novel. The essentialism of fetishism replaced the unity of appearance.

In worldly society sexual desire has its end in intercourse as opposed to marriage. We must now turn to the problem of how that desire is experienced. This is what Duclos wrote in the mid-eighteenth century:

> Je ne sais pourquoi les hommes taxent les femmes de fausseté, et ont fait la Vérité femelle. Problème à résoudre. On dit aussi qu'elle est nue, et cela se pourrait bien. C'est sans doute par un amour secret pour la Vérité que nous courons après les femmes avec tant d'ardeur; nous cherchons à les dépouiller de tout ce que nous croyons qui cache la Vérité; et, quand nous avons satisfait notre curiosité sur une nous nous détrompons, nous courons tous vers une autre, pour être plus heureux. L'amour, le plaisir et l'inconstance ne sont qu'une suite du désir de connaître la Vérité.[26]

Sexual desire has become a search for truth—or rather Truth—and, as in the bourgeois patriarchy, women are the repository of the Truth. The difference is that, unlike in bourgeois society, marriage does not function to confine and fix intercourse as Truth. In worldly society Truth only appears in the structure generated by desire. It is guaranteed by the female control of *le monde* in the *salon* system. As Brooks explains in detail, and as *Les Liaisons dangereuses* illustrates, in worldly society where the appearance is the Real, the important thing is to be able to fix that appearance permanently. This is achieved through a person's ability to understand and act upon the nuances of etiquette and ritual which make up the Reality. The greater one's understanding, the greater one's power. This attempt to penetrate and fix the individuals in their appearance is the defining feature of the portraits of the *précieuses*. It is very different, as Braudy[27] points out, from that leading to recognition of the person as individual in bourgeois society. The power of intercourse here exists only in the potential rupturing of the reality of appearance which the revelation of intercourse might bring.

The reality of the woman is guaranteed in her movement from the absolute reality of the convent in which, like Cécile Voulanges and the Marquise in *Les Liaisons dangereuses*, women are educated—a reality guaranteed in its turn by the Truth of the Church—by way of marriage to the realisation of worldly society. Always, however, the convent awaits; the punishment for adultery was a two-year confinement, possibly longer, depending on the husband's whim. This punishment was not just a threat:

> The files of Police Chief D'Argenson reveal that early in the century the high-ranking Duchesse de Mazarin (Marquise de Richelieu) unwillingly entered the Convent des Filles Anglaises, that the Chanoinesse de Bretteville went just as reluctantly to the Ursulines de Chateaubriant and Madame de Montonosency, niece of the Bishop of Montauban, to the Benedictine convent at Issové.[28]

There were others. The Church, then, also stands as a guarantor of the reality of worldliness. Interestingly, the term used when discussing the punishment of adulterous women was *authentiquer*, from the legal term *authentique*, which was associated with Justinian's reform in civil law. Now its original Greek meaning, 'of first-hand authority', can be seen changing in worldly society to its modern bourgeois meaning of 'genuine'. In this sense we may argue, as has for other reasons often been argued, that the Church gave an ideological legitimacy to the *ancien régime*. The position of the Church as outside the developing economic order was reflected in its exemption from taxation until late in Louis XVI's reign. Its convents were used as boarding schools for girls until they were to be married, and as places to which they could retire. The Présidente de Tourval in *Les Liaisons dangereuses* goes to one after her rejection by Valmont. These places of confinement, to become so popular in Gothic fiction, were perceived as extra-social places, a reality from which girls emerged to the reality of appearance in *le monde*.

Having mentioned this, I might just discuss the significance of the Opéra in worldly Paris as a place of assignation. The women who worked on stage at the Opéra were also well known as courtesans. As Lee notes, 'The term "filles d'Opéra" could always provoke a knowing smile'.[29] Brooks comments on the Opéra as it is used in Duclos's Les Confessions du Comte de ****: 'the Opera is a privileged space in a world seen as a theater, an illuminated stage demanding a performance the falsity of which is apparent to the penetrating and informed spectator who sees through the representation to the dissimulated emotion.'[30] (Intercourse in prostitution is another performance—this time desire is not rechannelled or repressed.) It is no wonder, then, that until late the audience was allowed on stage. The only difference (but a crucial one) between the play and worldly society was the acknowledgement that the former was a dissimulation. This acknowledgement reinforced the reality of the lived world. When the Marquise de Meurteuil discovers her social ostracism at the Comédie Italienne, it is an irony lost on bourgeois readers. It is in this context that we can view Diderot's discussion of acting, *The Paradox of Acting*, as a part of the on-going embourgeoisification of worldly society. Equally, we can now understand one reason for the taboo on portraying the clergy on stage; it would have threatened their claim to Reality. The association of acting with prostitution in bourgeois context I will take up in greater depth later.

If we turn now to specific comparison, we find that unlike Shamela, who moves from the world of sex to a sexualised world, the Marquise in Laclos's *Les Liaisons dangereuses* is the arch-dissimulator. Her power lies in her ability to understand the reality of appearances which surrounds her. Her reality lies in the distance this places between her and the world, a distance articulated in her individuality sited in her body, an individuality based not on essence but on non-essence, on dissimulation:

When have you known me break the rules I have laid down for myself or betray my principles? I say '*my* principles' intentionally. They are not, like those of other women, found by chance, accepted unthinkingly, and followed out of habit. They are the fruit of profound reflection. I have created them: I might say that I have created myself.[31]

It is only because of her success at dissimulation that she is able to admit her desire to Valmont. We might usefully compare Shamela on her wedding night with the Marquise on hers:

Who knows where this desire [for knowledge of love/sex] might have led me; with my lack of experience at the time a single encounter might have been my ruin. Fortunately my mother announced a few days later that I was to be married. The certainty of learning before long what I wanted to know subdued my curiosity, and I proceeded a virgin into the arms of Monsieur de Meurteuil.

I awaited the moment of enlightenment with confidence, and had to remind myself to show embarrassment and fear. The first night which is generally thought of as 'cruel' or 'sweet' offered me only further opportunity for experience. I took exact account of pains and pleasures, regarding my various sensations simply as facts to be collected and meditated upon.[32]

For the Marquise there is no reality other than the reality of signs. There is no elusive essence to which the signs may be a key. However, her tragedy is that she must still be fixed, penetrated, by men. In this sense she is still dependent; she can only defer her real—that is, male defined—reality. It is, for her as for the men, a knowledge of the organisation of the signs which allows her the possibility of desire. (Shamela is able to comment on the quality of her intercourse to her mother; in the novel of worldliness nobody comments on the sexual experience itself because, as an act in its own right its importance lies in its repression. It is only important for its signification, and for the French novel of worldliness it signifies nothing except the end of a reality.) In the British bourgeois novel intercourse has a power of signification precisely because of its repression. For the people in this fetishised world where the body/the individual is becoming the site of contradiction and reality, it is desire, which is called love, which is becoming important in structuring the world,[33] and marriage which is important in fixing that structure. In *le monde* marriage and the domestic domain do not have the same importance. The fetishism might be said to be generalised and desire is lived as the key to a meaningful existence based in the playing with appearances.

In Richardson's proto-Gothic novel *Clarissa*, Clarissa's rape is so shocking for the bourgeois reader precisely because Clarissa's drugged state enables the Cartesian essentialism at the foundation of bourgeois individualism to be made explicit through what would seem to be her waking state during the rape. The rape represents a violation of her valorised body. In worldly society penetration refers to an understanding of the representation; in bourgeois society penetration refers to the physical act of intercourse where the body as container is penetrated.[34] Hence, once again, we are returned to the importance of female virginity in bourgeois society.

In London there was never an attempt to preserve the world as an experiential unity. Fielding could write *Shamela* because he could find a legitimate world of meaning, a real world, outside, or rather inside, Pamela. Pamela and B.'s social world is structured by his desire, but also by her virginity, a coupling fixed socially by their marriage. In *Les Liaisons dangereuses* there is not a concern with people as bodies or as individuals in the book nor a concern with marriage as fundamental to the construction of the social world. It is this which forms the link between Richardson and Jane Austen. The constituting desiring structure of the book is that of Valmont for the Marquise. It is in the space of this desire that the novel exists. They have had an affair before, but Valmont wishes to have another. Actually it is a wish for intercourse, as the Marquise explains in a letter to him: 'I am perfectly sure that for a single night we shall be more than sufficient for each other; and I don't even doubt that we shall enjoy it too much to see it end without regret.' The Marquise also understands the importance of desire, if not its origin, in their *monde*, for she goes on, 'But let us keep in mind that this regret is necessary to happiness. However sweet the illusion, let us not believe that it can last.'[35] It is only desire which structures this world; intercourse destroys it. Defloweration here is only an initiation into a reality which exists solely at the moment of its destruction. Marriage is only a mark of establishment, positioning a person in *le monde*. The true reality of this world is the appearance of the object and its signification. As the Marquise remarks of her entry into *le monde*,

> I paid little attention, in fact, to what everyone was anxious to tell me, but was careful to ponder what they attempted to hide.
> This useful curiosity, while it increased my knowledge, taught me to dissemble. Since I was often obliged to conceal the objects of my attention from the eyes of those around me, I tried to be able to turn my own wherever I pleased; from that time I have been able at will to assume the air of detachment you [Valmont] have so often admired.[36]

In this world where appearance is reality, the appearance of desire is love. *L'amour*, as the Marquise understands, lasts until intercourse. From this point on, as she demonstrates in her relationship with Belleroche, strategies must be used to recreate desire. Her promise to Valmont (to spend a night with him should he succeed not only in seducing the Présidente de Tourval but also in gaining a letter proving it) is never kept. It is made as a counterpoint to his statement that after finally succeeding in his pursuit of the Presidente de Tourval, 'Intoxication was complete and reciprocal and, for the first time with me, outlasted pleasure. I left her arms only to fall at her feet and swear eternal love; and to tell the truth I meant what I said.'[37] Valmont's discovery is a threat to *le monde*, where life exists in desire not in an overdetermining permanence.

One of the interesting aspects of Valmont's pursuit of the Présidente is that she is not of his world. She is a bourgeois. Once this is realised her distress at the potential loss of her virtue—to be lost through her unfaithfulness to her husband—becomes much more understandable. For her, love and intercourse with Valmont would be, and indeed are, more real than they are for him. Love is not merely a sign of desire and intercourse; it involves a giving of the self rather than simply the end of desire. The death of the Présidente, delirious and in a convent, is a function of her realisation that Valmont does not love her as she understands the term; although, as we have seen, Valmont comes close. The echoes of Clarissa's death in that of the Présidente may be deliberate;

twice *Clarissa* is mentioned in the book. Once Azolan, who is spying for Valmont, his master, tells him that *Clarissa*, volume I, is one of two books that the Présidente has taken to her boudoir. Once Valmont himself remarks that he does not wish to 'succeed' with the Présidente in the manner that Lovelace succeeds with Clarissa. The Présidente, like Clarissa, is a bourgeois and her death counterpoints the killing of her social reality by Valmont just as Clarissa's death counterpoints the rape which makes an acceptable bourgeois reality impossible for her. For Valmont this would be no success because the body is not important. What Valmont requires is that the Présidente should live in his reality of desire and of appearance. This makes his relationship with her much more complicated than Lovelace's and Clarissa's relationship. Lovelace's background is not so different to Clarissa's that he cannot appreciate her problem. Indeed, precisely because he does understand it he is able to use his knowledge to his own ends. *Les Liaisons dangereuses* might be read as a morality tale illustrating the dire consequences that could attend the involvement of a worldly aristocrat with a bourgeoise.

Love/desire in *le monde* realises the world through its structuring effect. As one of Crébillon fils' characters says on hearing that her love is reciprocated, 'Il me semblait que je commençais à vivre que de cet instant, qui me paraissait le seul heureux de ma vie'[38] It is desire, male desire, which gives life by animating the world. Male desire is potent because, as the Marquise explains, women have to appear passive where appearance is reality.[39] It is the desire for women which structures that reality: 'Je voulais métourdir en vain sur l'ennui intérieur dont je me sentais accablé; le commerce des femmes pouvait seul les dissiper.[40] Without desire there is *ennui*, boredom, a state of emptiness. Desire fills the emptiness, the paradox of intercourse is that penetration recreates it. We should also note that in this French structuration of desire, while the social person is important for the instatement of the structure, the body is only important as the *locus* of desire. Hence Madame de Meurteuil's remark to Valmont about the Comte de Gercourt, to whom Cécile de Voulanges is promised: 'You have been irritated as often as I at the importance Gercourt attaches to the kind of wife he wishes to have, and at the stupid presumption that makes him believe he will escape his inevitable fate.'[41] That Madame de Meurteuil wishes Valmont to seduce Cécile tells us exactly what it is de Gercourt is after: marriage to a virgin, which, as we have seen, is a wish (desire) more in keeping with the bourgeoisie than *le monde*. Knowing this we are now able to understand why Valmont and Madame de Meurteuil find de Gercourt's predilections concerning whom he will marry so irritating.

Desired people are not individualised by their bodies. Just as, though for different reasons, Shakespeare's men and women cannot tell each other apart in the dark, so the pornography of Crébillon fils and of Laclos lies not as in bourgeois society in the detailed description of bodies and of intercourse or its variations, but in the descriptions of desire which disrupt the fetishised world of appearances.[42] Here we may contrast the pornography of *Fanny Hill* based on voyeuristic physicality with that of, for example, Crébillon fils' *La Sopha*. This book consists of a recounting of numerous sexual adventures from the point of view of a person whose soul is trapped in a series of sofas. It describes not the bodies or intercourse but, like *Les Liaisons dangereuses*, the desire which surrounds sex. This is the pornography of *le monde*. In these French works the people only exist in their world when they are structured into that world by desire. I would suggest that under the *ancien régime* there were two types of pornography, each supplementing one of the types of novel discussed earlier. One form of pornography was based on desire and written for consumption in *le monde*. It is illustrated by *La Sopha* and *Les Liaisons dangereuses* and the impact of these works may be measured by their problems with the censors. *Les Liaisons dangereuses* was not actually banned until after the Revolution in 1824, but it was not a book to be read in polite company. The other type of pornography emphasised the act of intercourse and the fetishised body. It was for the consumption of the bourgeoisie. It is this tradition which runs from *Escole des filles*, published in 1660, to *Le Gazetier cuirassé* and on to the Revolutionary works of de Sade.

To sum up, then, we can say that in the French epistolary novel the letters which repeat the desire give it reality. The letters are the structure and, in turn, are the reality—a truth the Marquise learns when the dying Valmont, rather than returning her letters to her, allows them to be revealed to *le monde*. The one who (re)made herself as dissimulation is fixed in the reality of her letters by a man. As if to emphasise this point, Laclos marks the *locus* of sexual desire; her body is badly disfigured by smallpox. The reality now truly is the appearance. The story of the Présidente and Valmont, and her subsequent death, is not the central plot of *Les Liaisons dangereuses*. Unlike *Clarissa* where Clarissa's death effectively produces the novel, in *Les Liaisons dangereuses* the death of the Présidente is a by-play to the central concern which is the socially deadly game played between Valmont and the Marquise. Whereas intercourse in *le monde* destroys a reality which is given existence by the structuration of desire, the bourgeois siting of reality in the sexualised body entails the realisation of individual incompleteness through the impossibility of the practical accomplishment of the bourgeois Romantic mythos of love.[43] The bourgeois belief in essentialism is the other side of the perception of the individual as incomplete. The essence can never been incorporated. It is always Other.

The shift into a classical bourgeois society was accomplished in France for all practical purposes during the period of the bourgeois Revolution which marked the end of absolutism. It is then that the body as fetish makes its appearance, later of course as in Britain, to be fetishistically concealed:

A woman's body under the *ancien regime* was a mannequin to be draped. In the first year of Thermidor, it was undraped to the point of near nudity and became flesh. The *merveilleuse*, the woman of fashion, dressed this way, wore a light muslin drapery which revealed the shape of her breasts fully, covered neither her arms nor her legs below the knees. Audacious women like Madame Hamelin took promenades in the public gardens completely naked, covered only by a thin shawl of gauze. Madame Tallien, the leader of fashion in Thermidor Paris, appeared at the opera wearing only a tiger skin. Louise Stuart wrote from Paris that these 'transparent dresses ... leave you certain there is no chemise beneath.[44]

At this same time de Sade is cataloguing the parameters of bourgeois pornography. I should add that it is not just that the body becomes fetishised during the Revolution. Sexual desire is also given its bourgeois ratification. McManners, for example, writes that:

> Some day a thesis will be written about the French Revolution's naive enthusiasm for sex—about Sylvain Maréchal's Temple of the Hymen, where young lovers kiss the transparent urn containing the ashes of the two most virtuous spouses of the canton, where the only vows are against abstinence, and the only penance is to 'make love again better'; about Fouché's Temple of Love at Nevers where husbands and wives swore eternal fidelity, like Baucis and Philemon ... There was a spirit of sexual release in the Revolution.[45]

There was indeed, but it was a release counterpointed by an emphasis on the fundamental importance of marriage. Maréchal, the anti-cleric, for example, was married in church in 1792. Marriage as preserving the family as the fundamentally important unit is merely transformed; it is not disposed of. The new concern is not with intercourse *per se* but with intercourse as a function of lasting love in marriage. There was the ever-present bourgeois excess of desire which was satiated by the large number of prostitutes who were present in Paris just as they were in London. In the *Encyclopédie* we can see this change in operation. In the secton 'Mariage (Jurisprud)' we find, 'Le mariage est d'institution divine, aussi est il du droit des gens y en usage chez tous les peuples, mais il s'y pratique différemment.' Further on it is stated that 'Le contract civil du mariage est la matière, la base, le fondement y la cause du sacrement de mariage, c'est pourquoi il doit être parfait en foi pour être élève à la dignité de sacrement'.[46] Marriage may be a divine institution, but its sacramental status is determined by the degree of practical success that the participants achieve in living by the civil contract. Marriage is becoming the fundamental contract in a market economy based on contract and ordered by that transcendental contract, so beloved by Hobbes, Locke and Rousseau, among others, which brings society into existence in the first place, namely the Social Contract.

In England by the mid-1790s the female fashion was also a

'flowing see-through style in which women floated about in diaphanous veils with their bosoms exposed or lightly covered, and the contours of the body fully displayed.'[47] In the *Ladies' Monthly Museum* of June 1802 the French fashion was described as 'the close, all white, shroud looking, ghostly chemise undress of the ladies who seem to glide like spectres, with their shrouds wrapt tight about their forms.'[48] On the whole it would seem that the fashionable Englishwoman revealed slightly less of her rather more fetishised body than her French counterpart. It has been suggested that this style was brought to England from France by the famous Parisian dressmaker Rose Bertin, who went to London during the French Revolution.[49] This, however, does not, on its own, account for the success of the fashion there. In England, where the body had by now become concealed, the revelation of it would appear to have been a transient fashion accepted from a Paris pruriently celebrating the female body. Even in post-Puritan England, however, the body was not yet totally concealed. For example, naked female sea-bathing was still permissible.

Most important in this history of concealment was the introduction of drawers for women. In the fetishistic concealment of the body, the most important area to be concealed will be that which produces and realises the woman as female. In bourgeois society the vagina is the ultimate metaphor of confinement. It must be confined but it is argued by patriarchy that it is, in fact, the vagina which confines. (It is B.'s argument, which we have already examined that it is Pamela who has trapped him in marriage not she who will now be confined in the domestic domain.) Drawers, as we would expect, began to become popular in England among the middle and upper classes from about the turn of the nineteenth century onwards. In other words, their introduction paralleled the fashion for bodily revelation.

Their introduction was not altogether smooth. In a book in 1800 a Dr Willicks wrote that 'In High life many women and girls wear Drawers, an abominable invention which produce disorders in abundance.'[50] The wearing of drawers was something else which spread down the social order. In *Public Purity, Private Shame* Pearsall quotes from *The Mysteries of*

Verbena House by Etonensis: 'Peasant women, who are chaste enough as times go, don't wear drawers; and when they stoop you may see the bare flesh of their thighs above their ungartered stockings.'[51] There were two other reasons why the introduction of drawers was not without problems. In the first place drawers had previously only been worn by prostitutes. Whether there was a practical reason for this I cannot determine but certainly it makes sense in the context of the bourgeois system of signification. Coarsely, it amounts to wrapping up the goods. Prostitution was structured into the bourgeois system of fetishism at the moment when desire and capitalism met. In the use of drawers by prostitutes we can see the vagina as fetishised commodity being concealed to stimulate desire. The second reason given for the lack of acceptance of drawers was their connotation of masculinity. Drawers were perceived as being a garment allied to trousers. Their acceptance with this overtone is a realisation of the general truth that the female was being confined by the male. I should add that the origin of the female use of drawers is obscure but it is agreed by authorities in this area that Italian bourgeois women were using them well before their sisters in northern Europe started to use them. It is a sign of the singular social importance of drawers ('knickers' was a word first used in 1881 according to Pearsall) that, from being a fashion, they became an essential and necessary garment throughout the bourgeois world.

From the French Revolution onwards bourgeois society and its literature follow the same fetishistic systematisation in both France and England, a fetishisation constructed in the division between public and private domains. The acceptance of drawers in both countries is a symptom of their subsequent similarity. Drawers also mark the completion of the metamorphosis of clothes from their use as signals of social position to their importance in sexualising the (female) body. In literature the nineteenth century saw the culmination in France of a bourgeois realism typified in the works of Balzac, Zola and Flaubert. During this period the novels of France and England are not only structured similarly but evidence many of the same preoccupations summed up in the generic term 'realism'.

CHAPTER 5

Reality and Displacement

The novel has the choice of either representing the real or articulating the repression on which the real is founded. In either case marriage and the act of intercourse provide the constituting basis of the novel. It is Gothic which utilises the repression of the domestic domain. The horror the bourgeois finds in Gothic is the horror which consists in confronting manifestations of that primary experiential displacement, which, in the normal course of events exists—or does not exist—in the place of repression. Not that Gothic should be classified as revolutionary, or progressive, because it explicates, the displacement; it does not do this. Gothic replicates the displacement rather than replicating the bourgeois ideology which is founded on it. It does not escape the displacement; by utilising it, Gothic provides the possibility for commentary on it.

Tompkins describes the advent of Gothic as being: 'Like a beanstalk, it sprung up overnight into redundant vegetation, and enterprising novelists thronged to its stem.'[1] Walpole's *The Castle of Otranto* was published in 1764 but it is not until the 1790s that Gothic becomes a popular form with Mrs Radcliffe's *The Mysteries of Udolpho*, published in 1794, and Lewis's *The Monk*, in 1795. At the same time, to quote Tompkins again, while 'there is no sudden demand for realism in the seventeen-eighties, and no demand at all for realism unadulterated ... there is a gradually increasing proportion of common-sense ... greater probability of detail ... wider range of character.'[2] In short, there was a steady movement towards that formal realism defined by Watt as being based on:

> the premise, or primary convention, that the novel is a full and authentic report of human experience, and is therefore under an obligation to satisfy its reader with such details of the story as the individuality of the actors concerned, the particulars of the times and places of their actions, details which are presented through a more largely referential use of language than is common in other literary forms.[3]

Thus, historically, we may pair Gothic and realism. Realism may then be viewed not as the expression of reality but the expression of a specific constructed reality, that of bourgeois capitalism founded on repression. This is not a new argument. Leo Bersani and more recently George Levine came to a similar conclusion:

> Leo Bersani, *A Future for Asyntax* (Boston, 1976) sees realism as a strategy to serve society by 'containing (and repressing) its disorder with significantly structured stories about itself' (p. 63). I would revise this by adding that while it struggles to contain what it imagines as monstrous, it also devises the strategies to imagine and release it.[4]

One of the implications of Bersani's argument is the conclusion I have already drawn with the aid of Baudrillard's work; the development of the realist novel marks a completion of the signifying system of bourgeois society. The Other is successfully repressed and literature and society mirror one another as object and object, literature always searching for a more faithful re-presentation. The other implication of Bersani's argument is that if realism represses 'disorder', then the Gothic expresses it. I believe Levine to be closer to the truth when he suggests that the practice of realism carries within it the possibilities for the articulation of the monstrous. However, the argument would seem to suggest that Gothic can release the repression by manifesting it. This ignores the already determined position of reader and text. The text is already an object; it already has a repressed sexuality. The text is already written—and read—as a place of confinement. If, at one end of the spectrum, the realist novel attempts to 'involve' the reader, and by the exposition of a 'complete' world tries to persuade him/her that the containment does not exist and the fantasy is real, then, at the other end of the spectrum, 'pornography' assumes it fantasy involvement by generality. As Marcus puts it, 'although on first inspection pornography seems to be the most concrete kind of writing—concerned as it is with organs, positions, events—it is in reality very abstract. It regularly moves toward independence of time, space, history and even language itself.'[5]

Pornography does not escape repression by writing the socially repressed. It merely denies confinement by a generalisation of the fetishistic formulation of bourgeois realism. In this sense it is equally confined. The female, asexual, text is placed as the literary equivalent of the prostitute, credited with asserting a sexuality which the female is not supposed to have. The involvement of the reader with a pornographic text specifies the reader as confined in the generalised structure evoking specific sexual experiences which even when articulated in the texts are always replications of the Other, the non-existent experience which can only be articulated as repression. Moreover, even as bourgeois society in general considers that prostitutes may only be female so that the client—the person on the active end of the cash nexus, the person with realising power in a society where money is the universal significatory and the structuring device of the fetish system—may determine them by his use of money in a market exchange, so the reader of pornography is inevitably positioned as male in relation to the passive and female text. The conclusion of this argument is that feminist pornography could not exist in bourgeois society. It is a contradiction in terms. That some pornography appeals to some women is indisputable. However, I would argue that these are the women who have most accepted the dominant (male) sexual ideology with its positioning of 'women' as object and, in turn, as fetish. This argument would seem to be borne out by the results of the limited amount of research that has been done comparing male and female attitudes to pornography. Goldstein, Kant and Hartman sum up these results:

> Results ... showed that *all* women reacted more strongly to male pictures than to female pictures, but the ... subjects with greater masculine tendencies had a significant reaction to *all* the pictures representing some degree of nudity. In other words, women who resemble men to some extent in their interests and values will probably respond, like men, to all kinds of erotic photos.[6]

This is not just an argument about that pornography designed to appeal to the heterosexual male but also to the possibility of *any* female pornography. The existence of the text as female inevitably positions the bourgeois reader as voyeur and as male.

This returns us to the problem of the Gothic. Ellen Moers in a perceptive piece called 'Female Gothic' writes:

> We are ... familiar with Victorian cliches about women being by nature (and women writers, therefore, being by right) gentle, pious, conservative, domestic, loving, and serene ... But to confront the long engagement of women writers with the Gothic tradition is to be reminded that its eccentricities have been thought of, from Mrs. Radcliffe's day to our own, as indigenous to 'woman's fantasy'.[7]

Jane Austen obviously felt the same when she wrote *Northanger Abbey* and gave to the heroine the ability to create the Gothic. (Conventional Gothic themes are the stock of Catherine Moreland's fantasies about the abbey.) Gothic exists at a mid-point between realism and pornography. In *Wuthering Heights* it shades off towards the former while in de Sade's works it shades towards the latter.[8] Gothic manifests the forbidden, the monsters of the Other. This is really to say no more than Levine says, that Gothic and realism call each other into being as strategies of literary practice. However, Gothic also is subject to the determination of the text. Gothic does not express repression; it replicates it.

The importance of Gothic as 'woman's fantasy' is, in the first place, as an expressive cathartic cathexis not available in the realist fiction which reproduces reality as fantasy. The escapism of realism is an escape to a more completely objectified world because the individual as reader is collapsed into the generalised narrational third person. The escapism of Gothic is an escape into a Freudian playing with the formulations of repression. In an interesting article on the

different dominant readings which males and females in our
society give to Gothic literature Holland and Sherman
suggest that:

> In gothic, it is the male villain who usually represents sexual desire ... ,
> the villain makes available to [the predominantly female readership] the
> dark, asocial world of fantasy, dream, and the unconscious, a subversive
> attack on the bourgeois values embodied in the heroine ... He ...
> expresses what she dare not, her sexual desires, perhaps even sado-
> masochistic desires, in the gothic paradigm of the young heroine and
> middle-aged sexual villain.[9]

The text is still female and the reader is still positioned as
ideologically male. It is important that, in addition to
suggesting the link between pornograpy and a male
understanding of society, Goldstein, Kant and Hartman
report that the results of available studies indicate that
women in American society require a degree of fantasy in
order to precipitate sexual arousal. By this they mean the use
of a story context in which the female may immerse
(immure?) herself. Here, again, fiction provides the
repressive escape from repression.

Gothic can operate to comment both on the structural
determination of the text and on the repressive nature of
society. Perhaps one of the most interesting examples of this
is the Gothic birth myth because it can be made to operate in
both ways. Moers discusses the production of Frankenstein's
monster in Mary Shelley's story in relation to Mary Shelley's
own experience of pregnancy at sixteen and almost continual
pregnancy for the next five years. Moers identifies
Frankenstein as women's myth-making because the emphasis
of the story is on the trauma of the post-natal period. A part of
the specifically female understanding of the story may be
found in its commentary on birth, the production of
'something' from one's own privatised and valorised body.
However, Moers does not go on to comment on the
transposition of sexes in the person giving birth. At this point
the Gothicness lies in the articulation of a more general social
metaphor. It is men who give birth to society; the writer is
positioned as male. Frankenstein not only creates/produces
the monster—in doing so he creates/produces the story.

Frankenstein becomes the socially produced Mary Shelley just as the monster becomes the articulation of repression. The monster is male, as is the action of repression. We might compare this reading of the story with readings of *Pamela* and *Clarissa*. Richardson (male) creates/produces in *Pamela* the archetypal bourgeois heroine. Clarissa, however, as Mario Praz argues in *The Romantic Agony*, is a Gothic heroine. One important twist of the story is her desire to write her own history. This is something she achieves by her death, which allows her correspondence to be collected, edited and published. Clarissa does not allow herself to be created; she wishes to create herself. From the point of view of the bourgeois reader, Richardson has attempted to usurp the male position as creator and give it to a female, thus creating a 'female' writer and a 'male' text which might assert the reader as integrally female. But a text cannot create itself so *Clarissa*/Clarissa exists as both determined and determining, the text as female and determined, struggling to be really *sui generis* and determining, Clarissa attempting to be male in order to produce herself as a female. In this way *Clarissa* may be read as a commentary on the possibility of the production of a feminocentric novel.

Another birth myth is worth noting here and that is the creation/production of Heathcliffe in Emily Brontë's *Wuthering Heights*. Heathcliffe is a foundling picked up by Mr Earnshaw on a journey to Liverpool. He is birthed into the Earnshaw family from beneath Mr Earnshaw's coat. It is a kind of male Caesarian—a more recent and more literal example of the same myth may be found in the film *Alien*. It is Heathcliffe who then becomes the monstrous Other writing the destruction of the Earnshaws and the Lintons only, in the end, to submit before a female power, Catherine, who must be dead, like Clarissa, before she can control the destiny of the text. At this point it is worth remembering Mr Lockwood's dream when he first visits Wuthering Heights and stays the night. He dreams of a girl, Catherine Linton, excluded from the room but attempting to enter it. Catherine, then, is both child and sexed, as signified by the use of her married name. In the male Lockwood's dream, Emily Brontë is able to express her own repression by creating/producing the independent woman in a unity of child and adult, 'innocence' (asexuality) and sexed marriage, and demonstrate that repression by excluding her from the domestic environment. In the case of Wuthering Heights it is a domestic environment ruled by the male and the monstrous. Wuthering Heights is to Thrushcross Grange what Gothic is to realism. Catherine, who is excluded at the beginning of the book, enters at the end as an Absence to end Heathcliffe's Gothic destruction enabling Emily Brontë to marry her daughter (Catherine) and namesake from the Grange to Hareton Earnshaw from the Heights. Uniting the repressed with the real, they are sent to live, one assumes, happily ever after at Thrushcross Grange in an unrepressed bourgeois idyll. In the context of my argument, this reading places Emily Brontë as a revisionist rather than a full-blown feminist. This does not matter. The book, by its use of Gothic metaphors, calls into question the nineteenth-century understanding of women.[10]

Wuthering Heights will, however, still be read as a novel, as fiction, as the Other, the escapist fantasy which provides the reader with relief from what Wright called 'the strenuousness of her life'. The text is inevitably female and readers will continue to exact vicarious, voyeuristic satisfaction from it. Thus the writer, and reader, is trapped. To write a book accepting the *status quo* merely reproduces the ideology; to write a book challenging it provides voyeuristic cathexis. The nature of the bourgeois reading process determines this choice of apprehension.

In *Pamela*, B. is the guardian of his child by Miss Godfrey. Much can be said about this. In the first place we have an example of the excessive nature of male desire. We now, at the end of the book, have evidence of B.'s overdetermining sexual demands which have from the beginning constructed the text. B. acts as the sole parent, although the child calls him uncle. The child is female and we find explicit the male myth of conceiving/producing the female. The text is not disturbed, the female child aligns itself with the feminine text. By contrast, feminine, Gothic texts give us male creations who come back to rupture the social reality of their texts. I am thinking, for example, of Heathcliffe's birth when he is first brought to Wuthering Heights and of Frankenstein's monstrous' creation. B.'s child in *Pamela* is called Miss Goodwin; she does not have an inherited name, only the name given to her by her mother. The text is rescued from Gothic disruption by a female and preserved as female. Finally, the child's mother has gone to Jamaica—a place external to British bourgeois society and a place whose connotations of sensuality would have, for *Pamela*'s readers, reflected, back on the unchasteness of the woman herself. Jamaica, of course, is the home of Rochester's first wife in *Jane Eyre*. The secret of B.'s sexual excess is kept by B.'s sister, Lady Davers, until she alludes to it in a moment of anger. Still the sensuality of the female remains a secret until Richardson/B. reveals it. It is the climactic excess of the novel. However, Richardson does not disturb the smooth flow of the novel's, and Pamela's love, idyll by this eruption of unlicensed sensuality which is the dark secret of B. and, more generally, the final expression of the secret of the sexuality of the novel. Pamela concentrates her interest on the child, and in the process elides the problem of her mother and, in turn, of B.'s sensuality. As a consequence, the reader is also directed towards the child and away from B.'s sensuality and its victim. Just as, in the end, Lady Davers kept her secret, so too does the text for the uncritical bourgeois reader. The unnamed male threat birthed by a male of the Gothic novel is here safely repressed into a named female with a merely absent mother. Pamela accepts the child and the textual idyll is saved—as, one might add, is the realist novel.

Both Punter and Jackson argue, though from slightly different positions, that Gothic and Fantasy present, or rather re-present, areas of repression in the post-eighteenth-century European *Weltanschauung*. This still suggests that realism is somehow the touchstone. I am arguing precisely the reverse of this: that the realist novel is fantasy, not just in the sense that it articulates a bourgeois ideology but because it has within its own conceptual structure no *locus* of reality except that of the alienation implicit in the omnipotent and omnipresent third person narrative. The acceptance of this use of alienation/distantiation may reasonably be compared with the assumed link in post-eighteenth century science between 'reason' and the scientific method. In England we look to Bacon for this link; in France, to Descartes. Reality from this period exists as a produce of that discourse of sexuality which is simultaneously articulated and displaced. The importance in all fields of the idea of method becomes a metaphor for this displacement; it is, if you like, the distance between articulation and repression. This distantiation is often concretely replicated in the Gothic novel where either the Other, like Dracula, comes from a far-off place or where the story is set elsewhere. Again we find Gothic is a mid-point between the immediacy of realism and the absolute Otherness of pornographic pornotopias. It is, perhaps, more than just intriguing that so many British Gothic stories are set in Italy. The first country to raise a bourgeoisie is also the one which most often in the eighteenth and nineteenth centuries embodies the site of repression. It becomes truly the place of the Other. The focus of this repression may be found, as I have explained, in the conjunction of sexual intercourse and marriage where the former is discursively allied to changing ideas about the body, the individual, the private, and the latter to society (the state), the social, the public.

Foucault has suggested that from the eighteenth century on, discussion of matters which we would call sexual was not so much repressed as rearticulated in other discursive areas such as child-rearing and medicine.[11] The realisation of this has blinded us to the further ramification that post-eighteenth-century 'sexuality' is always already displaced. It is not that sex is simply reclassified, rather sex itself is (re)created and (re)located in the object-full world as fetish. The problematic area of the 'socialised person' forms the meeting/dividing point of the structure fundamental to, and created by, displacement. As a consequence it would be true to say that fantastic literature is more 'real' than realist literature. While realist literature accents the displacement and creates/conceives a sexualised, objectified world which has its sexuality repressed, fantastic literature attempts to displace the realist world onto the primary, transcendentally signifying displacement by utilising forbidden motifs which express that repression. Todorov makes a similar point in *The Fantastic* when he writes about *Louis Lambert* by Balzac and

Gautier's story *The Hashish Club*. They are both 'works that initially offer themes of the self, [and] define from without—as though modelling around a hollow center—this new theme of *sexuality*.'[12]

As the bourgeois world becomes more solid, the horror is achieved increasingly by not articulating the structure of desire which is repressed. Rather the horror lies in the absence as Jackson notes of Victorian horror fiction. With this in mind, if we take Richardson's pair of 'female' books, *Pamela* may be read as realist, indeed as containing the bourgeois love myth,[13] while *Clarissa* may be read as fantastic, indeed as possibly the first Gothic novel. As I have already argued, one example of the repression that inheres in *Pamela* may be found in the large number of 'Anti-*Pamela*'s which were written, including, of course, Fielding's *Shamela*.[14] Not that these works come any closer to revealing what is 'really' happening in *Pamela*; the 'clean' view of the work and the 'pornographic' view cohere in articulating the essential displacement of sexuality in a bourgeois world. However, by comparison there were no 'Anti-Clarissas'. Clarissa as book and person stands astride, structurally and sexually, the displacement which articulates it/her and of which it/her is an articulation.

I have mentioned the importance of method in post-eighteenth-century society. The seventeenth- and eighteenth-century French and English philosphers' concern with reason sought to establish it as the foundation of method, and from there as the basis of human society. Mathematical and geometrical reasoning was justified as being both the foundation of capitalist economics, indeed of the new discourse of economics, and of the social order. It is interesting to speculate on the repression which underlies capitalist economics as a discourse. In Adam Smith's *The Wealth of Nations* published in 1776 the most well-known image is that of the invisible hand which regulates the capitalist economy. This may or may not be a conscious echo of an image which occurs in Horace Walpole's *The Castle of Otranto* (1765). In this story Alfonso, who has been wrongfully killed, returns as an armoured giant and, at the end, forces Manfred, whose line has usurped his own, to reveal his wrong-doings. It may be said that Alfonso is the driving force of the story, and indeed towards the conclusion, more parts of Alfonso's armoured body are revealed to people in the castle. At one point Alfonso's giant hand in its armour is seen by Bianca, a servant of Manfred, on the uppermost bannister of the stairs. Previously, two other servants had seen a foot and part of a leg. At the end the walls of the castle are thrown down and the form of Alfonso 'dilated to an immense magnitude, appeared in the ruins'. Alfonso then announces his true heir and ascends heavenwards. Manfred's confession follows. Smith's invisible hand, implying an invisible person, seems to have the same purpose as Walpole's use of Alfonso. The job of both is to ensure the normal functioning of society. Right at the start of (bourgeois) economic discourse we find recourse to a metaphor of explanation which is Gothic. The difference is that Smith regards the hand as natural and normal while Walpole uses it as an unnatural but necessary intervention to realign society to its proper, just order.

Method, as the structure of reasoning, was experienced as the practical reality of the alienation inherent in the living of displacement. The acceptance of such an understanding of reason in the public sphere underscored as problematical the life of the individual in his/her private day-to-day existence and, of course, the 'character', essentially self-determining, in the realist novel. *Clarissa* confronts this problem for, as Punter notes in a statement with which I can only agree in part: 'Richardson's whole project was founded on an investigation into the emotions, into the strength of those feelings which the rationalist tried to suppress.'[15] Punter's argument is that it is this concern of Richardson's which makes him important as a forerunner of the new non-realist fiction given the name Gothic. However, Gothic and realism are not two different plants, they are both branches of the one tree. Punter has also argued, in the context of Walpole's *The Castle of Otranto*, that 'Walpole's affinities with pre-eighteenth-century writers hinge not on any wish on his part to write like them but on his need to use their example to give himself licence forbidden by realism. Contentual and formal taboos merge.'[16] The mistake lies in considering that, in this case, contentual and formal taboos were distinct in the first place. The repression which underlies and articulates realist fiction is the same which Gothic strives to discover.

Jackson notes that 'The fantastic gives utterance to precisely those elements which are known only through their absence within a dominant 'realistic' order.'[17] However, again, this linkage of realist and non-realist does not go far enough. The primal, transcendental structure of displacement is not articulated by the fantastic because it is the structuration itself which gives the fantastic and the Gothic the possibility of existence; if realist fiction exists as the product of the acceptance of displacement, non-realist may be understood as the interrogation of that displacement. Frankenstein's monster, Dracula and the Alien, to name but three, all provide the necessary Other to question the taken-for-granted reality of bourgeois society. Richardson's concern with the emotions in *Clarissa* does not mark him as not being concerned with the rational, as Punter argues; rather the emotions and the rational each generate the other's existence as articulations of structure. *Clarissa*'s Gothic qualities reflect Richardson's attempt to interrogate the limits of the structure which was his world. It is this, by the way, that enables us to do away instantly with the argument that Lovelace is simply a manifestation of misrule.[18] In ideas of misrule the point is that the practice of misrule is an inverted reflection of the dominant order. Lovelace is more than this; he and Clarissa are both premised on the bourgeois structuration of displacement. It is this which gives the couple their equal realism, and Lovelace's behaviour does not, as a result, exist in its own right for the reader but only as a function of that of Clarissa—and *vice versa*.

Clarissa was published in 1747–8; Hardwicke's Marriage Act was first promulgated in 1753. Both reflect the drastic changes which were occurring in attitudes towards marriage and intercourse. In a now essential paper on *Clarissa*, Christopher Hill draws attention to the increasing importance of property settlements in the developing bourgeois practice of marriage.[19] However, property transfer is only one part of the problem. The shift in orientation from concerns with lineage to concerns with property disguises in a more fundamental shift in the capitalist reorientation of society around what is socially constructed as 'reality' and on what that reality is considered to be based. One sign of the changed importance of marriage was its shift from a predominantly community ritual to an act which, in order to be legitimate, required the acknowledgement of the state. Here we can see how bourgeois marriage, which establishes the nucleus of the domestic domain, requires the sanction of the state as the embodiment of the public domain. In addition to its role as an institution which organises the community, marriage starts to take on an extra symbolic loading. This is not to deny the increasing importance of the property aspect of marriage but more to suggest that what was understood by the term 'property' had been changing with the consolidation of the market economy. Not only did the woman as wife become property but she was a conveyor of property who was not, as wife, allowed to own property. In England until the Married Women's Property Acts of 1870 and 1882 all the goods held by a woman became on marriage the property of her husband. It was not even possible for a wife to make out a will.

Previous to the passing of Hardwicke's Marriage Act in Britain there was much confusion over what constituted 'marriage'. In addition to its task of legal clarification, the Act also shifted responsibility for the execution of the law concerning marriage from the ecclesiastical courts to those of the state. The confusion that had surrounded marriage arose from the perception of it as an act concerned with the ordering and preservation of the community.[20] The conceptual strength of this perception of marriage may be gauged by noting that the Church did not give marriage the status of a sacrament until 1439. Moreover, Church courts had a long tradition of hearing marriage cases where the marriage had not been conducted in church. Previously, the basic form of marriage was by spousal, that is either an agreement between the two parties alone to marry at some future date or an agreement of marriage between the two partners in front of witnesses. The latter form of spousal was generally considered more binding but, one suspects, only because the presence of witnesses made denial harder. It has been argued by Stone that the former spousal type was strengthened by consummation; that is to say, sexual intercourse following the declaration. However, Quaife suggests the firming up of the spousal was probably more to do with practical community problems relating to the upkeep of bastards. Indeed, cases are extant where the reverse was practised; that is to say, where the spousal was nullified if subsequent intercourse did not result in pregnancy, and it is often suggested that premarital intercourse as a fertility test was common. Of course this was a complete reversal of middle-class practices and was probably one factor in the perception of the lower classes as immoral.

The change in attitude to bastardy is a good index of the change in attitude towards marriage. While historically Europe has always had a definition of bastardy, its stigmatisation comes late. As Laslett, following Goody, has pointed out,[21] bastardy is an understandable category when taken in relation to the problem of inheritance. Moreover, the variability of the definition is always in relation to the community's definition of what constitutes marriage. Bastardy, as a practice in medieval Europe, was unsocial because of the drain on the community's resources when it came to upkeep. This was not a stigmatisation of bastardy *per se* but was a reflection of the obligations which were considered incumbent on married couples. However, provided upkeep was acknowledged, bastardy does not seem to have carried its modern stigmatisation. We might, for example, refer to the French ruling classes where bastard children were commonly brought up by the father along with his legitimate children. The most famous example is that of William the Bastard, conqueror of England. Stone suggests that as late as the sixteenth century in England, 'husbands felt free to take lower-class mistresses and to beget bastards without any sense of shame and any attempt at concealment. The children of these unions were frequently mentioned in wills and open provision made for their upkeep and education.'[22] However, with the new Puritan attitude towards marriage, bastardy comes to be stigmatised *in its own right*. The cause, though, is not Puritanism, for in France, too, there was a general tightening up of attitude towards bastardy.

What seems to be occurring is that as marriage becomes the point of contact between the state and the nexus of social reproduction, so bastardy becomes not so much a possibly unsocial act but more a political act. To view bastardy in a non-commital manner would call into question the paramount role being given to marriage and its hidden other, intercourse. Moreover, bastards become a living acknowledgement of the lack of success in keeping desire harnessed within the domestic domain. The fear of conceiving bastards was a much more important check on illicit intercourse during a period which did not have our modern range of, and access to, contraceptive devices. The social stigmatisation of bastardy *per se*, then, becomes a function of the ideological importance of marriage.

The absoluteness of marriage in bourgeois society creates the family as the *locus* for an internalised set of desires. The intercourse which is legitimated by marriage is repressed and the illusion of the domestic sphere is that the satisfaction of desire in marriage—something insisted on by Puritans and Jansenists alike—creates the domestic sphere as an area of life free from desire. Incest, then, is the functioning of an illicit and, from a bourgeois point of view, illogical desire. As Deleuze and Guattari have pointed out, the Freudian myth of the Oedipus complex functions precisely as a commentary on the creation of desire and on its function within the bourgeois family.[23] This gives us the key to the importance of incest in Gothic fiction.

The public nature of marriage in its new guise was replicated in the public form of its celebration. Marriages were no longer legal with purely verbal contracts; they had to be written down, registered with the state. Marriage, then, shifted from being a reinforcement of the community and an assertion of community order, to being the most important point of connection between the imposed law of the state and the day-to-day lives of the people. Those lives were conducted in the new private domain, an arena defined in opposition to the public domain of the state. In the process of this shift the significance of sexual intercourse was altered. Simultaneously, Hardwicke's Act gave sanction to the new capitalist understanding of the woman not just as the bearer of property but as object and property in her own right. Foucault has commented that:

> Perhaps the emergence of sexuality in our culture is an event which has several levels of meaning: ... it is (among other things) linked to something which is still obscure and tentative—a form of thinking in which an interrogation of *limits* replaces a search for totality and in which a movement of transgression replaces a movement of contradictions.[24]

Marriage became the outward, public sanction for intercourse, legitimating the private sphere in terms which gave it a matching continuity with the public while removing from sight the activity itself. Bourgeois sexuality thus implies an interrogation of limits because its generation at the moment of unity and separation of the two capitalist spheres of influence is what articulates the two domains as Real.

The pansexuality which Freud saw in society is actually the pansexuality of bourgeois capitalist society. The lived experiment of the expression and repression of sexuality is of displacement, of an absence which the person is always trying to fill. This is the experience of the Romantic individual. It is, as we shall see later, Werther's problem in *The Sorrows of Young Werther*. The counterpart of this absence is the certainty of an individual essence which may be called Other but which can never be known and assimilated. The knowledge of oneself as having an essence is always the knowledge of oneself as other.

Lacan has noted that:

> In any case, man cannot aim at being whole ... , while ever the play of displacement and condensation to which he is doomed in the exercise of his function marks his relation as a subject to a signifier. The Phallus is the privileged signifier of that mark in which the role of the logos is joined with the advent of desire.[25]

We should not take Lacan seriously; the individual in capitalist society aims at nothing except being whole. It is, as Lacan well knows, the achievement of that aim which is impossible because it is the aim itself which is brought into existence by, and which may be said to be, desire.

Lacan describes the primacy of displacement when he

writes that it is 'as desire of the Other that man's desire finds form',[26] and it is the Other which is the *locus* of the signifier. As he says elsewhere of the Other:

> the subject has to emerge from the given of the signifiers which cover him in an Other which is their transcendental locus: through this he constitutes himself in an existence where the manifestly constituting vector of the Freudian area of experience is possible: that is to say, what is called desire.[27]

The reality of the signifiers, which is a function of the Reality of the Other, exists as the articulation of the absolute structure of sexuality in capitalist society. In Baudrillard's terms it is the completion of the systemisation of fetishism. Both Foucault's understanding of the problem of 'limits' in sexual society and Lacan's notion of the Other are manifestations of this generative displacement. It is not that Freud's, and Lacan's, work is wrong for other societies, it is rather that the full plenitude of meaning is only realisable in a fully sexualised society where desire is, in a total sense, the desire for the absolute Reality of the subject as fetish. This is a desire impossible of fulfilment as Goethe shows well in *The Sorrows of Young Werther*.

In the mirror stage Lacan postulates precondition for the individual's placing as a person in society. The importance of this stage lies in its existence as the moment when the individual both loses and gains him/herself:

> [The] jubilant assumption of his secular image by the child at the *infans* stage, still sunk in his motor incapacity and nursling dependence, would seem to exhibit in an exemplary situation the symbolic matrix in which the *I* is the precipitated in a primordial form before it is objectified in the dialectic of identification with the other, and before language restores to it, the universal, its function as subject.[28]

In its necessity for the functioning of Lacan's general theory the importance of the mirror stage far outstrips empirical questions about when babies first view themselves in a mirror and what happens when they don't, much as the importance of the Oedipal complex in the functioning of Freud's theory forced him to shift from a claim that the paternal seduction was empirically real to a claim for its symbolic reality. Lacan's problem is to create the human as individualised when she/he is decentred and awash in the symbolic order of language. The mirror stage gives him/her (both Lacan and the general individual) that moment of structure when she/he is realised as *I* and Other, while Lacan's Imaginary order may be identified as the on-going activity of mediation, which (literally) makes up a person's life. The problem with the mirror stage is that it is overloaded; Lacan forces his individual to make him/herself alone in his/her Cartesian fullness. But the individual in bourgeois capitalist society is the member of a family, if not of a 'real' one then always of one which approaches or substitutes for a 'real' one.

Shorter's argument, in *The Making of the Modern Family*, is that the uniqueness of the bourgeois family lies in its separation from other aspects of society. Whereas the medieval *domus*, based on a material place, contained a variable number of related and non-related people from grandmothers to servants and apprentices, society and family interpenetrating in a manner so complex that no distinct line may be drawn, the modern 'nuclear' family is clearly demarcated as consisting of mother, father, children and other, specifically acknowledged kin. The society becomes Other to the unity of the family. Thus we may argue that the Lacanian mirror stage is itself a part of a structure, that of family/society, which is a lived but ideological experience. The recognition of the individual as *I* is dependent on, and a function of, the family as a unit—subsequently, of course, challenged and its strength thus affirmed in the Oedipal complex.

Lacan has spent some time talking of anamorphosis in relation to sight—his chosen example is Holbein's 'The Ambassador'.[29] He might have been better employed remarking on the peculiar vogue for convex mirrors in bourgeois households. The endurance of these mirrors may be illustrated by the early example in Van Eyck's painting known as the Arnolfini portrait. The convex mirror throws back the adult as Other and as *social*. The magnification of the image which is the result of convex mirroring is one articulation of the individual's giantising of his or her social world. It also emphasises the 'objectness' of that world of products. The bourgeois society is perceived as predatory on the domestic environment, the only environment in which the individual can relax and 'be him/herself'. This phrase, in common use in Britain, demonstrates the taken-for-granted assumption that the individual does indeed have an essence, and one which is congruent with the domestic domain where the individual can act naturally. Of course the true structuration is somewhat different with the domestic environment parasitic on the socio-economic reality of the bourgeois public world. The family recognises itself as a haven in an unknown (or misknown) world. The family, given birth in the domestic private sphere by capitalism, perceives itself as the defender of the individual and the Real against the encroachment of the public, capitalist sphere. The *I* thus precipitated is therefore a historical *I*, both Cartesian and Freudian, and, in day-to-day practice, Individualist. Moreover, this *I* is articulated with reference both to itself as other and to society as Other, both these Others comingling because the individual is social.

To exemplify this experience from the realism of Gothic fiction, we may take that figure so beloved of bourgeois mythology—Frankenstein (so beloved that a checklist gives sixteen feature films as having been made in America and England which make use of the name 'Frankenstein').[30] In his discussion of the book Brooks writes, 'In the narrative situation of the Monster facing and speaking to his creator, we have an instance of what we might call, in the terms of Jacques Lacan, the imaginary versus the symbolic order.'[31] Meanwhile, Daniel Cotton, elsewhere, suggests that the 'physical monstrosity of Frankenstein's creature is related to problems in the representation of man as a species, a social figure, an individual, a creature of reason, and a being in the contexts of science and political economy.'[32] Both are agreed that Frankenstein's creation/production is the Other. However, for Brooks, following Lacan, the monster is a personal Other residing in the Imaginary; for Cotton he is a social Other reflecting, like the convex mirror, the threatening, giant Other of society. The monster is both, just as Superman is both Clark Kent's Other and the society as Other looking after the individual and defending the family life that Frankenstein's monster attacks. For the bourgeois reader the horror of *Frankenstein* is analagously constructed to the construction of the comfortable reassurance that the bourgeois gains from *Superman*. For the bourgeois for whom the Other holds all that is repressed, the mirror which signals the Other has become a thing of mystery fraught with danger. Alice, remember, actually went through the looking-glass. The medieval metaphor of the *speculum*, which suggested that in a unified world everything partook of everything else, is transformed in the bourgeois world where the mirror becomes a metaphor of difference. In *The Monk*, for example, Lewis has Matilda give the lecherous monk Ambrosio a mirror in which he, and the reader, is able to watch Antonia undressing for her bath. The mirror here has magically become the window for voyeuristic lust. We should not forget that a part of vampire mythology is that vampires do not reflect from mirrors. The mirror constructs the self as Other; it does not enable the Other to become a part of social reality. Bourgeois society requires that the Other remains different. In this context we must not forget that the realist novel is often considered, as Stendhal suggested, to hold a mirror up to nature.

Since Ian Watt's book on *The Rise of the Novel* it is standard practice to associate the development of the novelistic form with a particular notion of realism based in objective description. The *locus classicus* for this is Defoe's *Robinson Crusoe*, but Richardson's work with its minute description of individuals' feelings (sentiment) does for people what Defoe does for 'objects'—or so Watt would have us believe.[33] The problem is that this understanding of realism is predicated upon the assumption that the alienation inherent in giving 'reality' to material appearance is normal. This alienation leads also to a shift in understanding of the composition of the 'people' who inhabit the new externalised world. Cixous describes the development like this:

> The ideology underlying (the) fetishisation of 'character' is that of an 'I' who is a *whole* subject (that of the 'character' as well as that of the author), conscious, knowable; and the enuciatory 'I' *expresses himself* in the text, just as the world is *represented* complementarily in the text in a form equivalent to pictorial representation as a simulacrum.[34]

The 'character' as individual is called into being by the alienating action which articulates him/her to the reader as different, as Other. It is the opacity of the realist novel which gives the bourgeois reader an illusion of depth where 'characters' may be read as being the signatures of personalities. 'Characters' appear to be knowable as personalities precisely because of their creation as objects fetishised by the displacement which is desire. The Reality of the realist novel, its acceptance by the reader as a meaning structure coterminous with the reality of the world in which she/he lives, lay/lies in the acceptance of the underlying displacement as taken-for-granted, as natural and, in the end, as real in its own right. It is, after all, only very recently that Freud's work has been suggested to be historically specific.

I have suggested that realist works are, in reality, works of fantasy. Warner[35] has, correctly I think, explained how *Clarissa* is a book without meaning and how it may be read as a book constructed by Clarissa the realist/fictional individual. *Clarissa* and Clarissa are at the same time unified and displaced by the sexualised writing/reading in a constructed, fetishised world. If one problem of *Clarissa* may be read as Clarissa's attempt to be an individual, then simultaneously the book operates to deconstruct that individuality. One place from which to start an examination of this problem is Clarissa's name. In general the problem of names in the book is an interesting one. Watt suggests that while Richardson bowed to the tradition of giving names which signified the type of person, he utilised names as significations of individuality.[36] In fact, the problem is more complicated than this. While Richardson places himself solidly within the tradition of apposite rather than opaque naming, he does this by giving individuals names appropriate to them alone as individuals rather than by giving them names which fitted the characters into generic types. Not only does Lovelace's name 'mean' something (this is picked up from his association with Restoration drama figures) but all the names of the major protagonists are, in this sense, transparent. The list runs from Morden, whose name marks him as the carrier of death—a death deferred from the duel, which James, Clarissa's brother, loses at the beginning of the book—to Dorcas, whose name is taken from the Bible and signifies a doer of good works. Morden the carrier of the end of the male signifier and also of the confinement which presages the end of the novel, is in fact also the only person whose name is not an ironic commentary. Clarissa lives a life governed by dissimulations through which she is unable to see. The transparency of her name gives it a remarkable (and no doubt from Richardson's point of view, ironic) opacity, while the house/brothel in which she is confined and raped is run by a Mrs Sinclair; a name which more plainly, and yet for Clarissa so opaquely signifies her real role, would be hard to find.[37] Dorcas too, of course, deceives Clarissa. The good works she does are, in fact, for Lovelace.

In this list we should not leave out Arabella, whose skin-deep beauty causes such confusion at the beginning of the book, or Clarissa's confidante Anna, whose surname, Howe, amply expresses her inquisitional role. Lovelace himself though, the dominant male real-iser of the book, carries the most ambivalent name. He may well attempt to fix reality through his sexual penetration[38] of Clarissa, but his reality can only be fixed in relation to her; is he 'loveless' in the active or the passive? The metaphorically blind Clarissa cannot tell, and because she cannot, neither can the readers. These names are not, in the normal use of the term, allegorical. The people concerned do not represent types. The 'meaningfulness' of their names gives them a transparency in the bourgeois world of objects and presents an ironic commentary on the action which once more opens up the structure of displacement. These characters are not individuals inhabiting a fictional world; they are names dependent on the other name *and* the reader for their meanings—dependent, of all the characters, on the one confined by a bourgeois world of appearance who cannot tell (in the full sense) when that world is real(ist). Hence the irony of their names. This is an important point because it bears upon the changing usage of names in the developing bourgeois society.

The modern association of a person's full name with the identity of that person as an individual[39] is a development which we can see occurring in the early bourgeois period. In both France and Britain the aristocracy used a system which ensured the continuity of their titles. Basically this was brought about by an association of the title not with a particular line of descent but with an estate. Title and land went together; in the later period of the *ancien régime* hereditary titles went with particular positions in the government service. Flandrin has demonstrated this complex intermeshing of descent and title/land with respect of France.[40]

This tie of name with land becomes more understandable when we remember the late medieval manner of defining a family as being composed of all the members of a specified domicile. One would be known not by one's family name but one's estate name—what Flandrin rather confusingly calls the name of one's paternal house. Hence what was important was the continuity of the place name. When it is remembered that untitled—and non-estate owning—peasants used an analogous system the reason becomes much more obvious. In an immobile agricultural society, what is important is not an individual's social position with respect to the rest of the population but a system which made sense of, and gave continuity to, land transferral. Moreover, in a pre-money- and pre-market-economy society the unity of the family group and their land was unsundered by the fetishised reality of a market evaluation. People did not 'own' their land; people and land intermeshed in what, for us, consists of an overlapping of concepts. The only name which truly 'belonged' to a person was that given to him or her when they were christened. However, the true process was a movement in the other direction. Christening was a major sacrament (unlike marriage) which brought a person into the Christian Church and designated him or her as a member of the society understood to be generally coterminous with the Church, *societas christiana*. One's Christian name, then, gave one a place in God's order; it did not assert a person as an individual. An interesting demonstration of this may be found in the period immediately following the French Revolution. During this period of dechristianisation, the designation of a child's forename was not solely a matter of choice; it was a reflection of the parents' ideological commitments. Thus, as McManners has pointed out,[41] among the *sans-culottes* of Paris the names Brutus, Marat and Peletier figured prominently as their children's forenames.

The rise of the bourgeoisie entailed a complete change in the attitude towards names. Giving to a firm one's own name does not make for the same unity with the person that is present in estate names or those given to one because of one's occupation, such as Carter or Wheelwright. Names became the sign of the person as individual and as a member of what was perceived generally as a limited kinship system, the nuclear family and its immediate relations. This can be illustrated by the modern example of referring to a family as 'the Douglases' or 'the Davises'. The encroachment of bourgeois society, and the realist novel, can be seen in the way Laclos takes a leaf from Richardson's book and gives his characters names which resonate with their personalities. Having already noted in the introduction that the Marquise de Merteuil's name suggests her ability to use the fixing eye of death which eventually brings about her social death, I will just add that Madame de Rosemonde's name is an obvious echo of her position as repository of wisdom in *le monde*, as she also becomes the literal repository of knowledge when the Chevalier Dancerny sends her Valmont's entire collection of letters. Madame de Rosemonde, by suppressing the contents of the letters, preserves the reality of appearance. It remains, for all who deserve it, a rosy world.

In Britain, the new attitude towards names developed faster than in France. In novels the opacity of names reflected the essentialism being granted to individuals attributed to the text. A parallel may be made with how today we assume each person has an idiosyncratic way of signing their name—of signalling themselves as an individual essence. Through the feudal period when different scripts were used for different purposes, people used signatures appropriate to each script. The bourgeois signature brings together the expression of individuality as an aspect of writing and the expression of individuality inherent in the bourgeois name. The name in a novel signals an individual who exists only in the novel. The reader conceives the individual in the linear and constituting process of reading.

The new debate centres over modes of address. Stone, in

commenting on the British eighteenth-century development of the companionate—that is to say, sentimentalised—marriage, notes that 'More concrete evidence of change is provided by the abandonment in many circles of the formal seventeenth-century modes of address between husband and wife of 'Sir' and 'Madam', and the adoption of first names and terms of endearment.'[42] Names have become important as designators, not of rank, but of familiarity. Names now signal the person as individual with one's surname being more formal because it is more general as it refers to one's family, and one's Christian name designating one as unique, and being, therefore, more intimate. Names, then, come to focus in from the family to the individual. In bourgeois society an individual's name locates him/her as a person, indeed as real. The loss of one's name loses a person their claim on the social world. A modern example of this may be found in the often enunciated fear that as computers take over, individuals will be given numbers rather than names. In Gothic novels we can now understand why the carrier of the repressed so often goes unnamed. The classic example must be Frankenstein's monster which is so often mistakenly familiarised—in both senses of the word—by people who think that it/he was called Frankenstein. Once again the modern film *Alien* gives us another example. If we return to *Wuthering Heights* we will note that Heathcliffe has no second, family name. He is, if you like, only half-human, which is to say half-real—even the name he has refers not to the domestic but to that Romantic Other, nature.

For the eighteenth century the debate was around the organising of this new order; who should call whom what. In his fiction Richardson very often takes the problem further by interlinking the name and the character. The uniqueness of his characters is asserted, and their functions as pieces in an *exemplum* proclaimed, by the use of names which have no allegorical heritage and which appear to give the characters the opacity of real individuality while giving them a general quality through the use of names which could be taken to 'mean' something. In some later Gothic fiction such as *Vathek* names become important as opaque signifiers of strangeness. This may be found in the use of Eastern or

Italian names. In *Clarissa* the bourgeois namings which aid the opaque appearance of individual objectivity are, at the same time, transparent signifiers of a displaced Other.[43]

Another aspect of naming in novels of the period is the large number having names as their titles. All three of Richardson's novels are named after their main protagonists while Fielding not only wrote *Shamela* but also *Joseph Andrews*, *Tom Jones*, and *Jonathan Wilde*. Defoe wrote, among other novels, *Robinson Crusoe*, *Moll Flanders* and *Roxana*, and we should not forget Sterne's *Tristram Shandy*. This list is a collection of some of the most well-known titles. By no means all novels of the period linked character and title but many more than would be suggested by chance and many more than would be the case in the nineteenth century. If names signal the veracity of people, then when a novel is given a name it partakes of the veracity which readers, suspending disbelief, give to the characters contained within it. In other words, giving a novel a name reinforces the inappositeness of making a distinction between real and fictional.

Titles are one element in the confinement of the text. Similarly, the bourgeois opaque name does not sum up the individual; it confines him/her. The bourgeois illusion is that naming frees an individual; it is the same illusion which suggests that titles are gateways into unrestrained worlds. In both cases the name is a (re)presentation of the fetishised object. The importance of repression in the construction of bourgeois reality is articulated in the significance which the figure of confinement takes in the construction of bourgeois literature and in the contents of that literature. In *Clarissa* Richardson problematises bourgeois sexuality and does so by utilising the new significance which bourgeois society had given to confinement. There is, it should be remembered, only one act of coitus in the novel and that is a rape. Clarissa is one of the longest novels in English and one aspect of its Gothicness, as has been well examined by Doody,[44] is to be found in the motif of confinement which runs through the work: Clarissa confined first by her parents, then by Lovelace and finally by her coffin, and all the time asserting herself as a mind confined by body. She is also confined in writing by Richardson, the male writer.[45] All this confinement focuses on her body and in the process sexualises it as Other, as object/fetish in structured opposition to 'Lovelace' who generates the confinement as the patriarchally dominant male. Perhaps it is necessary to say here that patriarchy is not a product of bourgeois social order but it has been appropriated and reworked by that order.

One way of understanding the change in the discursive understanding of confinement is to look at its history. The phenomenon of confinement was not new. The act of locking away individuals whom the state considered had transgressed the law lies, in origin, well back in the early Middle Ages in Western Europe. In England the first documentation which refers to incarceration as a form of punishment may be found in the laws of Athelstan (925–39). However, the acceptance of imprisonment as a way of dealing with malefactors did not occur until about the time of Henry III (1216–72) and was not consolidated until Edward I (1239–1307).[46] Compared to most societies even the act itself, without its later discursive connotations, was unusual. If we turn, for instance, to Gluckman's work on law in societies studied by anthropologists we find that confinement is not an option.[47] In such societies reparation is not made to an alienated state but to the offended lineage within the group. The alternative to such reparation is the exclusion of the offending member from the group. This may be accomplished by death. This is not the death of reparation (a hangover of which we find in the vendetta) but a method of ridding the society of a person who is a threat to the society and, being now outside it, may be destroyed. The advent of the option of confinement evidences a change in the rules of this game. If previously reparation was aimed at preserving a harmonious functioning of parts within a taken-for-granted social order, confinement reflects the awareness of the physical limits of the social order by physically partitioning individuals within but away from it. The correlative of this idea is the increased use of banishment in the later medieval period.

The gradual solidification of state frontiers was reflected in the gradual concentration and hierarchisation of power in the 'state' as an administrative and executive body and in the consequent development of the European idea of the nation-state. We cannot, then, say with Foucault that 'In England the origins of confinement are no more remote [than in the rest of Europe]. An act of 1575 covering both "the punishment of vagabonds and the relief of the poor" prescribed the construction of *houses of correction* to number at least one per county.'[48] This does not represent the origin of confinement as a practice but rather as an extension of confinement from transgressors of the law to groups now perceived as transgressing the encompassed social order. What we have is a new positioning of confinement based on an assumption of the socialness and essential humanness of all people. The limitations which are articulated in confinement are the metonomic presentation of all the other differences which are coming into being during this period: individual/society, public/private, public/domestic, and most important, the new definition of male/female. All these require a common factor which will give validity to the structuring of difference. It is this which sexuality brought, providing a fetishistic base for the developing market economy. I have earlier quoted Foucault as suggesting that the new sexuality lacked limits. We are now able to understand how this may be the case.

The notion of confinement is an idea of exclusion which demands in the first place an assumption of inclusion, and then spills over to include the new attitudes towards intercourse as created in the fetishisation and repression of the sexualised body. A common metaphor for the body became the prison. John Donne, for example, in the early seventeenth century wrote in 'The Progresse of the Soul' of 'Prisons of the flesh'. The voyeuristic nature of the confined and hidden criminal is confirmed by the late-eighteenth-century obsession with hiding the criminal and observing him/her. The most well-known example of this new concern is Jeremy Bentham's plan for a new prison structure called *Panopticon*, in which, as its name suggests, all the prison's inmates would be open to the view of one central supervisor.

This new confinement is not an exclusion of the person from society; it is the assertion of the essentially social position of the individual. This new understanding of confinement is coupled, as Foucault has pointed out, with a shift in the nature of crime. The majority of crimes become no longer the effect of large gangs of ex-soldiers or deserters but change to become the individual act of property appropriation.[49] We might add that this new crime is crime exercised within the social order, and it is the system of commodity fetishism which gives meaning to these crimes. The new criminal works within the assumptions of the state-encompassed social order.

Clarissa is a figure of this new understanding of confinement both as the novel *Clarissa* and as the character in the novel. Gothic texts comment on their own otherness, their own confinement, and it is this property of *Clarissa* to which I now want to turn. The book itself is Clarissa in a way that character and book are not co-substantial when considering *Pamela*. In *Pamela* book and character form a structure isomorphic with, and the same as, the structure of sexual (dis)placement within which they operate. In *Clarissa* the work itself (re-)presents the displacement and, in doing so, spreads out to contain the world pivoted upon the rape. As *Pamela* demonstrates, marriage (and bourgeois legitimated coitus) reproduces bourgeois reality from the inside. Clarissa's rape is not simple intercourse with a person against their will; it is experienced by Clarissa as a violation of her individuality as physically manifested in her body. The inescapability of bourgeois sexualised reality is validated by its transgression. Clarissa's rape is not outside the socially constituted reality; it is experienced by her as an articulation of it. Rape and 'legitimate' intercourse in bourgeois society become two sides of the same coin. Intercourse, as the assertion of male-created sexualised reality, cannot occur as rape within marriage.[50]

Pamela turns about Pamela's and B.'s marriage. The social displacement of intercourse in *Pamela* reflects the sexual displacement and the writing opens a structure for the bourgeois love idyll and, simultaneously, accusations of dissimulation. In the Gothic fantasy it is the structure of displacement which is the absence often articulated as chaos. *Clarissa*/Clarissa succeeds only in encompassing that displacement. Whereas the writing in *Pamela* replicates and articulates the structure of displacement and, in doing so, becomes transparent (clear) to the reader who takes it for granted, in *Clarissa* the writing becomes more opaque. Pamela, like Clarissa, is abducted but when B. tries to rape her, unlike Clarissa, she faints. B. then halts in his attempt. It is as if the fainting is a metaphor for the suppression of the repressed aspects of bourgeois sexuality. The climax of the novel is deferred until it can be suppressed by the act of marriage. As Clarissa moves towards the (sexual) climax, the temporal disjunction between action and description increases and, indeed, when Clarissa finally describes the events which surround the coition, the act itself is not described:

> I remember I pleaded for mercy. I remember that I said 'I would be his—indeed I would be his to obtain his mercy. But not mercy found I.' My strength, my intellects failed me—And then such scenes—followed—O my dear, such dreadful scenes!—fits upon fits (faintly indeed and imperfectly remembered!) procuring me no compassion—But death was withheld from me. That would have been too great a mercy.[51]

Of course, were it to be described Richardson would, in bourgeois society, run into accusations of pornography. What is not suppressed for Clarissa remains so for the reader. A question which must be asked is at what point the writing/reading of *Clarissa* becomes the writing/reading of *Fanny Hill*. Richardson is caught in the paradox of bourgeois society—how to express sexuality without sexual overtones. The temporal displacement is finally replaced by a real (written) displacement. The one event upon which, in Clarissa's and Lovelace's socially constructed reality, both are in substantial agreement, and out of which in general terms, their reality is constructed, is not described. The death which Clarissa desires and which counterpoints the rape, of which she has previously dreamt, is also displaced, emphasising the absent rape as the still centre of her/the book's confinement.

In the sensualising of death *Clarissa* again evidences the new Gothic and bourgeois reality. Clarissa 'dies' twice in the book, once before the rape in a dream in which Lovelace stabs her then buries her body and tramples on her grave,[52] and once in 'reality' of unknown causes but as a climax of a decline, the point of origin of which is the rape itself. The transgressive coition is thus bracketed. On the one side there is Clarissa's dream, a figuring of her death but in a language which lends itself so easily to a Freudian sexual decoding that further evidence of repression would seem unnecessary. The dream unites the two acts which in the later novelistic reality are separated in time in the one act in which Lovelace stabs her through the heart. On the other side there is Clarissa's real death. Clarissa recognises the coming of her death and prepares for it in a way which calls to mind the medieval understanding of death as a moment of transition lubricated by the fulfilling of ritual such as confession and the distribution of one's goods. Yet this is not a private and uninvolving death. Clarissa's dream already has shown us that her death is tied to the actions of Lovelace. If we understand the dream as an illustration of the process of male domination, then Clarissa's death may be seen as a function of this. Lovelace exclaims to Hickman, Anna Howe's fiancé, 'Ay sir, we have all heard of him—but none of us care to be intimate with him—except this lady—and that as I told you in spite to me. His name, in short, is DEATH! DEATH! sir.'[53] Here we must follow Warner's argument that Clarissa's death is actually an exercise of strategic power on her part which enables the text of Clarissa to give her view of the events. It is her wish that after her death the letters should be collected and published. Here we can see the way in which the reader is implicated as the site which gives reality and truth to the novel. Clarissa (and Richardson) is arranging a 'correct' reading in which the reader, through the epistolary method, is involved as she/he tries to construct the novel's world. Giving less real-ism to the work, it might similarly be argued that Richardson makes use of Clarissa's death to confirm Lovelace as the anti-social being which it was his original intention to portray. Either way Clarissa's death would not be the simple, easy passing over which is recounted in the work. She, personally, might approach her death easily but not so the Others with whom she is caught up. And, if in her dream sex and death are united, so they are also in Lovelace's perception of her death.

In the previous quotation Lovelace's personification of death allows a mingling of imagery: Clarissa cares to be 'intimate' with death. (The sexual overtones of 'intimate' were fully formed by this time—the *Oxford English Dictionary* gives 1637 as the date of its first extant written use in this sense.) Clarissa, in being intimate with death, is 'spiting' Lovelace and here is the tone of a male hurt by a female's faithlessness.

The linking of sex and death was a new phenomenon. Aries has traced its beginnings to the sixteenth century and illustrates this shift by Durer's Fourth Horseman of the Apocalypse, the leanness of whose horse 'emphasizes the size of the genital organs in a contrast that is certainly deliberate',[54] and by the work of Nicholas Manuel in which 'Death no longer merely points out a woman, his victim, by approaching her and drawing her away by an act of will; he violates her, he plunges his hand into her vagina.'[55] It is important to see here that death is characterised as male. Historically this was the case. The Reaper, for example, was male. Now, though, the masculinity of death takes on new meaning. In the bourgeois period the most shocking death is that of a beautiful young woman. Ophelia, with the sexual overtones involved in Hamlet's attitude towards her, was reconstructed as an *exemplum* of this *topos*. Millais's picture of the dead Ophelia captures the image perfectly. The importance of the link as a modern theme, in particular for women, may be exemplified in the popularity of the print of the painting among young females. The woman is not only produced as the bearer of sex, she is also the repository of reality. The image which links sex and death in a woman therefore becomes a myth of great power. The figure of death becomes a kind of anti-male conceiving the destruction of (bourgeois) society in bringing death to the eligible virgin. Intercourse, after all, is often characterised as a kind of death. The anti-male and the male both bring the destruction of female autonomy.

Todorov views the linkage of desire and death in this way: 'Their relation is not always the same, but one may say that it is always present.'[56] The obviousness and prevalence of the theme in Gothic literature seems to suggest to him that it is a universal link. In a society the reality of which is dependent on the creation/repression of desire, if intercourse marks a person's fixing and realising of that reality then death marks the person's exit from it. Moreover, if the reality may be experienced as a confinement, then death becomes the moment of liberation from that confinement. Again, we must think of the importance of the body as a fetish. The body is both a prison in which we are trapped and something which may be confined, as in Poe's stories of people being burned alive. Of course, this is not to say that death is perceived as something to be wished for. The true success of the bourgeois Realisation of the world lies precisely in its ability to persuade its inhabitants that there is no alternative to the reality of their confinement. Death marks the end, not just of the sexualised, individuated individual, but of the only possible individual— hence the importance of the link between sex and death in Gothic literature and the fact that it is, from Clarissa onwards, the woman who dies.

For these reasons the rape becomes the absolute confirmation of Clarissa's confinement within bourgeois reality. Her death, when it does occur, is the necessary beginning to the process of decarceration for the reader which includes, but does not require, the death of the male signifier in this world of signs, Lovelace. Clarissa, of course, remains permanently confined, permanently asserting the realism/reality of the bourgeois fetishised world. Warner, in his book on the inclusive meaning of structure of *Clarissa* notes that 'Clarissa dies so that she might produce the book which will guarantee her triumph. Death is the crucial initial act in the generation of this book.'[57] But this book is not just Clarissa's book, that is, the book Clarissa requests be created from her letters. It is also Richardson's written and published book which, unlike *Pamela*, he acknowledges to be not real but fiction. By contrast in *Pamela* it is the male, Squire B., who wishes to turn Pamela's letters into a book. Clarissa's request is another example of the Gothicness of the book. Clarissa's death, in (de)constructing her as the individual which she has struggled to be allows the text as the sexualised writing of displacement to be (re)created as meaning, the writing becoming transparent, that is to say, easier to read and therefore more taken for granted. Richardson in the Preface which states the book as fictive and simultaneously operates as his (as opposed to the publisher's) first confinement of the work writes thus: 'All the letters are written while the hearts of the writers must be supposed to be wholly engaged in their subjects (the events at the time generally dubious): so that they abound not only with critical situations, but with what may be called *instantaneous* descriptions and reflections.'[58]

Letters in general were becoming identified with the newly developed bourgeois individual. As such they were seen to be expressions of the individual and a part of the private domain in which she/he lived. Richardson himself wrote in one letter, 'when I follow not my correspondent's lead, [I] write whatever, at the moment, comes uppermost trusting to the heart, and regarding the head',[59] and in another, letter-writing 'is friendship avowed under hand and seal'.[60] The publication of letters, with their real/fictive ambiguity, becomes another assertion of the public/private division. It is only at the event of the rape that Richardson departs from his own policy, the instantaneous giving away to the deferred. Only in Clarissa's ravings written very shortly after the rape—and given to us enclosed in one of Lovelace's letters—is the taken-for-granted organisation of the printed book ruptured. Only here is reading, and in turn writing, problematised as an activity. Not only is [are] the meaning(s) of these passages obscure, opaque, but also the writing itself. The paradox is that the (re)instatement of displacement only articulates the displacement upon which the sexualised, fetishised world operates. Clarissa and the written text exist each as a function of the other—both located and realised within the structure of sexualisation which locates also the bourgeois reader.

CHAPTER 6

Rape and Virtue

In this chapter I want to examine various forms of sexual activity which are considered to be transgressive from within the reality of bourgeois society. Such an examination will allow us to shed light on the dual relation between sexuality and virtue and sexuality and capitalism. The form of transgressive sex which causes the most horror within bourgeois society is rape, and it is to this that I wish to turn first.

Like all bourgeois crime rape operates within the system. The popular mythology of it shows this. Rape, it is assumed, tends to happen to unmarried girls who 'flaunt' themselves. Moral: they should be married and in the safe, 'sexless' domestic domain. The horror of rape is analogous to the horror of conservative reading of Gothic literature. In both cases the moral lies in the acceptance of bourgeois values and bourgeois reality. The illusion of rape is that it is not in any sense a social construction. The universality given to rape reinforces the universality given to its Other, intercourse in marriage.

Within marriage intercourse exists so that it may be denied. Not only the act itself but how the act is conducted is important. Darkness and privacy become signs of confinement and repression, the act being carried out in the missionary position, itself confining for the female. Because of Victorian repression, we have little knowledge about that period's practice of marital intercourse. In late-1940s America, Kinsey and his co-researchers discovered that 'For perhaps three-quarters of all males, orgasm is reached within two minutes after the initiation of the sexual relation',[1] and there seems little reason to doubt a historical continuity here. Certainly, it reflects the prevailing bourgeois perception of marital intercourse as an activity which relieves male desire through orgasm. The woman, on the other hand, is constructed as asexual and does not require satisfaction in the act. In a book published in 1893 Lombroso and Ferrerio wrote that 'Woman is naturally and organically frigid.'[2] The ideal of a female virginal ignorance on coital matters until the consummation of the marriage night was conducive neither to female enjoyment nor to female knowledge of the sexual possibilities of their bodies. A male correspondent of Havelock Ellis wrote of his wedding night like this:

> The first night she found the act very painful and was frightened and surprised at the size of my penis, and at my suddenly getting on her. We had never talked very openly about sex things before marriage, and it never occurred to me that she was ignorant of the details of the act. I imagined it would disgust her to talk about these things.[3]

Wives cannot be raped, though in many cases the activity of the wedding night at least would look remarkably like rape. Rape exists where marriage does not. From a male bourgeois point of view rape may occur only when either of two factors is not present. One is marriage and the other is the exchange of money for sexual access. Since it is around these factors that the sexual economy of the male is elaborated, any definition of rape must be female. When the first secular divorce act was passed in Britain in 1857, as I have mentioned, while the wife could be divorced on the grounds of adultery, the husband could be divorced only for either aggravated adultery such as incestuous or bigamous adultery or for unnatural sexual activity such as sodomy or bestiality. Incest and bigamy problematise marriage much more than simple adultery while sodomy and bestiality call into question the basis of bourgeois sexual intercourse. The one other ground was rape, which calls both normative marriage and normative intercourse (which in one sense are the same thing) into question. It is fitting that, in the phrasing of the Matrimonial Causes Act, it came between bigamous adultery and sodomy.

The male sexual economy works with a definition of woman as object, as commodity. De Sade clearly understood rape as a function of the woman as property. He wrote, 'It is certain, however, that rape, an act so very rare and so very difficult to prove, wrongs one's neighbour less than theft since the latter is destructive to property, the former merely damaging to it.'[4] Here the woman is not only property, she is so much an object that she does not have a point of view. In terms of the logic of this system, males cannot be raped because rape defines a passive experience and males operate with an active excess of desire. Prostitution under capitalism provides for the relief of that excess. The principle of excess here is the equivalent of the capitalist preoccupation with growth. In the bourgeois marriage the woman, as property, becomes an extension of her husband. Should he desire intercourse, she is automatically called upon to provide the opportunity.

At this point we must not forget love. In bourgeois society it is assumed that the male and female both love one another, otherwise they would not have married. In the act of intercourse the male demonstrates his love in the loss of himself in ejaculation. For the female, as we shall see, Romantic love requires her loss of herself in the act of loving. In prostitution the sexualised female is able to lose herself in the act of intercourse, something illustrated in pornography's myth of the orgasmically satisfied prostitute. The operation of the cash nexus legitimates her in this freedom. The same, by the way, might be said for texts. The possession of a text always entails its retrieval from the public domain. The text always obliges its reader, its reader always desires the text. The important point in the bourgeois reading experience is the reader's involvement. The same determinant underlies love. In the ideal structuration of bourgeois society love is the third factor, the absence of which would determine an act of intercourse as rape. It is no wonder that the critical reading of texts is such a frowned-upon activity. The illusion of the bourgeois reading practice is that the meaning of the text is always the same as the reader's meaning. (In the analogous formulation in bourgeois marriage the myth is that the wife is always in agreement with her husband.) The meaning is in the text, but it is activated by the reader. In this sense the reader may be said to write the text in the process of reading. Clarissa, unlike Pamela, returns at the end of her book to assert that she wrote the text through the request that her collection of letters be published. By making the text self-referential in this way Richardson distances it from the reader. The reader can no longer claim to be the repository of its meaning. The transgressive act of intercourse which makes the marriage of Clarissa and Lovelace an impossibility produces Clarissa's textual death and the conception of the novel. The rape in the text mirrors the reader's problematic comprehension of the text. To carry the analogy to the bitter end, once the reader has deflowered the text she/he finds that, like Clarissa, it is still asserting its independence. It is a truly worthy attempt at a bourgeois feminocentric novel, something which, as we have seen, is a contradiction in terms because of the overdetermined construction of writer, text and reader in this society.

In *Clarissa* the rape is surrounded by a dissimulation which signals her confinement. Although it is difficult to tell, the impression that Clarissa's description of the rape gives is that during it she is conscious. The drug which Lovelace has administered to her seems only to have incapacitated her. Certainly, she pleaded with him and then she writes of 'such dreadful scenes! ... (faintly indeed and imperfectly remembered!)'. Clarissa's suppression of memory here is the image of Richardson's puritanical suppression of sexual description. The impression, nevertheless, is that she was conscious. This corroborates what we find Richardson doing in *Pamela*. Twice when B. is about to rape Pamela she faints, and each time B stops. If B. had consummated his rape while Pamela was unconscious, much of his, and the act's, power would have been dissipated because the violation of Pamela's individuality would not have been total. The act would not have been the transgressive equal of marital intercourse. In *Clarissa*, with Clarissa awake, it is exactly that. Clarissa's ultimate confinement, her functioning mind in her incapacitated body, becomes a synecdoche of the female's absolute confinement in bourgeois society. Clarissa's rape is exactly what makes her subsequent marriage to Lovelace impossible; in a terrible and inverted manner she is already married to him. Lovelace's use of a drug is a potent image for another reason. Unlike the drug administered to Clarissa, the nineteenth and twentieth centuries see more and more wives turning to drugs in order to suppress the confined action of their minds. In 1871 a doctor wrote of the cause of female drug addiction that:

> Doomed, often, to a life of disappointment, and it may be, of physical and mental inaction, and in the smaller and more remote towns not infrequently, to utter seclusion, deprived of all social diversion, it is not strange that nervous depression with all its concomitant evils, should follow—opium being discreetly selected as the safest and most agreeable remedy.[5]

Lovelace's drug incapacitates the body, increasing the bourgeois horror and setting the drug up as the opposite in function to the use to which opiates, and more recently such drugs as Valium, are put.

The rape acts as the moment of bourgeois realisation and as the moment of the realisation of absolute confinement. Previously, Clarissa is trapped in a set of appearance/reality transitions which she does not understand until the rape. Lovelace, the more aristocratic and old world figure, as the history of his name reflects, creates a world of appearance in which Clarissa believes. Within Mrs Sinclair's house (she retains her transparent/opaque name), Barbara Wallis becomes Lady Betty Lawrence and Johanetta Golding becomes Miss Montague, Lovelace's aunt and cousin, respectively. Both are prostitutes repetitiously performing (note the idiom) coitus for money. The domestic sphere in this case is not in opposition to the capitalist economy; it is, in fact, a part of the cash-nexus structure. Intercourse in the brothel is a function of money, not love, a dichotomy the equivalent of commercial/domestic. Love may be defined in terms of wholeness, an unreflexive feeling of unity; money, the cash nexus, operates to distantiate the individual. In the sexually active female, as in the male, orgasm becomes a sign of involvement and a substitute for love. Both the prostitutes are old partners of Lovelace. During this period it was often thought prostitutes enjoyed intercourse with their clients.

Whether or not it was true—or the extent to which it was true—it was what the clients wished to believe. As a result the prostitutes dissimulated, like Shamela on her wedding night, to please. The dissimulation of the brothel as household images the prostitutes' dissimulation of sexual pleasure. This provides an ironic commentary on the position of prostitutes as a sexually active Other counterpointing the asexual passivity of the classical bourgeois wife, and also on Lovelace's understanding of intercourse as the functional relief of desire as suggested by his relationships with the prostitutes. In turn it highlights the absolute honesty with which Clarissa experiences the rape.

If we recognise sexual need, we can understand the existence, and acceptance, of brothels in patriarchal, medieval society. Prostitutes:

> were frequently sent to welcome distinguished visitors. In 1438, for example, the protocols of the city accounts of Vienna read: 'For the wine for the common women 96 Kreutzers. Item, for the women who went to meet the king, 96 Kreutzers for wine.' Or the mayor and council gave distinguished visitors free access to the brothel. In 1434 Emperor Sigismund publicly thanks the city magistrate of Bern for putting the brothel freely at the disposal of himself and his attendants for three days.[6]

At first sight it seems strange that the death of the municipal brothel in the sixteenth century seems to have been caused more by a decline in clientele than by a rise in Christian fundamentalism. However, when we remember that the period saw the advent of the new, privatised view of intercourse in which prostitution came to be viewed as a 'necessary evil' but one which should remain obscure and repressed, it becomes more understandable that the old municipal institution should lose its customers. The new brothel would be a capitalist private enterprise based on the cash nexus.

Prostitution's loss of position has often been put down to the final success of Christian moralism. Flandrin, for example, links Protestant and Catholic moralists with their emphasis on premarital celibacy and seems to suggest that by the seventeenth century they had finally prevailed on public opinion, one evidence of which is the increasing

unacceptability of prostitution.[7] Certainly we know that in
Protestant England:

> In April 1644 Parliament closed all whorehouses, gambling houses and
> theatres. The players were whipped at the carlt-arse, fined for using
> oaths, or sent to prison. The may-poles were pulled down wherever they
> could be found, on the ground that they incited the peasantry to lust.
> Nude statues, when not broken up, had their genitals covered with
> leaves and scrolls; some were clothed to hide their nudity.[8]

However, the question which must be confronted is the
degree to which this movement was a purely Christian
success story and the degree to which these Christian
concerns, many of them new—such as the proscription on the
theatre—were in their new elaboration and success an
articulation of other, more profound, shifts in the social
order.

As for the individual's attitude we have Pierre Vidal of
Montaillou's statement that sexual intercourse with a
prostitute or with any woman provided that it 'pleased' both
parties was innocent, that it was not sinful.[9] I don't think that
the differentiation which Le Roy Ladurie perpetuates here
between intercourse for money and intercourse as 'pleasing'
is significant. In pre-capitalist, pre-market-economy,
medieval Europe, money operated simply as a more liquid
bartering device. The acceptability of prostitution can be
related to the acceptance of sexual needs. Other Montaillou
residents equated sex with prostitutes with such other
activities as stealing 'fruit, hay and grass from meadows' and
'making dishonourable suggestions to married women, and
even virgins. I was sometimes drunk. I told lies. I stole
fruit'.[10] Such is the significance of the other activities with
which visiting prostitutes are here associated that, assuming
we can generalise, at most it was viewed as a venial sin, and, of
course, it was not a crime at all. The seventeenth-century
change in attitude towards prostitution occurs at the same
period that both Protestant and Catholic wings of the Church
(though the former earlier) are beginning to lay great stress on
the new bourgeois concept of marriage. In earlier times the
Church appears to have reached an accommodation with lay
society on sexual matters. Just as marriage had not been a

sacrament, so prostitution, while considered a sin by the Church, was not the focus of a morals campaign. The legitimising of intercourse as a satisfier of desire within marriage entails its absolute proscription outside marriage, otherwise the absolute nature of marriage would be lost—hence the stigmatization of bastardy, fornication and female adultery. The horror of female adultery with the associated destruction of the domestic domain is well illustrated in Augustus Egg's trio of paintings called 'Past and Present' (1858). Here the effect would seem to be the death of the father, the abandonment of the daughters and the reduction of the mother to living under the Adelphi Arches. Extra-marital sex must be proscribed because it challenges the restriction of desire which forms the repressed basis of bourgeois marriage and society. No longer can prostitution and 'pleasing' consensual sex be viewed as equivalent. While in one way prostitution is extra-marital sex and therefore a threat to the absoluteness of marriage, in another way prostitution is legitimised by its placing within the market economy—hence we find the modern bourgeois rationalisation of prostitution as 'a necessary evil'. It is within this series of inverse significations that Clarissa has been placed without her knowledge.

In *Clarissa* both prostitutes have as a result of such commercial intercourse, according to Lovelace, lost the innocence with which they were born. Here is Lovelace teaching Johanetta Golding her part: 'O Lord! Lord! that so young a creature can so soon forget the innocent appearance she first charmed by; and I thought born with you all!—Five years to ruin what twenty had been building up! How natural the latter lesson! How difficult to regain the former!'[11] Innocence, then, is *real* in the female at birth. It is lost through coition. Specifically, as the rape scene acknowledges, it is lost through a coition which is a product of bourgeois society and is the price women pay for the male validation and reproduction of that society's reality. In this case loss of innocence is reflected in the ability to dissimulate. The paradox here is that the innocent female is not yet a full member of society. Innocence is actually a state of not having experienced, and by extension not having knowledge of,

sexual intercourse, just as in the bourgeois understanding of
the Garden of Eden story the gaining of knowledge requires
the loss of innocence. The lack is turned into a positive
condition—innocence. Virginity becomes a guarantor of
innocence and, once again, we find another overtone in the
eighteenth- and nineteenth-century male obsession with
defloweration, one which makes understandable the
construction not only of the child but of the child as innocent.

That the prostitutes 'used' by Lovelace are actresses
reflects their liminal position within the society. Acting, then,
becomes the mark of the public, of appearance, and at this
time we find a change in the attitude towards the theatre in
both France and Britain. The realisation that appearance may
be separated from some other absent but more profound
reality is at the heart of the idea of a lost innocence. The body
is fetishised as a function of the repression which aids the
production of bourgeois sexuality. It is no wonder that in the
'world of its own', which is the bourgeois theatre, the key
problem should concern how to resolve the importance of
appearance with the acknowledgement of individual essence.
Because of these new dichotomies the close relation between
actresses and prostitutes, which has a long historical
precedence, took on a new significance in the bourgeois
period. For example, while the Puritan government of the
Commonwealth banned the theatre, the Restoration saw a
vogue for voyeuristic, overtly sexual theatre in which female
parts were played by females rather than, as in Shakespeare's
time, by boys. The culmination of this new theatrical
sexuality may be found in a play, attributed to Rochester,
entitled *Sodom*.

The change to this new understanding of theatre was best
demonstrated in Diderot's *Paradox of Acting*, here summed
up by Sennett:

> At best in a world where sympathy and natural feeling govern, if there is
> an exact representation of an emotion it can happen only once.
>
> Diderot then asks how an expression can be presented more than once
> ... [*That can occur*] when a person, having ceased to 'suffer it' and now at
> a distance studying it, comes to define its essential form.[12]

This, as Sennett goes on to emphasise, does not do away with the importance of feeling; rather feeling is redirected into the reflexive playing of a particular emotion. The emotion is validated as real by the ability of the actor to make the appearance convincing. Lovelace sums this up nicely when, again in his role as director, he says, 'Airs of superiority as if born to rank.—But no overdo!—Doubting nothing. Let not your faces arraign your hearts.'[13]

Clarissa is ensnared, unable to tell appearance from reality. The bourgeois is able to tell appearance from reality, play from life, and the intercourse of prostitution from the intercourse of marriage, if all else fails, by its relation to the cash nexus. Clarissa remains confused because she does not know how she is positioned in relation to the cash nexus of the market economy. In the case of the play, the actors are able to represent emotion with the audience secure in the knowledge that the theatre (and its cash-nexus transaction) ensures its final illusionistic quality. In the same way, the capitalist reification of the book as object ensures the illusionistic quality of the realist novel. In the case of prostitution the cash nexus determines that no demonstrated emotion is Real. In bourgeois society both actor and prostitute are unable, in their roles, to be real; all they can do is re-present to the society those things which that society considers to be Real. The similarities between acting and prostitution are many; the crucial difference lies in the act of intercourse itself not because of the act but because of its association with bourgeois Reality. For the audience, as with the reader of a novel, the difference lies in the distantiation of voyeuristic involvement. Prostitution and acting operate within the same parameters in bourgeois society and, as the English legislation of 1644 showed, are often judged by the same criteria. That they are often considered to be overlapping activities is evidenced by the pervading belief that, for women, a career on the stage is tantamount to a decision in favour of, at best, a sexually dubious life. This has some basis in truth; the theatre as a place of assignation was common both in pre- and post-Commonwealth England and in *ancien régime* France.

Lovelace, like Clarissa, is also caught, unable to use/create Clarissa as object to replicate the patriarchally signified reality of the object because Clarissa, living in a world of sliding significations, is unable to determine what are criteria for judging reality, for realising herself—or, properly, being realised—as object. It might be argued that Clarissa's problem is to realise herself not as an object. In bourgeois literature her only hope would seem to become a monster, a Gothic artifice. After the rape Lovelace gives the impression that this is what he thinks she has become, but in the end, instead of becoming unnatural she simply dies. The novel accepts the bourgeois criteria which underlie the realist novel.

The individual's concern with the dual development of public and private areas of life is in the appearance that she/he makes in the public arena and, simultaneously, the meaning which she/he is able to find in his/her own individual life in private. It was Mandeville who first acknowledged this distinction and utilised it to show how Hobbesian vices might benefit the Commonwealth if checked appropriately. Mandeville is in fact restating in an economic context what we have already seen argued in a sexual context. Desire must be repressed in order to generate virtues. As we shall see, Mandeville's starting point was itself the problem of desire ad repression. The individual is created as the mediation of this twin development. This is one way of talking about the problem of *Clarissa*/Clarissa. Clarissa's desire for appearance to be absolutely Real marks her not just as being unable to cope with the new bourgeois distinctions but as attempting to live outside them. The reality for which she struggles is one composed of unity not separation, one where public and private are not just in harmony but are one. This is what will subsequently be called the Romantic attempt to call back pre-bourgeois society. In this sense *Clarissa*, and Gothic, represent a critical commentary on bourgeois society. Lovelace's world is the reverse; it is a world where reality is constructed through the difference between public and private. He writes to Belford:

> As to the manner of endeavouring to obtain her, by falsification of oaths, vows, and the like—do not the poets of two thousand years and upward tell us, that Jupiter laughs at the perjuries of lovers? ...

> Do we not then see, that an honest prowling fellow is a necessary evil
> on many counts? Do we not see that it is highly requisite that a sweet girl
> should be now and then drawn aside by him? And the more eminent the
> girl, in the graces of person, mind and fortune, is not the example likely
> to be the more efficacious?
> ... At worst I am within my worthy friend Mandeville's assertion, that
> *private vices are public benefits.*[14]

The furore over Mandeville's book *The Fable of the Bees*
was precisely because he suggested that such 'vices' as luxury,
avarice and greed in the individual worked to the benefit of
the state. Mandeville's work was the reverse of the Augustan
and Puritan idea that the sum of individual virtue was a
virtuous state.[15] Rather, he considered that people should be
taken as they are, by which he seems to have meant that they
were like Hobbesian individuals in need of state control to
keep them within socially acceptable limits. Hobbes's vision
of men in a state of nature was, however, a vision of fear; his
wish was for harmony. Mandeville sees his individuals as
beneficial to the Commonwealth through the employment
their vices bring. In the early days of the *ancien régime*, as the
culture of worldliness was beginning to take hold, we find La
Rochefoucauld moving in the same direction. As the
prefacing aphorism to the *Maximes* (1685) we find, 'Nos
vertus ne sont le plus souvent que des vices déguisés!'[16] There
is here, however, not the split between individual and state,
vice and virtue (desire and marriage?) which Mandeville
emphasises. The essence of worldly culture was the attempt
to preserve the illusion—and thus the reality—that this split
did not exist. Moreover, for La Rochefoucauld vice and
virtue were personal and cultural attributes and were not
connected with the economic order. It was the placing of the
old medieval *topoi* of vice and virtue as associated with the
economic order which was one of Mandeville's most original
moves.

One more step is important. Mandeville's work was, in
origin, an attack on that late-seventeenth- and early-
eighteenth-century development, the Society for the
Reformation of Manners.[17] These societies were primarily
concerned with the suppression of bawdy-houses, which
provided a place of work for prostitutes. Thus what becomes

a capitalist argument concerning trade has its beginning in an argument about the societal repression of socially unsanctioned sexual intercourse. Mandeville touches on this:

and it is Wisdom in all Governments to bear with lesser Inconvenience to prevent greater. If Courtezans and Strumpets were to be persecuted with as much Rigour as some silly People would have it, what Locks or Bars would be sufficient to preserve the Honour of our Wives and Daughters.[18]

Prostitution and women who are free with their sexual favours are a good thing or the domestic, private household would be threatened. It is the domestic domain which is fundamental to capitalist economic practice. Lovelace's argument takes this one stage on: sexual virtue is preserved as the obverse of intercourse outside marriage. The old medieval municipal brothel was returning in a new guise as a form of nationalised capitalist industry. In France in *La Pornographe* (1770) Restif de la Bretonne argued for the same thing as Mandeville had in his *A Modest Defence of Public Stews*. But the era of such total state intervention in either sexuality or economics had to wait until the post-war period in Holland and Germany for sexuality and, in economics, until the acceptance of the work of Keynes. Mandeville's argument about the utility of prostitution is based on an assumption of the importance of sexual intercourse for the public/private division. It is this acknowledgement and problematisation which gives *Clarissa* its Gothic centre articulated not as pure absence (that degree of repression comes later) but as rape manifested in a delayed and repressed form. It is the rape as a bourgeois act which fixes the reality of the book's world for its characters.

Many of Mandeville's vices point to economic considerations in the health of the state in their concern with employment and consumption. Mandeville's linkage of the social and the economic prefigures the mercantilist arguments about the role of trade and the acceptance of the public/private split upon which it operates. Hirschman has ably demonstrated that the seventeenth century saw the burgeoning of a philosophical tradition of the idea of balances in which 'one set of passions, hitherto known variously as greed, avarice, or love of lucre, could be usefully employed to oppose and bridle such other passions as ambition, lust for power, or sexual lust.'[19] The capitalist making of money is thus transformed from its Augustinian position as a vice to a new acceptability placing it as virtuous alongside correct bourgeois sexual behaviour. This is exactly what we see happening in Mandeville's work. Indeed, the making of money is made an individual virtue which underpins the socially prescribed virtue of chastity, which represents a code to be followed for acceptability into society. Hence, the vice of sexual lust is not held in check by the virtue of a passion for making money. The semantic focusing of virtue onto sexual matters enables, subsequently, the making of money to be seen as an inevitable part of society, neither good nor bad, as in Adam Smith's *The Wealth of Nations*. This fundamentalist view of capitalism lends its authority to the virtue of chastity which, in turn, functions as a determinant of the new sexualised structure of society. Money, as Simmel following Marx noted, it not itself an object which can give satisfaction; it is a *means* for acquisition and it is acquisition which creates objects. Money enables the capitalist desire for objects to be fulfilled. This desire is a product of the new developed sexualised desire. Money itself is the articulation of desire in the commodity fetishism of capitalism because it is a *means* to satisfaction in objects. As a consequence the uses to which individuals put money not only lend themselves with ease to Freudian-style analyses but actually are 'Freudian'.

At the level of practice the sexual economy of the male body became integrated with the monetary economy of capitalism. We find William Acton writing that over-indulgence in sexual intercourse leads to 'simple ruin'. The body has 'spent' too much and consequently the individual has become bankrupt. Even more obvious in its connotations is the activity occasionally indulged in by Walter in *My Secret Life*:

> I told her one evening how I had turned N**le L**l*e's cunt into a purse, and she wondered if her own would hold as much. ... The silver was carefully washed, and the argental stuffing began. ... I prolonged the work, not putting in five or ten shillings at a time as I did with the other, when my lustful curiosity was to ascertain a fact, but a shilling or two at a time only.[20]

Here the vagina literally becomes the site of money. We have travelled a long way and yet no way at all from B. in *Pamela*, who offers Pamela money in exchange for sexual favours. Walter is conflating the power of patriarchal desire and the power of money in a capitalist world of commodity fetishism. He is spending; at the end of the exercise the woman concerned acquires all the money her vagina can hold. Moreover, the implication is that, this time at least, he finds the exercise an erotic experience.

Harrison has summed up the interpenetration of sex and money in bourgeois Victorian England like this:

> The penetration of sexuality by money was the factor which determined the character of relationships between middle-class men and women. The sexual appeal had become indistinguishably associated with their material worth and, similarly, male virility was identified with monetary power.[21]

In sex as in capitalism only males were allowed to spend. Semen and the orgasm with which it was associated were male attributes just as surely as only males were allowed access to money and ownership. Whereas the male sexual economy had to be strictly regulated, evidence for which could be found in the limited number of ejaculations a male was able to have in any one period, it was considered that females could have a limitless number of orgasms. This myth is still perpetuated in many books on female sexual enjoyment. The sexualised female becomes a threat not only to the (male) sexual economy but, by analogy, to a (male) capitalist economy whereby both economies are based on thrift and hard work. Once again the female must be confined, unaware of her potentially destructive capacity.

Walter in *My Secret Life*, has shown us how the phallic presence of money commoditises the sexualised female. This commoditisation may be taken one step further than the woman selling her own body. She may be bought and sold as a body in what was called the white slave trade. Terrot has remarked that 'Throughout the Middle Ages the sale of young girls flourished everywhere; in many countries it was not merely tolerated but licensed and regulated by law. In the twelfth century, white slave markets on a large scale were established at Toulouse, Avignon and Montpelier.[22] This activity was not viewed as wrong. In a patriarchy where women were simply viewed as inferior, the sale of them, again *not* within a capitalist structure, was not a shocking event. Women, like men, were not yet individuals let alone fully commoditised objects; the sale of a human being for sexual purposes was as little objectionable as slavery. As has been well documented, the transformation in attitude towards slaves was an effect of capitalist market economics and bourgeois individualism. The slave was transformed from a member of the *domus* (family) to an expendable part of the means of production, in the process of which there developed a series of legitimating ideologies concerned with, for example, the natural inferiority of black races. As late as *Robinson Crusoe*, Crusoe accepts his role of slave and is treated as a member of the household. Similarly, the sale of girls for primarily sexual usage was not only socially acceptable but, like the municipal maintenance of brothels, something with which the authorities involved themselves. The capitalist history of the white (sexual) slave trade is another example of the history of bourgeois repression.

The medieval state withdrew from the trade gradually, Nuremberg closing down the last municipal market in 1552. From this time on, the trade is privatised in the sense of being operated within the new state structures but without their support. By the early seventeenth century (1635) France had advanced to the stage of condemning men concerned in the traffic, to the galleys for life. However, in France we get an example of the ossification induced by absolutism—in 1684 Louis XIV repealed this ordinance. In Britain the trade was suppressed by the Puritans alongside all other activities threatening the sanctity of marriage. With the return of the monarchy the rigour of Puritan suppression was replaced by an aristocratic sexual indulgence. English aristocrats bought mistresses and auctions of women were being held. In *ancien régime* France Louis XV built up a large harem. Now, though, as Terrot writes, 'Generally speaking, a veil of reticence and secrecy was flung over the white slave markets of Europe ... Brussels and Antwerp became the busiest centres of the trade—largely as the result of extremely corrupt police'.[23] The new market is a clandestine one. The buying and selling of women threatens the production of the domestic domain. In the same way that incest threatens the supposed asexuality of the domain, so the real commoditisation of women threatens the supposed a-capitalism of the domain. The Gothic horror of incest may be equated with the Gothic horror of female slavery. In the latter case male fantasies tend to preserve the domestic domain and the attractive female slave is portrayed as an adjunct to it rather than as a threat. Popular fiction about the ante-bellum American South is a good example here. In the context of the feminisation of the text we might draw a parallel between the proscription on women as actual commodities and the perjorative attitude which society has towards novelists who write for money rather than art. The penetration of money into the asexual text is also proscribed.

The added horror of the white slave trade lay in the threat which such implied intercourse contained for the bourgeois—the shock of not just the buying and selling of the sexualised act but the buying and selling of the object which enables that act to be performed. Here we find ourselves with the key to one of the bourgeois male's most repressed obsessions, the conversion of women into an overt part of the capitalist economic order. The impossibility of this final conversion is caused by the construction of the bourgeois world in the fetishised but not commoditised female. Love, but more particularly marriage, are the mainstays of Reality, and these are experienced as operating outside the economic order.

In the new world of objects, intercourse places the woman as object but not as commodity—as an asexual, a-commercial 'absence' determined by (though apparently determining) the sexual, commercial world. Arabella, Clarissa's sister, with the real physical beauty of appearance, reflects this when she writes to Clarissa rejecting her overtures for a reconciliation:

My uncle Harlowe renounces you for ever.
So does my uncle Antony.
So does my aunt Hervey.
So do *I*, base, unworthy creature! The disgrace of a good family, and the property of an infamous rake, as questionless you will soon find yourself if you are not already.[24]

Arabella has appropriated the kin structure and also, therefore, Clarissa's original domestic domain. The last phrase implies the signification of sexual intercourse in this context. Clarissa will become property, the bourgeois property, as Arabella knows, becomes appearance and is judged by exchange value. Clarissa, once she is made real by Lovelace, will realise little because of *his* value. Clarissa's position, had she married Lovelace, would have been different. Lovelace's sexual activity is notorious in his unmarried state. Marriage would have made his social position more important, because of its bourgeois displacing action, than his unmarried sexual encounters. Arabella emphasises her rejection of Clarissa by listing the kin of the domestic group who also reject her. She is expelled from the private family, expelled from the asexual Eden. Her only alternative is the sexualised world of commodities, which Arabella thinks she has already joined.

Clarissa is thrown out of the bourgeois Eden with none of her belongings except her clothes; and her clothes only because 'my poor mother cannot bear in her sight anything you used to wear.'[25] Here the emphasis is on sight which, as I have commented before, is the most important sense in the bourgeois world of objects. Clothes are so personal because they reveal/conceal the individualised, fetishised body. Bourgeois realism is triumphant. At a later date Goethe, in *Elective Affinities*, will write, 'A woman expresses her natural beauty in her clothes; we imagine we see a new and lovelier person whenever she wears a different dress.'[26] A more explicit example of the bourgeois understanding of the relationship between body and dress would be hard to find. A woman has 'natural' beauty, beauty which is immanent in her body and clothes should be used to express this. Clothes are no longer viewed as expressing one's position in society, sumptuary laws for example died out in Britain from the 1630s onwards,[27] rather clothes enhance the body while hiding (and confining) it.

Intercourse in this world where sex is displaced into sexuality is the producer of reality, but bourgeois reality is the realism of the appearance of the object—hence the new importance of clothes. The paradox of rape as transgression lies in its inevitable enclosure within the bourgeois sexualised world. In other words, while what is defined as rape may be experienced within the ideological structure as challenging the sexual order of bourgeois society, in fact it asserts that very sexualised structure as Real which is transgresses. Rape is not perceived/experienced as the same in all societies. If, for brevity, rape may be defined as sexual violation, usually of a 'woman' by a 'man', then in practice it involves the forcing of a person to do something socially defined as sexual which they do not wish to do. In bourgeois society this something is focused on intercourse, but a penumbra of 'sexual' activity may also be claimed. The significance attached to rape in bourgeois society is the obverse of the fundamental importance given to agreed-upon sexual intercourse in a society where coitus affirms the person as fetish and as individual. Early in his journal for the period 1405–58 the young Aeneas Sylvius, who later became Pope, records that when some Englishman with whom he was staying went to take refuge at night from possible Scottish raids, 'They could not be persuaded to take him with them, although he earnestly besought them nore yet any of the women, although there were a large number of beautiful girls and matrons. For they think the enemy will do them no wrong—not counting outrage a wrong.'[28] This society did not regard the limitation of sexual access to be important.

One of the most intriguing things about much rape in medieval society was its 'public' form. Both the cases documented by Flandrin involved a number of local males breaking into a house and abducting a single woman, who was then beaten and multiply raped in the open. Without unfortunately giving his figures Flandrin claims that 80 per cent of rapes of which he has evidence were group rapes, and that they conform to this structure.[29] Since these rapes also involved beating, it might be argued that the excuse for the bachelor groups' action was that it was a form of punishment metered out to unmarried women of marriageable age who, by not getting married, were reducing the number of possible spouses. My emphasis is on the public nature of the rape, which goes along with the publicness of all intercourse in medieval Europe. In a society where, according to Flandrin, 'nearly half the dwellings of craftsmen and workers only had one room',[30] privacy for intimate sexual relations must not only have not been possible but is unlikely to have been considered important. If it had been, we should surely have some evidence of the provisions made. We might add to this extrapolation the case of Margeurite, who brought a legal action against her seducer Pierre Pellart. A girl of eighteen testified 'that one night, when she was in bed with Margeurite in the latter's room, the accused came there and had carnal knowledge of Margeurite. She knows this because she was lying beside Margeurite and was touching her.'[31] Here we have a concrete example of normal peasant life. Beds were not private places and intercourse was not a private act. Equally, intercourse was not a public act to be voyeuristically consumed. Margeurite's friend seems to have been quite unconcerned at what was going on beside her, though one can hypothesise that she would not have been too happy at being kept awake. Hence forced public intercourse would not carry the overtones of shame which it carries in our society. The real punishment is likely to have been considered to be the beating, the rape merely the manifestation of the bachelor groups' wish to assuage their sexual needs—something which the patriarchy accepted. Women's challenge to this would have been more likely to be in terms expressing inconvenience and disregard for their wishes than Clarissa-like horror at their violation as individuals.

In *Montaillou*, Le Roy Ladurie comments on the constant possibility of rape. In general those guilty of rape were not severely punished—something which would also seem to point to the lack of significance attached to the sexual act (certainly by the males). One statement adds to this image. In Montaillou we find Raymonde Testanière stating, 'One evening the shoemaker Arnaud Vital tried to rape me disregarding the fact that I had children by Bernard Belot who was his first cousin. So I stopped Arnaud getting his way, although he kept on saying that I would not be committing a sin if I slept with him.'[32] Raymonde Testanière seems to oppose this intercourse because it would have been, in her eyes, incestuous. The decision to give in to the male to make life easier in a patriarchal society where sex has little significance makes the distinction between seduction and rape far less than it is in our society. Indeed, the distinction itself may be culturally relative. The privatisation of rape goes along with its stigmatisation, and this occurs in Europe around the sixteenth century concurrently with the beginning of the change in attitude towards intercourse and the body. The new social importance of rape is validated by its central and determining position in *Clarissa*, Clarissa dies as a counterpoint to the rape rather than marrying and giving life to a domestic domain. The importance of rape as a counterpoint to marriage in bourgeois society is highlighted by the punishments which it came to warrant. In fourteenth-century Bologna, for example, rape was punishable by death.

While satisfactory intercourse in bourgeois society, which is certain to encompass male orgasm, is defined by its spontaneity and lack of reflexivity (note how this definition can apply to love as well) which affirms the person as individual, then the same also goes for unsatisfying intercourse. Rape in bourgeois society affirms the individual as Real because of the degree of reflexivity engendered in the 'woman'. Castiglione set the scene when, having stated that 'a gentleman that is in love, ought as well in this point as in all other things, to be voide of dissimulation'[33] (dissimulation requires reflexivity), he goes on to say, 'and for part truely (were I in love) I would like it better to know that she whom I loved and served, loved me againe with hart ... then to enjoy her, and to have my fill of her against her owne wil, for in that case I should thinke my selfe maister of a deade carkase.'[34] This is the ideal—unreflexive love leading to unreflexive intercourse—but another of Castiglione's characters gives us the dark side of the equation: 'alwaies he that possesseth the bodie of women, is also maister of the minde'[35] In this way Lord Casper justifies rape. The argument is that exercising sexual domination over a women creates the woman both as fetish and as individual, in turn affirming the real-ness of the male and the social world. This fetishisation of the body through intercourse is reflected in the Gothic preoccupation with incest, where desire and/or intercourse realises a strange Other world through the sexual juxtaposition of kin bodies unacceptable to bourgeois society.

The displacement which gives the real is the same in Gothic as in realist fiction; it is the relationship to the displacement which is potentially different for the reader. Lovelace writes to Belford before the rape of Clarissa:

> But as to Miss Betterton—no rape in the case, I repeat: rapes are unnatural things, and more are than are imagined, Joseph. I should be loth to be put to such a straight; I never was. Miss Betterton was taken from me against her will. In that case her friends, not I, committed the rape.[36]

Rapes are unnatural and, because of this, are more real because they cannot be so well encompassed by the mind.[37] Rape transgresses all the bourgeois notions of the relation of virtue to virginity; in doing so it also transgresses the absence which separates the private and individual from the public and social. It is a very popular motif in pornography where the end of the rape is the realisation by the woman that she really does desire intercourse. Here it tends not to be the rape itself which is the fantasy, though at times this can be the case when intercourse is translated simply into a power relation. The realisation by the woman—often a virgin—that she 'likes' it duplicates the power relation by confirming the male in his ability to produce reality. In his attempt to increase the horror of Clarissa's rape, Richardson has Lovelace denounce rape. Lovelace does not view rape as 'real' intercourse because it does not involve the woman's freely given consent—or involvement. Similarly, Valmont in *Les Liaisons dangereuses* writes:

> There would be no difficulty in finding my way into (La Présidente de Tourval's) house, even at night, nor yet again in putting her to sleep and making another Clarissa out of her: but to have recourse after more than two months of toil and trouble to methods which are not my own! To crawl slavishly in other's tracks, to triumph without glory! ... No, I shall not allow her the pleasure of vice with the honours of virtue. It is not enough to possess her; I want her to give herself up.[38]

Here, again, Valmont is echoing Mandeville's problem. If Valmont rapes the Présidente, she will be able to keep her private virtue. Valmont wants to have her willingly so that she will be totally possessed, and totally ruined. In this he succeeds. With Clarissa, Richardson is operationalising a different principle. His concern is with the absolute wrongness of extra-marital intercourse. Although there is much talk of love by both Clarissa and Lovelace, when the rape takes place it is unequivocally a physical act counterpointing the union of bourgeois marriage.

We may contrast Clarissa's rape with the attempted rape of Fanny in *Fanny Hill* while she is still a virgin. Here is perhaps the first English example of this pornographic motif. The reality of this act is to be found in the inversion caused by the cash nexus. Fanny's virginity has been sold to a rich, but to Fanny 'old and ugly', man by Mrs Brown without Fanny's knowledge. The legitimation of the rape lies in the cash transaction. Rather than Fanny becoming property by means of marriage, she (actually, her virginity) has become property through its entry into the capitalist system. Fanny has already been realised as object; the man is simply attempting to claim the purchased commodity. Fanny is also realised as object in the text where the attempted rape is described in graphic detail from 'his pestilential kisses ... to ... his hand on the lower part of Fanny's naked thighs'.[39] The transgression of rape may be more real, but it is a 'reality' defined in opposition to the real(ism) of bourgeois society.

Clarissa is trapped: to give herself in love, willingly, to Lovelace—she was, she acknowledges, once in love with him—would be to lose her self-defined individuality; alternatively, to break off all relations with Lovelace would lose her the man she loves(?). She has no way out except to displace intercourse continually in time. The rape, the intercourse, finally makes it impossible for her to marry and to have legitimate sexualised intercourse with Lovelace because it demonstrates the impossibility of the resolution of her problem in a male-realised world. It does, however, at last realise that world. Miller has described rape in the eighteenth-century novel as 'the hyperbolic index of a society so turned in upon itself, so enamoured of its own rigidity and fascinated by its own rules, that it is unable to imagine and hence integrate a self that is not coded.'[40] Intercourse, by consent or not, codes a person into such a society. Individuals need to be positioned within the sexualised world and all intercourse is a function of that sexualising process. Lovelace expects Clarissa to be 'his' once he has entered her body, once her privateness has been violated. She refuses, threatening suicide when he tries to rape her again. Her refusal of the domination he has taken loses her a reality in the bourgeois world in which she lives, leaving her exit from the world she has created for him her only choice. The irony of *Clarissa*/Clarissa is that she can only exist in opposition to Lovelace because she lives for her virginity (virtue), which she thinks keeps her intact—an individual. In fact, the value she places on virtue is defined by Lovelace (males in general) in the first place. Similarly, the text does not give us a feminocentric novel because the position of the reader has already been determined. Richardson's failure and Clarissa's failure is the same failure. One cannot accept bourgeois values and then use them as the basis of a critique of bourgeois society.

CHAPTER 7

Love and Death

For the Romantics the ambiguities which surrounded the epistolary novel no longer existed. Fact and fiction were as clearly demarcated as were the domestic and public domains. Fact was to be read analytically and critically in the same way that science was to be practised. Fiction, however, was to be read synthetically, by a process founded on involvement. The importance of emotion in the domestic domain was replicated in its importance for reading fiction. Similarly, the importance of reason in the capitalist, public domain was replicated in the critical approach required for the reading of fact. Pornography may be classified as a special case which articulates reading as desire and is considered to legitimate its existence by commodity value rather than aesthetic value. The socially acceptable bourgeois novel articulates reading as an emotional response. Both are constructs of our sexualised interactions. We might ask, for example, why it is that readers refer to books (and other objects) with the same language that is used for people; they say, 'I loved that novel' or, perhaps more interestingly, 'I really enjoyed that story'. Whereas in other objects the fetishism is in the concrete thing itself, in the 'novel' or other textual construct the fetishism lies in the alien, fictional thing (re)constituted by the voyeuristically lived experience of the reader. Hence the paramount critical importance of the realist novel. The importance of a hero or heroine is that they become vehicles for involvement, points of easy contact. They also constitute points of easy contact between the writer and his/her text.

The conception and birth of the text are charged

experiences in which the writer as bourgeois individual divests him/herself of some of his/her 'personness'. The writer 'spends' and therefore must be male. Abrams, in *The Mirror and the Lamp*, writes of the new sense of unity between writer and text and sees it as reaching its first fruition in the theory elaborated by Hazlitt. Rousseau and Goethe provide steps on the way to this:

> To [Byron's] theory, that at least some literature is a form of *Wunschbild* Hazlitt adds the doctrine that it provides an emotional catharsis for its author. Rousseau had already confessed that *La Nouvelle Héloïse* originated in the compulsive daydreams in which he compensated for his frustrations as a lover, and Goethe was soon to describe in *Dichtung und Wahrheit* how his youthful despairs and disappointments had transformed themselves into *Die Leiden des Jungen Werthers*, which he wrote in four weeks 'almost unconsciously, like a somnambulist'.[1]

There are many points of connection between Goethe's own life and *The Sorrows of Young Werther*. Goethe gives Werther the same birthday as his own, 28 August, and Werther's relationship to Lotte has marked similarities to Goethe's with Charlotte Buff, who subsequently married J. G. Kestner, a friend of Goethe. Goethe literally translated his own unfulfilled desire into writing. Friedenthal tells us that when he was a student in Leipzig Goethe had consciously attempted to contrive his life as 'un roman'.[2] In *The Sorrows* he reproduced his life as a book. When the book caught its readers' imagination they searched for the originals of the characters. The grave of the suicide, Jerusalem, whose death Goethe appropriated for Werther, became a place of pilgrimage. The connections between Goethe and Werther mark the fictional text as a fantastic attempt to appropriate reality. We can see that the world of *The Sorrows* is Goethe's Other world in which he cathetically articulated his repression. Rousseau once remarked of St Preux in *La Nouvelle Héloïse* that the character was not what he had been but what he wished to be. The production of fictional Otherness is, itself, a function of desire in the bourgeois world.

This is true of all forms of fiction, not just novels. In Christina Rosetti's poem 'Goblin Market' it is men who are

constituted as the Other. This poem is founded in the
sexuality of the bourgeois writing system. Although it may be
given a radical, critical reading, it appears to be a poem about
children and goblins and ends with a moral which extols the
virtues of sisterhood:

> For there is no friend like a sister
> In calm or stormy weather;
> To cheer one on the tedious way,
> To fetch one if one goes astray,
> To lift one if one totters down,
> To strengthen whilst one stands.
> (Lines 562–7)

Utilising a Gothic framework, Rosetti wrote a children's
poem in which not just the market economy but the men who
run it are perceived as alien. The men are goblins who sell
fruit; Laura and Lizzie are sisters who seem to live a self-
sufficient pastoral existence. If anyone buys and eats the
goblins' fruit, as their friend Jeanie did, they waste away and
die:

> Do you not remember Jeanie,
> Took their gifts both choice and many,
> Ate their fruits and wore their flowers,
> Plucked from bowers.
> Where the summer ripens at all hours?
> But ever in the moonlight
> She pined and pined away;
> Sought them by night and day,
> Found them no more but dwindled and grew grey;
> Then fell with the first snow,
> (Lines 147–57)

Jeanie's malady (and even Clarissa's), like that of Dracula's
victims, which I shall discuss later, could well be diagnosed in
the real world as hysteria. The inversion of the Garden of
Eden motif similarly calls up the idea that it is sexuality which
the goblin men are selling. The description of the fruit itself is
so sensual as to dispel any doubt. Laura gives in to temptation
and:

> Then sucked their fruit globes fair or red:
> Sweeter than honey from the rock,
> Stronger than man-rejoicing wine,
> Clearer than water flowed that juice;
> (Lines 128–31)

Having tasted the fruit it is impossible for the female to hear the cry of the goblin men again. The victim wastes away. Laura is saved, however, by the self-sacrifice of Lizzie, who goes to the goblin men to buy her some fruit. The goblins are angry when they realise it is not for her and in the ensuing fight try to force her to eat it. She returns safe to Laura but with her body covered in juice, which Laura sucks. Laura is saved, she:

> ... clung about her sister,
> Kissed and kissed and kissed her:
> Tears once again
> Refreshed her sunken eyes,
> Dropping like rain
> After a sultry drouth;
> Shaking with anguish, fear and pain,
> She kissed and kissed her with a hungry mouth.
> (Lines 485–92)

Laura paid for her fruit with a golden lock from her hair. Lizzie tried to pay with money. Sexuality is 'owned' by men—they 'spend' it after all—and Laura buys it with her body. Having succumbed to lust, Laura can no longer be tempted, but she must die for women are not allowed to be sexual, to partake in the goblin men's fruit. Here we have the symbolism of sucking, the male draining and sexualising the female, and the symbolism of blood:

> The wicked, quaint fruit-merchant men,
> Their fruits like honey to the throat
> But poison in the blood;
> (Lines 553–55)

Both of these ideas we will find reappear in the Gothic vampire myth. The blood here becomes polluted by the goblin's sexuality. In the end the story may be read not only as an asexual children's story but also as a story of sisterly love, of the saving of the domestic domain from the predatory male sexual capitalist domain. The male sexualising experience is anaesthetised when it is carried by a woman. At the end of the poem the two sisters have grown up to tell the story to their own children in their own safe domestic domains. Between them they have sustained the domestic domain since they do not have a sexual relationship. Incest is negated by the horror of it for the reader—Lizzie's act saves her sister rather than destroying her—and by the bourgeois belief in the impossibility of female/female sexual relations. Women must abstain from predatory male (capitalist) sexuality and remain as Other just as the sexuality on which the poem is constructed is repressed. The poem, after all, is Gothic, not pornographic. It is acceptable reading for children because it replicates the repression of bourgeois society. The 'innocent' child is able to 'innocently' read an 'innocent' poem. The excavation of the sexuality in the poem equates with the recognition that both children and the activity of reading have sexual components to their construction within bourgeois society.

For the asexual female, love is a much more important concept than for the male. Love may be said to be constituted in the fetishistic repression of the sexualised female. In fact, the effect of love on a person is remarkably similar to the effect of an orgasm. In pornography people have orgasms— sometimes simultaneously—as the repressed Other of love. Similarly in patriarchal mythology prostitutes are considered to enjoy sex with their customers, but while they may well have 'a heart of gold', they are not considered to be capable of falling in love.[3] Lovelace's actresses realise innocence by a control of their hearts, and it is to feeling, seated in the heart, that we must now turn.

Mrs Haywood in *Love in Excess*, one of the three most popular novels of the eighteenth century before *Pamela* (the others being *Gulliver's Travels* and *Robinson Crusoe*), writes thus:

Those who have the Power to apply themselves so seriously to any other Consideration as to forget him [i.e. Love], tho' but for a Moment, are but Lovers in Conceit, and have entertain'd Desire but as an agreeable

Amusement, which when attended with an Inconvenience, they may, without much difficulty shake off. Such a sort of Passion may be properly call'd *Liking*, but falls widely short of *Love*. Love is what we can neither resist, expel nor even alleviate, if we should never so vigorously attempt it.[4]

Love, then, is a feeling generated within the individual but over which the person who feels it has no control. Indeed Mrs Haywood would argue, in true Mills & Boon fashion, it is something over which the person should have no control. The last three decades of the eighteenth century, as Richetti tells us, was the period when the amatory novel took off, and also when the bourgeois marriage, based on property concerns, was both consolidated and threatened by the new individualist ideology of Romantic love.[5]

In the early seventeenth century the theme of love was of concern only to those in the new bourgeois Court of Manners, while in the eighteenth century they become of interest to a much wider group.[6] In order to understand bourgeois ideas of love we must look at the history of the idea. Stone suggests in *The Family, Sex and Marriage in England 1500–1800* that there was a spreading out of the notions of the importance of affection which had its origins in the twelfth century courtly love tradition. This ideology of affection becomes more important with the development of the capitalist ideology of individuality. Neat as this idea is, and useful because it emphasises the continuity between the two traditions, it does not take into account the new eroticisation which was taking place. The courtly love theme was principally concerned with the legitimisation of relationships (both sexual and non-sexual) outside aristocratic marriages contracted by people more concerned with the affairs of their lineage than with the happiness of the couple concerned. The fundamental difference in the case of Romantic love was that it was articulated teleologically as legitimising itself by virtue of its very existence. Love is considered to be a feeling and therefore to be natural. This enabled it to operate independently of marriage, though with marriage as the consummatory aim. The idea that Romantic love was spontaneous—and therefore good—allowed it a place not as supplementary to marriage but as something on which marriage could, and indeed should, be based. We must not forget that the domestic domain, like women, operates on feelings while the public, capitalist domain, like men, operates on reason.

Earlier forms of marriage, both aristocratic and peasant, were essentially instrumental. To justify this I will take but two examples from Shorter's study of landholding peasantry in France, remembering that I have elsewhere demonstrated the lack of repressed sexuality and therefore of eroticism to be found in such societies—a point, I should add, which Shorter also makes. After marriage in this French society women would not use the familiar form 'tu' to their spouses.[7] This new politeness, as well as demonstrating the subservient position of the woman, showed there to be an unbridged division within the relationship. That this division is a product of instrumentality rather than a lack of affection is shown in the proverb from Britanny: 'Mort de femme et vie de cheval font l'homme riche.'[8] Rather than belabour this point I would suggest even a cursory reading of Le Roy Ladurie's *Montaillou* demonstrates well the instrumental nature of peasant relationships in a medieval village. The shift was this:

> Affection and inclination, love and sympathy, came to take the place of 'instrumental' considerations in regulating the dealings of family members with one another. Spouses and children came to be prized for what they were, rather than for what they represented or could do. That is the essence of 'sentiment'.[9]

Bourgeois Romantic love is an artifice which unites the individual with his/her essence and Other. The reflexive fracture of the bourgeois individual is healed in the desirous union of two individuals. Shorter gives credence to this idea of Romantic love when he writes that 'affection and romantic love have wellsprings in the unconscious, and in the beast's nature lie unpredictability and transitoriness.'[10] The new truth, on which Romantic love is based, is that spouses and children really *are* something. This is the experiential basis of fetishism.

We may compare this idea of love spontaneously coming into being in both male and female with the courtly love tradition, which as we have seen has, historically, a claim to be its antecedent: 'In every love relation in the courtly lyric, the living lady, universally esteemed, reflects that idealized image of the man who consecrates himself to serving her.'[11] Love here is not the mystical conjoining of two minds but rather is a term used to describe the knight's use of the lady as a mirror which throws back to him an image which enhances the meaningfulness of his society. We should remember here the earlier discussion of Lacan. As Goldin points out, from the medieval perspective the decline of Narcissus was not the result of loving himself but was occasioned by the fact that that self was only an image. The modern accounts of Freud and Lacan emphasise the predicament of the person as individual; the medieval account emphasised the problem of empirical reality and representation in a world where all mirrors mirror the Reality of God. In that world the worthy individual must, as St Augustine wrote, love his own mind as he loves God. The person who is complete, then, loves himself—hence the mode of functioning of courtly love in which the woman makes the man more worthy. Bourgeois society interrupts this endless flow of reflections making love into something which dyadically moves from one person to another, essentialising the person as individual in the process.

Just as the earliest usage of drawers by women may be traced to sixteenth-century Italy, so too, and for the same reason, we may go to Italy to find the first example of this new notion of love. Castiglione devotes almost all of the fourth and last book of *The Book of the Courtier* to a discussion of love and how it should and should not be practised. Such a lengthy discussion in a book which achieved instant popularity would itself suggest that the bourgeois reading public in Italy—and in thirty-three years Britain as well—considered love to be a problem in its relation to the new bourgeois code of behaviour, the code which mediated the meeting point of the new private body and new public society. Castiglione's argument is that real love, as opposed to sensual love, which he regards as pardonable in young people, is only attainable in later life when 'the soule is not now so much wayed downe with the bodily burden, and when the natural burning [i.e. physical lust] aswageth and draweth to a warmth'.[12] In this condition, 'if they [i.e. those of a "more ripe age"] be inflamed with beautie, and to it bend their coveting, guided by reasonable choice, they be not deceived, and possess beautie perfectly'.[13] Already the opposition is set up between lust and love. It is reason which harnesses sensual lust which enables love to flower. If, having thoroughly examined this emotion reflexively by means of reason, the courtier finds that it is still present, then Castiglione advocates sexual abstinence: 'But in case it continue or encrease, then must the Courtier determine (when he perceiveth hee is taken) to shunne throughly all filthinesse of common love, and so enter into the holy way of love, with the guide of reason.'[14] Here, at the very beginning of the bourgeois tradition, we find the displacement articulated. The courtier is, in the first place, attracted by the woman's physical beauty. However, the strength of his attachment to her must be equivalent to his repression of any physical, sexual, feeling for her. The mediating structure which exists within this displacement is the code of manners which it is Castiglione's purpose to elaborate. His ability to differentiate is founded on the newly important notion of reason. In Castiglione's system man is 'of nature indowed with reason'.[15] Real love, like real society, is the harmonious uniting of these two aspects. The historical justification for this perception of human beings is well known.[16] Castiglione's emphasis, however, is new. His saw is social customs, indeed society, and his description of 'man' becomes a justification for repression, a repression from which springs both society and love. The essentialism which is credited to Romantic love affirms for the individual his/her reality. In turn, the reality of that society is the point of contact with the structuration of displacement (the Absence) upon and with which bourgeois 'reality' exists.

Love is defined as unreflective, undistanced, undisplaced feeling; feeling which is instantaneous, like Richardson's ideal mode of writing and the bourgeois ideal mode of reading. Love is experienced not as sexualised desire but as uncontrollable longing. For Mrs Haywood's heroines and heroes, however, the effect is the same:

> What now could poor Amena do, surrounded with so many Powers, attack'd by such a charming force without, betray'd by tenderness within: Virtue and Pride, the Guardians of her Honour fled from her Brest ... Dressing that Day, she had only a thin silk Night Gown on, which flying open as he caught her in his Arms, he found her panting Heart beat measures of consent, her heaving Brest swell to be press'd by his, and every pulse confess a wish to yield[17]

Feeling becomes not just the affirmation of the person as an individual but also the assertion of the individual in a social world where appearance is separate from but images reality.

Feeling also governs coition. Just as intercourse generates reality, love guarantees the reality of intercourse. Richetti notes, 'We noticed as well that only Amena's palpitations are described. She vibrates, he controls. But his pleasure, even though he is the aggressor, is irrelevant to Mrs. Haywood's readers.'[18] It is irrelevant because he *appears* to be there to serve rather than to master. The predominantly middle-class female readership of Mrs Haywood would identify (unflexively and with feeling, of course, as is expected of bourgeois readers of fiction) with Amena as the experiencer of pleasure, not as the person whose reality is created by the male, D'Elmont. In the 'pornographic' *Fanny Hill*, Cleland makes this loss of reflexivity the test of good coition; for example, 'she went wholly out of her mind into that favourite part of her body'.[19] *Fanny Hill* emphasises the body as the seat of feeling; *Pamela* and *Love in Excess* emphasise the heart, or rather the mind as the seat of 'Love'. Intercourse, as the moment of displacement, of the (re)creation of the real, carries also the moment of its own materialisation as a social construction, as a simulacrum of reality. Whether intercourse is 'felt' or not, the individuals involved—and particularly the woman—are lost. They become objects.

Love in the bourgeois world is the permanent attraction of a single woman and/or single man. Pamela is concerned with the fixing power of love. Rousseau found in *Clarissa* the critique of *le monde* which he desired precisely because it can be read as a story of everlasting love (as reality). *Pamela*, as Fielding demonstrated, may read as dissimulation, as myth. *Clarissa* cannot be read as dissimulation because it is dissimulation. Desire and love pervade the text as twin structures of myth and reality, each revealing the other for an appearance in the day-to-day (re)constructions of existence. In the truly bourgeois *La Nouvelle Héloïse* Rousseau decentres the bourgeois preoccupation with intercourse which is so crucial to *Clarissa* and replaces it with the 'individual' and love. The repression of the text which is present in *Pamela* is completed in the later bourgeois novel in which the concern is for individuals who love one another.

La Nouvelle Héloïse may be read as a commentary on this change. Tony Tanner ends a fine piece of writing on this book, saying, 'This enormous book is for the greater part concerned with an extensive dream of union whereby the family house can be extended and modified so as to contain within it everyone (and everything) that Julie loves in different ways'.[20] Julie's dream is to be able to reconcile the bourgeois (signifying) Wolmar and the desired/loved (realising) Saint-Preux in a Real union of love. This 'love triangle' is a commonly occurring theme in bourgeois fiction. In *The Sorrows* for example Lotte's dream is to reconcile Albert and Werther, while in *Wuthering Heights* Catherine is torn between Edgar Linton and Heathcliffe. The bourgeois myth is the union of this irreconcilable duality in an idyll. The end of *Wuthering Heights* with the uniting of the two opposing forces in a new generation is an example of this in practice. The substitution of the fetishised individual within his or her body as the focus of the novel—a substitution extended and developed by Goethe in *The Sorrows of Young Werther*—for the desire for intercourse, is in this sense only a shift in emphasis. Homologously to the body in bourgeois intercourse Julie's love is, but contains more than, sexualised desire. As a consequence, it is not stable; the idyllic quality of the book is to be found in the assertion that it is.

La Nouvelle Héloïse starts on a high point of personal anguish reflected in—or rather articulated for the reader by— a use of language designed to express a heightened emotional state. To appreciate its full effect one must read the French. However, in translation the feeling is there: 'I must fly, from you, Mademoiselle, I know I must. I should not have waited so long, or rather, I should never have seen you. But what can I do now? How shall I begin? You have promised me your friendship; consider my difficulties and advise me.'[21] Here we find that involvement so important to Romantic love transposed to the reader's relationship to the text. The use of sentiment is a strategy for generating involvement. Moreover, the result of both Romantic love and literary involvement is the same: the validation of the lover and the reader as real. Below I will discuss the relation of love and writing in *The Sorrows*. In *La Nouvelle Héloïse* the space which is the place of desire between Saint-Preux and Julie as well as Julie's ambiguous desire for Saint Preux is filled by a continuous outpouring of sentiment which provides a location for the reader's emotional involvement. The material success of the book—it went through seventy-two editions in French alone between 1761 and 1800—points to Rousseau's successful understanding of bourgeois sensibility. In *La Nouvelle Héloïse*, as in most epistolary fiction, the reader's involvement is achieved through his/her relation to the letters. In the more completely self-contained novel the reader's involvement is achieved through an emphasis on character. Here the reader can find a focus for identification. In *The Sorrows* Goethe attempted to produce a piece of epistolary fiction in which, nevertheless, the reader was supposed to empathise with Werther as a character. Werther's letters are important not as contributions to a structure of desire and meaning but as descriptions of Werther's emotions. The letters affirm Werther as an individual. The novel confirms this by only giving us Werther's letters. Werther lives within the letters. There is only one way out of the novel—the cessation of Werther's letters. There is only one way out for Werther—his death. Clarissa dies as a counterpoint to her rape and as a function of her appropriation of the novel. Werther dies so that the novel which is him may end.

In *Pamela*, near the beginning of the genre, the majority of letters were written by one person; in *The Sorrows* all the letters are written by Werther. Here, however, the similarity ends for whereas Pamela's letters describe events and objects, Werther's letters use events and objects (in particular Lotte as woman-as-object) to elaborate (for us) his own emotional state. As a consequence, the reader is established as a voyeur and participates in Werther's emotions. The prerequisite for this involvement is the objectness of the novel's world and of the people who compose that world. Existentially, the reader apprehends the world of the novel as object. Werther's emotional expression of love provides the basis for the reader's emotional involvement. In the process Lotte's objectness is duplicated and confirmed as she becomes both Werther's validating object for the reader in this Other world, a fetish twice-over. Pamela's letters structure her world through her presentation of her knowledge and her perceptions. The illusion is Richardson's that it is a real world represented by her real letters rather than an illusory world presented by fictitious letters, which in the strict sense are not even letters at all. That world is not a private world of thought; it is a public world in which the individual participates through events.

Werther's letters show us a very different world, the world of the individual. Pamela's letters structure the world by the fact of presentation. Werther's letters structure the individual—Werther, who exists between the first letter and his final suicide note. Pamela's world exists for Werther only outside himself, an unstructured world which Werther attempts to structure not by his actions but by his being, his existence; a success achieved by Goethe—with a little aid from the letters and 'editor'—but not by Werther. His death signals Goethe's success and his own failure. The degree of Goethe's success depends upon the reader's belief in the illusory world created, dependent on the realism of Werther. However, the world which is generated in this fashion is a world split between the individual and the world around him. Goethe can only resolve this split with Werther's suicide. It is at one and the same time the final assertive act of the individual—Werther himself has already said this—and the moment when the separating power of the individual's reflexivity, the force which generates the individuality of Werther, is lost. The person, no longer individual in this special sense, and the world are thus united. It is then no irony that while Werther considers that Lotte has 'touched [his] heart'[22] and that 'since [seeing Lotte] sun, moon, and stars can do what they will—I haven't the faintest notion whether it is day or night. The world about me has vanished',[23] he nevertheless continues to use Lotte to display his own emotions, indeed to create for him the emotions which articulate him as individual.

The fully developed bourgeois individual, male or female, is as the Romantics appreciated, a fetish marking the existential apprehension of difference, of lack of unity. The person becomes an individual striving for unity, a unity achieved either in orgasm, love or death. Freud remarked that 'In the opposed situation of being most intensely in love and of suicide the ego is overwhelmed by the object, though in totally different ways.'[24] The comparison is well made. The differentiation, for Freud, is that love, by which he means what I have called Romantic love, overwhelms the self-love of the ego enabling the individual to become fully involved in another individual. Similarly, for Freud, the act of suicide can only occur when the ego views itself, the individual, as an object. Hence, in both instances the ego is obliterated, on the one hand through the translation of individual identity into a dyadic union, on the other through the total objectification of the self. Both these possibilities exist as elaborations on the basic idea of the essential individualism of the bourgeois person. For suicide the new understanding of the individual as having final dominion over him/herself leads inexorably to the argument that that dominion should be extended to the possibility of taking oneself out of existence completely. The medieval Church was against suicide, calling it self-murder and relating it to the Sixth Commandment (Thou shalt not kill). By contrast the modern period tends to consider suicide a qualitatively different act to murder.

While we might argue that the rise of Protestantism and the decline in Christian authority might have led to a greater acceptability of the idea of suicide, it is asking a lot to argue that the rise in the rate of suicide in the post-seventeenth century period may be attributed to the loss of that authority. After all, if the Church achieved such little control over people's sexual lives, why should it have been able to control their attitude to death any better? Suicide itself is a word which enters the English language in the seventeenth century, about the same time that the act enters English literature. The *Oxford English Dictionary* finds its first use in writing in 1651, but Alvarez has found it earlier in Thomas Browne's *Religio Medici* written in 1635 and published in 1642.[25] It might be argued that new socio-economic conditions produced a rise in what Durkheim calls anomic suicide, and I would not disagree with this. My point is simpler—that the new acceptance of suicide sprang from a new understanding of the individual[26] and that the change in name was one reflection of this. The Romantics, who understood the power of love, also appreciated the power of suicide. At the Sorbonne in 1841 a group formed The Suicide Club. In the case of Werther we see both love and suicide utilised. Because Freud does not go on to look at the manner in which his views of love and suicide are similar, he fails to see that both may be experienced as expressions of bourgeois individuality. For Werther love and death are diametrically opposed but, structurally, they are the same; both validate him as individual.

It is in the context of love and death that we can understand some of the power of Dracula. Dracula exists between life and death; he is 'undead'. He does not age. He also exists between desire and love. He needs women because their blood enables him to remain stable between life and death. The mythography of Dracula is by no means this simple and involves many contradictions, but we can say that Dracula's Otherness consists in his being neither living nor dead, neither desirous nor loving. He is all these things. Indeed, he lacks emotions (emotions would give him life as a human being). Mr Spock in *Star Trek* has the same problem. Luckily for him he had a human mother (his father was a Vulcan), and every so often his humanness, his emotions, seem to show through. Dracula, however, is wholly Other. In Polidori's story *The Vampyre* the vampire, here called Lord Ruthven, murders his own wife between the marriage ceremony and the consummation. Frankenstein's monster murdered Frankenstein's wife at an equivalent moment. Just as, on the wedding night rape and consensual intercourse were often indistinguishable, so sex and death, in the Gothic commentary, also merge together.

Polidori wrote the first modern version of Dracula as his

contribution to a competition with Mary Shelley, Percy Bysshe Shelley and Byron to write a horror story. However, the myth of the vampire is more usually associated with Bram Stoker's novel published in 1897. The new feature which differentiates the modern vampire from his forbears is the eroticisation which, from Polidori onwards, comes to surround the subject.[27] Like that other great bourgeois horror figure, the nameless monster in *Frankenstein*, the vampire occupies a position as an Other to bourgeois reality. Just as the monster articulates the combination of concerns around marriage/intercourse and reproduction, so the vampire embodies the concerns which surround love/intercourse and death. In Polidori's story the victim wife's mysterious destruction is, in fact, a Gothic nuptial consummation. The ambiguity at the heart of bourgeois sexuality here Gothically consumes it as the climax of the story. The Other has penetrated to the centre of bourgeois society and destroyed it by destroying the dichotomy on which it was founded.

Polidori's story is more obviously sexual than is Stoker's. Lord Ruthven delights in ruining virtuous women. Ruthven quite clearly embodies the repressed Other of bourgeois sexuality. Moreover, in a straightforward fashion the end of the story and the climax of the story occur simultaneously. The repression of the sexuality of the reading process and of the sexuality in the story duplicate one another. In Stoker's novel the story of Dracula is framed on the one side by the engagement of Jonathan Harker and Mina Murray and on the other by their marriage. In both cases the text expresses the repression of bourgeois marriage as its reason for existence. The reading of *Dracula* is the articulation of a repression once more confined by the bourgeois marriage, but it is an articulation made safe for the reader by the conventions of the bourgeois reading practice.

Dracula and the other vampires are designated as the Undead; the kiss which they bring repositions a person as neither in the realm of the living nor the dead. Moreover, this kiss is the kiss of love as well as lust. When Dracula finds the three female vampires about to kiss Harker, he drives them away and is accused by them of never having loved. His reply is, 'Yes, I too can love; you yourselves can tell it from the past.

Is it not so? Well, now I promise you that when I am done with him you shall kiss him at your will. Now go! go! I must awaken him'.[28] The love which should bring one into the life realised by bourgeois reality, in this case, takes one entirely out of the realm of that reality. A part of Dracula's threat is that he sexualises the domestic domain. This sexualisation is reinforced by the sexual excess embodied in the hint of polygyny. Dracula's victims evidence a similar mixture of emotions to those expressed in the pornographic myth of the rape which turns into a desired lust. They begin by fearing him and trying to escape from him and end by offering him their necks to be bitten. Stoker, and his followers, have clothed the pornography with an acceptable level of repression.

The newly sexualised women sicken and finally become undead.

> The woman grows pale and thin, eats little, or if she eats does not profit by it. Everything wearies her,—to sew, to write, to read, to walk,—and by and by the sofa or the bed is her only comfort. Every effort is paid for dearly, and she describes herself as aching and sore, as sleeping ill, and as needing constant stimulus and endless tonics. Then comes the mischievous role of bromides, opium, chloral and brandy.[29]

This could be a passage from *Dracula* so accurately does it run through the symptoms of Dracula's victims. In fact, it is from a handbook written by S. Weir Mitchell and is his description of the typical suppressed hysteric. Female vampires bear a remarkable resemblance to women who have traversed the hysteric stage in which their sexuality is manifested within the bonds of bourgeois domestic confinement and, having been sexually liberated by Dracula, they become predatory beings in their own right. For Stoker, however, this is not a critical expression of radical values. The text of *Dracula* affirms Dracula and his activities as horrible. The reader is positioned in a conservative perspective and the better experiences the horror. The bourgeois reader is supposed to be thankful at the end of the novel that Dracula is destroyed and Jonathan and Mina are able to live out their bourgeois repressed marriage. In this sense the end of *Dracula* is more conservative than the end of *Jane Eyre*. The conservatism of *Dracula* is apparent in the one place where Stoker allows Mina to comment on the then current position of women:

> Lucy is asleep and breathing softly. She has more colour in her cheeks than usual and looks, oh, so sweet. If Mr. Holmwood fell in love with her seeing her only in the drawing room, I wonder what he would say if he saw her now. Some of the 'New Women' writers will one day start an idea that men and women should be allowed to see one another asleep before proposing or accepting. But I suppose the New Woman won't condescend in future to accept; she will do the proposing herself. And a nice job she will make of it too![30]

Mina goes on to be rescued from the terror that Dracula brings, but Lucy succumbs and becomes a child molester on Hampstead Heath. She accosts young boys and drinks their blood. Not only is she sexually active but she likes young males. Oh, the horror for patriarchy! Luckily, van Helsing is to hand and persuades Arthur Holmwood to drive the necessary phallic stake through her heart. He who would have been her husband becomes her murderer and saviour. Lucy is finally confined in a Gothic rewriting of the wedding-night experience.

The body, the site of the individual, is transformed by the kiss which draws blood, the same blood which was of such concern to Descartes, turning it into something human but not human, analogous to the body of Frankenstein's creation. For the Cartesian individual the circulation of the blood marked the isolation and unity of the person. Blood becomes an affirmation of life. However, blood is also conventionally an accompaniment of the defloweration of the wedding night and a sign of the male bourgeois preoccupation with virginity and its loss. If we go back to Fanny Hill we find her making use of a small phial of blood in order to convince her clients that she was a virgin. Throughout this period blood is also associated with menstruation, which was taken to be a sign of the imperfection of women. In 1859 Jules Michelet wrote, 'woman is forever suffering from the cicatrization of an interior wound which is the cause of the whole drama. So that in reality for fifteen days out of twenty-eight—one may say always—woman is not only invalided but wounded. She suffers incessantly from the wound of love.'[31] I have chosen this quotation because it sums up the male fantasy so well; extreme imperfection coupled with an overtone which suggests that the necessity of menstruation is somehow sexual—though (or perhaps because of this) intercourse during this period was taboo. Blood, then, was an evocative sexual image; more than this, it imaged a repressed female sexuality. Within this context the blood-sucking of Dracula becomes more understandable as a Gothic metaphor. Charlotte Brontë had already used it in *Jane Eyre*, however, when she made Bertha Mason suck her brother's blood and say that 'she'd drain my heart'. Bertha's sexuality here overruns into incest. Jane Eyre even says later than Bertha reminded her of a vampire. The vampire/female sexuality link is unmistakable. It is no wonder that during the early part of this century the term 'vamp' was used colloquially to refer to sexually liberated women.

The agelessness of the vampire precludes the bourgeois idyll of growing old as a loving couple within marriage. Just as love and suicide perform the same affirming function for Werther, so in *Dracula* unnatural love generates an unnatural, ageless death-in-life which, in the horror they produce in the bourgeois reader, go to affirm the safety of Romantic love and bourgeois marriage. *Dracula* ends with a brief note 'in which we find, seven years on, Jonathan and Mina married with a young son'. Marriage and reproduction are once again harmonised. Life and death, too, reoccupy their 'natural' places. Jonathan and Mina's son has the same birthday as that of Quincey Morris and is given his name. Quincey was the name of their companion who, though mortally wounded, had still managed to plunge his bowie knife into Dracula's heart. Now that the threat has been vanquished, the hero can live again as an average bourgeois.

The reality of Werther is for him a function of his (re)creation of Lotte, who like all the other characters we only know through Werther's writings, which are, in all but the case of one letter and the suicide note, not letters to her but letters to William *about* her. Werther, as a character, is one stage on from Lovelace. In *The Sorrows* Lotte has always already been appropriated by Werther just as we always assume Werther's essential existence. Werther's problem is to find unity not reality. Lovelace's problem was to assert his existence by relating to Clarissa. In *Clarissa*, as in *Pamela*, the reader is positioned within the structure; in *The Sorrows* the reader is positioned within Werther. Lotte is created as fetish by Werther just as Frankenstein literally (physically) creates the monster/human being. It is Frankenstein's creation which kills his spouse Elizabeth after the marriage ceremony but before the marriage night. The being, of human pieces but not of human birth, calls into question the fetishised construction of the individual and his liminal quality is reflected in his separation of the two components of bourgeois marriage, the public and the private, thus fulfilling the threat which has shaped Frankenstein's life from the moment the being first uttered it: 'I go; but remember, I shall be with you on your wedding night!'

It is a comment on what I have said earlier about names that the monster is not named. This also places it as outside human, bourgeois society. Moreover, in a world where everything is named and classified into a system—Linnaeus had published his now famous work in 1735—the lack of a name places the monster outside of nature as well. From this period on, Otherness must be unnatural; it must utilize the repressions of society itself. Thus while Lotte is defined as human and realises Werther's and the reader's world, the monster of *Frankenstein* produces horror by threatening the category distinctions by which bourgeois society operates. I should add that the being's ideas of love are themselves shaped by his reading of *The Sorrows*. The monster's gradual disabusal that the idea of love which he has picked up from the book actually occurs in real life may be read as a commentary on the notion of love by Mary Shelley herself. Her work can be regarded as a Gothic Other to *The Sorrows* in the sense that it is a story of frustration and exclusion, the obverse of the bourgeois love idyll.

In a later Gothic fantasy the sympathy and the horror which a bourgeois audience feels for King Kong exists because the monster behaves towards Fay Wray as should the ideal Romantic lover. In other words, King Kong switches genres. This is evident even in the early scene where he begins to disrobe Fay Wray (the film's suggestion is that he is

fascinated by clothes—something he has not seen before). In
its filmic structure, however, the bourgeois viewer—
positioned from a 'male' perspective—voyeuristically
watches Fay Wray's body being revealed. In this case the
tendency is for the viewer to read against the film. As the film
progresses King Kong's actions demonstrate more obviously
his Romantic attachment; he shows jealousy and he finally
dies in a vain attempt to keep possession of, and protect, Fay
Wray. What started out as a Gothic utilisation of repression
becomes, at the end, another celebration of the bourgeois love
idyll. Frankenstein never completes the mate his monster
requests and the monster kills Frankenstein's loved one.
King Kong loves a woman and is killed by the aeroplanes of
society, the revulsion the bourgeois feels at an unnatural love
affair is defused by society's triumph, thus permitting the
viewer to feel sorry for King Kong comfortably while
empathising with his emotional attachment. All these
monstrous Others are male. A female Other would be read as
male just as a radical text would be read as cathartic fictional
fantasy.

There is no horror attached to Werther's love for Lotte;
indeed, his suicide becomes a triumph for the bourgeois
reader who empathises with him. It is not a shocking act from
which the reader recoils. The evidence for this may be found
in the wave of copy-cat suicides which the book precipitated
and, more generally, in the cult which surrounded the
Werther character. Friedenthal notes that 'There was a
Werther epidemic; *Werther* fever, a *Werther* fashion—young
men dressed in blue tail coats and yellow waistcoats—
Werther caricatures—*Werther* suicides.'[32] The popularity,
and degree, of identification with Werther demonstrates the
acceptance of the ideology of Romantic love amongst the male
population of Europe. It equally demonstrates the
acceptability of suicide. The unity for which Werther strives
and which would reconstruct him as both individual and
whole and which Werther could not find in love, he found in
suicide.

I have argued that in the epistolary novel the letter is
written and read as a manifestation of desire. The letters
comprise an explicit structure. The reader is integrated by

means of the libidinal act of reading into the structure. In *The Sorrows* this does not occur. In *Pamela* and *Clarissa* the characters' logorrhoea, if anything, increases during periods of emotional tension. After the rape Clarissa sits at her table and writes disjointed notes. She articulates her emotional turmoil in writing, but in *The Sorrows* writing is not used as a means to involve the reader. The reader is expected to elide his/her awareness of the text itself in order to enter Werther's mental world. As a consequence, Werther himself has a very different attitude towards writing. For him writing is not desire; it is a pale imitation, indeed a sublimation, of desire. In his fourth letter Werther requests that William should not send him any books as 'I have no wish to be influenced, encouraged, or inspired anymore. My heart surges wildly enough without any outside influence'.[33] Werther reads to generate emotion, an emotion in which he will be asserted as an individual. At this time the letters to William are despatched thick and fast—4 May, 10 May, 12 May, 13 May, 15 May, and so on. However, as soon as he meets Lotte the letters stop. When, after a gap of sixteen days he finally does write, it is, we are again led to believe, in reply to a query from William: 'You want to know why I don't write? You ask me that, you who are supposed to be a learned man? You should know without a word from me that I am well and ... oh, let's not beat about the bush. I have met someone who has touched my heart.'[34] Not only has William had to spur him into writing but Werther suggests that being 'learned' given the status of literary education in bourgeois society (I assume he means well-read) he should know already why Werther has not written. What keeps Werther from indulging in literary activity, here of course writing rather than reading, must be something which excites his emotions more. Werther/Goethe is himself here commenting on the sexual nature of writing and reading. For Werther the only thing which could excite him more is love. Just as writing is a manifestation of sublimation for the bourgeois (in this case Werther), so in the act of reading the bourgeois suppresses awareness of the writing which separates the reader from the realist text's fictional world. The text which is produced as an expression of sublimation is repressed as it is consumed.

Pamela writes unceasingly when B.'s intentions are dishonourable, when honourable and she discovers she loves him, and when married. Clarissa and Lovelace, too, are forever writing letters. By contrast, as Werther becomes increasingly unbalanced he writes less. This correlates with his increasing obsession with Lotte. Werther's letter before the first intervention of the 'editor' runs thus: 'How the sight of her haunts me! Awake and dreaming, she fills my whole being. Here, when I close my eyes, here, behind my forehead, where we assemble our insight, I see her dark eyes. ... [Her eyes] fill my whole mind.'[35] Werther's love/desire for Lotte appears as a substitute for literary activity, but the reverse is the case. Werther realises himself in his relation to Lotte far better than in literary activity. His last action before turning Albert's gun on himself was to write a suicide note. Previous to this he had spent 'the rest of the evening going through his papers again, tore up many and threw them into the stove, sealed several packets and addressed them to William'.[36] Werther gives himself a literary execution before turning the gun to his head.[37] There is another connection here, not as esoteric as it might appear at first sight. Werther's literary execution was not just that, it was also a clearing-up of his bourgeois, capitalist affairs. Werther settles his contractual obligations with bourgeois society and thus no longer feels bound to that society. In England the debate on suicide moves from its medieval Christian basis to its mid-eighteenth-century legal basis epitomised by Hume's discussion on whether or not suicide is criminal. It does this by way of the new post-Hobbesian view of society as being based on contract.[38] In this argument the right to suicide depends on a person's ability to fulfil his/her contractual obligations to society. Werther literally does and therefore, in the most materialist sense, earns the right to opt out of the Social Contract.

Letters, for Werther, are the articulation of a distantiation which enables him to generate his own individuality. Literary activity in general has become the establishment of separation, alienation. Werther's desire for a union with Lotte, a union defined both sexually, as best exemplified in his final meeting with her, and socially, as best shown in his sense of disaster after he discovers that Lotte and Albert have married, transcends the emotional satisfaction he looks for in literary activity. The essential alienation which lies at the root of, and which is reinforced by, his desire for union/unity, is the fundamental separation which Werther attempts to overcome by his love for Lotte. However, Werther only succeeds in establishing Lotte as a fetish, an object. Werther's letters do not tie him to Lotte. They reach out as aspects of himself and establish her as Other, as separate and different just as, for the reader, post-epistolary fiction is separate and Other. Werther, and the bourgeois individual in general, is in the world but, as fetish, is not united with it. Werther's sketching may be read as a symbol of this. It is an attempt to capture a world from which he is estranged.

Werther's pastime is sketching; his ideal is to draw nature as it is, without adding anything:

> I sat down on the plough and began with great enthusiasm to sketch this little picture of brotherly devotion. I put in the fence, a barn door and a few dilapidated wagon-wheels—everything, just as it was—and found, after half an hour had passed that I had produced a very well-arranged and interesting drawing without really having contributed anything to it.[39]

The illusion in which Werther believes is that this nature, which he reproduces, is there in the first place. Werther's sight enables him to become a channel, a medium for the pictorial description. As he goes on to say, 'rules and regulations ruin our appreciation of nature and our powers to express it.'[40] Werther sketches with the same ideal in mind with which he reads and writes. These activities are not problematical for him; they are simply extensions of the individual which help to (re)produce the world as a means of realising the world. The importance of sketching is not limited to its use by Goethe; sketching, along with the ability to play music or sing, was one of the necessary accomplishments of the well-brought-up nineteenth-century bourgeois female. Within the limited context of the domestic domain the fantasy of female production is in this way extended.

Werther's eyes are his tool for union;[41] they are not a means for mind-disciplined use. Sight, as I have noted before, is the fundamental sense in the process of fetishisation. As a consequence, it is the most charged sense. Werther utilises sight, and eyes as its place of origin, as the medium for producing unity. In the Gothic mirror Dracula's eyes have a tendency to glow red the moment before he plunges his teeth into some unfortunate's neck. When Werther becomes obsessed by Lotte it is her eyes which 'fill [his] whole mind'.[42] Goethe associates eyes with the natural. In *Elective Affinities* the baby born to Charlotte has the Captain's features but it has Otillie's eyes, Otillie being the most 'natural' of the quartet—so 'natural', in fact, that she has to be taken away from the social, unnatural, school to flower in the natural setting of the domestic home, under Charlotte's tutelage. During the act of intercourse from which the baby was conceived, Charlotte was thinking of the Captain and Eduard of Otillie. Since capitalist society is built on fetishism, eyes and sight become an important signification of the natural. When Rochester's sight starts returning in *Jane Eyre* it is in the natural domestic domain sanctioned by his marriage to Jane. In *Dracula* the red glowing of his eyes asserts his essential unnaturalness.

Werther, then, approaches both his drawing and his literary activity in the same way and it is no surprise that as his letter writing declines so he finds himself increasingly unable to draw. It is not that these activities are displaced by his love/desire for Lotte, but rather that they are, themselves, cathexes, dropped when the real thing is offered. In the sexualised society Werther's need for an experience such as that manifested in his relations with Lotte is the description of the displacement which articulates Werther as individual and as real. Werther's other activities are palliatives, satisfying but not successful in illuminating and articulating the primary displacement which realises Werther's world. Werther's relationship with Lotte is a product of the displacement which produces bourgeois sexuality. Werther creates Lotte as fetish. Goethe's success in realising Werther is dependent on Werther's lack of success in realising himself. In our sexualised society the satisfactory reading of *The Sorrows* is dependent upon our experience of it as sexually charged writing. The story of Werther's love is, itself, a displacement of sexual desire and this desire is never consummated. From this perspective the book may be read as a gradual revelation of love as desire. Moreover, the reader's necessary deferral of gratification (a practice common among the bourgeois middle classes according to sociologists) implicit in the process of reading the novel is reflected in the lack of gratification available to Werther. The final substitution of suicide for marriage/intercourse validates the reader who, because of his/her voyeuristic position, can never be wholly satisfied by a love story. Both reader and Werther are, at the end, isolated and Werther's suicide presents the reader with his/her repressed climax.

The first time Werther, and the readers, meet Lotte it is in physical description: 'Six children, from about eleven to two, were swarming around a very pretty girl of medium height. She had on a simple white dress with pale pink bows on the sleeves and at her breast, and she was holding a loaf of black bread'.[43] Goethe/Werther, the sketcher, gives us a 'natural' description and the woman appears as object. Her dress is not seen in the social context of fashion but as an expression of her *persona*. If we return to Erasmus and his 'natural' etiquette we find that while the first chapter of *De civilitate puerorum* is devoted to the body; the second is concerned with dress. Dress, as I have noted before, is for the bourgeois a complex extension of the body. Later, Werther writes to William that he has asked repeatedly for one of the bows, and it is given to him as part of his birthday present. He has kissed it, he writes to William, 'a thousand times'. The dress is not just an extension of her *persona*, it becomes a fetishised extension of the fetish which is Lotte.[44] There is a similar scene in *Elective Affinities* when Eduard kisses a slipper belonging to Otillie. The connotations of the whiteness of the dress were, for Goethe's time, what they are now—purity and, in the new bourgeois society of which both Werther and Lotte are a part, virginity.

Lotte, as object is also placed as natural. She is surrounded by children and she is feeding them. This image draws on, and enhances, the ideology of the naturalness of domestic relations, the home as private. The *oekos* of the private domestic sphere is structured in opposition to the capitalist economic structuring of bourgeois society in the public market-place. The domination of the woman, wife, in the domestic sphere signals this by inversion, but it is of course only an apparent domination. The finance of the household is conditioned by the income of the male (husband) in the labour market. Capitalist society calls the domestic domain into existence, the production fracturing the previous unity. That it is only an apparent domination Goethe makes clear in the scene between the dying Frau M. and her miserly husband. Because her husband would not give her enough housekeeping money Frau M. regularly pilfered from his till. This negation of the structurally opposed spheres was felt by her to be so important as to warrant a death-bed confession.

Lotte is not married—nor, of course, is she a mother. The 'real' situation in which Werther finds himself is, compared to the bourgeois ideal type, un-real. But its reality resolves important disjunctures in the ideological *topoi*. Lotte is signified iconically both as virgin and as mother. She draws on and combines the signification of the sexualised mother and of the virginal blood kin sister. I have described how in *Wuthering Heights* the Catherine of Lockwood's dream is composed of an analogous sexual/non-sexual combination. Werther, too, is drawn into this system by Lotte's classification of him as 'cousin', a kin position which occupies the unsure border region for incest definition in bourgeois society. This was a common pre-bourgeois appellation but which now has a new effect. The equivocalness of the classification reflects and reinforces Werther's developing desire as both sexual and non-sexual.

In terms of the structure of the book its success in articulating the Romantic bourgeois ideology as Real lies not in Werther's desire but in the characterisation of Lotte as the fetishised object. Lotte's naturalness, in fact, is not a naturalness that stands outside society but one which is a product of a perfect integration of her actions with social convention. (Remember Werther calls her perfection.) Although Werther writes as if there were a radical discontinuity between nature and society (his letters from his time as secretary to the ambassador are the most obvious example), in fact it is the reflexive articulation of the social as artefact which he dislikes:

> How dreadful people are who have nothing on their minds for years but formality, whose every effort and thought are bent towards moving one place higher up the table!...
> If only the fools would realise that the seating doesn't really matter, that he who sits at the head of the table rarely plays the leading role.[45]

The problem as Werther sees it lies not in the unnaturalness of the social structure itself but in people's relationship to that social structure. When he is asked to leave Count von C.'s residence because the nobility who are gathered there think his presence wrong, he does not complain about it as a social injustice. He is upset because people thought he was social-climbing. Similarly, earlier on in the book, he comments:

> there are those who shrink from all contact with simple people, ... I know that we human beings were not created equal and cannot be, but I am of the opinion that he who keeps aloof from the so-called rabble in order to preserve the respect he feels is his due is just as reprehensible as the coward who hides from his enemies because he fears to be defeated by them.[46]

Werther's point is that the respect which is one's due will come *naturally* provided we believe in the social order. The social order is real. Peasants, simple people, are natural because they accept the social order. Werther's story about how he helped the servant girl place a pitcher of water on her head illustrates this well. She blushes, he helps and she goes on her way having thanked him. It is because both Werther and the girl believe in the absolute reality of the social order that they are able to behave so naturally. Werther's desire is to deny the social genesis and reproduction of the social order, as he ignores the economic structure which underpins it. This allows him to experience individual and social practices as natural. His Romantic idealistic dream is that as a result unity will be achieved as the private becomes public. We are returned to Julie's dream of the expanded home. It is in this conservative way that Romanticism rebelled against the capitalism which produced it.

Werther's denial of the socio-economic foundations of bourgeois society is justified in the idea of the correct social order as being natural, thus conflating it with the natural, that is to say untouched, nature of the world. This is, in fact, the end-point of Rousseau's philosophy. In education, for example, Emile is born natural:

> We are born sensitive and from our birth onwards we are affected in various ways by our environment. As soon as we become conscious of our sensations we tend to seek or shun the things that cause them. These tendencies gain strength and permanence with the growth of reason, but hindered by our habits they are more or less warped by our prejudices. Before this change they are what I call Nature within us.[47]

Unfortunately, the growing person enters a series of conflicts between his/her wishes and those of society, between, as Rousseau puts it, man and citizen: 'Drawn this way by nature and that by man, compelled to yield to both forces, we make a compromise and reach neither goal.'[48] The purpose of Rousseau's treatise is to demonstrate a form of education in which these self-contradictions will not appear; the individual and society will be perfectly reconciled producing the natural individual and, in the long term, producing the natural society advocated in *The Social Contract*. Rousseau's critique is not of bourgeois society as an ideal but of his own society in its real, mundane existence. His very use of the natural/unnatural distinction is predicated on the bourgeois conception of the natural. This is easily demonstrated by looking at how Rousseau differentiates male and female:

> But for her sex, a woman is a man; she has the same organs, the same needs, the same faculties ...
> Yet where sex is concerned man and woman are unlike; each is the complement of the other.[49]

Natural society is ordered around sexual difference, defined in the first place by physical difference. Rousseau is here putting forward the bourgeois assertion which I examined in Chapter 1 and compounding it with the patriarchal idea that women are somehow 'not-men'. We might sum up Rousseau's position by suggesting that it is an attempt to

harmonise the natural world and bourgeois society through a
new social order founded on an idealisation of bourgeois
sexuality. In this light we can now understand why
Rousseau's 'first and most painful step in the dark and miry
maze of [his] confessions'[50] is his revelation that he gains
erotic satisfaction from flagellation and that if this is not
available, he is happy 'to fall on my knees before a masterful
mistress, to obey her commands, to have to beg her
forgiveness, [these] have been to me the most delicate of
pleasures.'[51] Confession here is different from the Catholic
recapitulation, and the measure of that difference is to be
found in the fact that Rousseau begins with the basic
bourgeois repression—sexuality. Rousseau regards this as his
most painful confession. Everything which follows is
secondary and dependent. In his writing he is reversing the
conventional practice of the bourgeois text. His confession is
truly an expression of repression. Rousseau claims that his
sexuality is not what he, and bourgeois society, considers to
be correct. He assumes the naturalness of eroticisation. He
repeats that he has 'a sensual nature' but views his own
conduct as being unnatural. Rousseau's natural society is
based upon the ideal bourgeois sexualisation which he gives
to Emile and Sophie.

Nowhere in *The Sorrows* does Goethe/Werther
acknowledge the economic ordering of society. All economic
concerns happen 'off-stage'. Werther's entry into the pastoral
of the Wahlheim region is precipitated by problems with a
will, about which we hear no more. Lotte's father and Albert
both make trips to town, off-stage, to work. The stage shows
us only the social order. Goethe, then, represses the
economic, the capitalistic, just as he represses the sexual. The
'natural' in the Romantic bourgeois world is a function of this
dual repression.

The best demonstration of Lotte's social naturalness is in
the dance which is the reason for her and Werther's first
meeting. Lotte, we are told, loves dancing: 'If a passion for
dancing is sinful', Lotte said, 'then I cheerfully admit to it. I
don't know anything I would rather do than dance.'[52] But
mid-eighteenth-century bourgeois dancing was not
unregulated. Dances were separated from their

predominantly peasant origins precisely in their rule-governed restructuring which necessitated a high degree of control over the body. Werther describes Lotte's dancing like this: ' "You should see her dance! She is so completely absorbed by motion, she dances with her whole heart, body and soul. The result is harmony, so carefree and natural" '.[53] It is in this that Lotte's naturalness resides. She internalises bourgeois social mores during the day-to-day practice of her life. Her success in this sphere extends even to the waltz, a dance regarded as morally dubious at that time because it required the permanent holding of one's partner. Byron wrote a satirical poem on the waltz in which he pretended outrage:

> Say would you wish to make those beauties quite so cheap?
> Hot from the hands promiscuously applied,
> Around the slight waist or down the glowing side[54]

It is the waltz which Werther dances with Lotte. Her ability to be so natural in performing this artificial activity makes Lotte so perfect in Werther's eyes and thus suitable to be realised by his desire. We never meet Lotte except as fetish, Lotte as woman-as-object created for the reader by Werther's letters.

Just as Julie, as fetish, is able to ideally (idylly?) combine the rationalism of Wolmar and the desire of Saint-Preux, so Lotte combines in her person the analogous aspects of Albert and Werther. The lack of intercourse in *The Sorrows* is a repression which reflects the structuration of displacement which is embodied in Albert and Werther. In the one act of coition in *Elective Affinities* each partner (they are husband and wife) is adulterously desiring coition with someone else— Charlotte with the Captain, Eduard's best friend, and Eduard with Otillie, the girl of whom Charlotte is guardian and aunt. Moreover, to draw them up in structural oppositions Charlotte and the Captain are both 'rational' while Eduard and Otillie are more emotional and natural. The two desired unions never take place in reality. Charlotte has a child which looks like Otillie and the Captain, and this child becomes a

major factor in keeping the couples apart. The coition thus
may be read as a metaphor concerned with the importance of
repression in the sexualisation and realisation of the
bourgeois world. Implicit in this repression is the creation of
the fetish/individual. Lotte's unnatural position in the
household reinforces Goethe's claim for her naturalness. The
children, too, reinforce Lotte's claim to nature. She is, after
all, their sister. They act, in Werther's eyes, without the
constraints of society, they 'were swarming around [her]'[55]
and they 'jumped off happily with their supper or, each
according to his nature, walked away quietly in the direction
of the courtyard'.[56] Lotte only appears natural because she is
in an unnatural situation. However, once again, appearance is
reality. Here, however, the reality is also the appearance. The
natural, unsexualised Lotte which we are given is
bourgeois—Lotte as unmarried and virginal. As mother she is
sexualised; as sister she is not.

The dual positioning which articulates Lotte as the
bourgeois female ideal highlights the ambiguities present in
the bourgeois expressive/repressive constitution of sexuality
within the domestic domain. Incest is a favourite theme of
Gothic literature, but in the eighteenth century we find it
matter-of-factly pervading the not-quite-bourgeois literature
of Defoe. In *Moll Flanders*, Moll has intercourse with an
adopted brother, marries another adopted brother and
subsequently marries her blood brother. The incest here is
treated light-heartedly and realistically. By the late
eighteenth century the treatment of incest has been relegated
to the province of Gothic. Incest becomes an aspect of the
dark threat of sexualisation from which the domestic domain
must protect itself. At the same time adultery, the
'acceptable' face of bourgeois sexual excess because it shows
the excess turned outwards and therefore not threatening to
the asexuality of the domestic domain, starts to appear in
realist literature. From the concern with adultery in
Richardson's *Pamela*, Volume II, it reaches a climax in
Flaubert's *Madame Bovary* and Zola's *Thérèse Raquin*.
Mythologically speaking, the ideal married woman would be
a mother and virginal, unsullied by the sexuality which
occurs outside the domestic domain. Marital intercourse

would be a form of non-intercourse. The Other of this repressed sexuality may be found in the sexualising of an asexual person in the domestic domain—a sister/daughter (the kin position is the same) who is unmarried and therefore still has a sexual potential. The horror of maternal incest is defused by the fact that since the married woman constitutes the domestic domain, her illicit sexuality instantly destroys it. Thus her incest is, in one sense, not incest at all.

We might, then, identify two types of bourgeois, Gothic incest. In the first the woman herself is actively sexual. We might take Madeleine in *The Fall of the House of Usher* as an example here. Madeleine passes through her 'death'—we are not told what her illness is but once again it bears a remarkable resemblance to hysteria—to emerge, the suggestion is, as sexually active. In the second type it is the male father/brother who brings sexuality, horrifically, into the home. Ambrosio's kidnap and rape of his sister Antonia in *The Monk* can serve as an example here. Lewis slightly alleviates Ambrosio's guilt, however, by making him unaware until too late that Antonia really is his sister. Byron, with his usual good grasp of bourgeois repressions, climaxes the curse on the Giaour as vampire by saying that his own daughter would be his final victim.

The bourgeois ideal is to make the world safe by expanding the domestic domain outwards to encompass it. This leads to continual literary attempts to construct relationships and marriages which partake of the asexuality which, it is believed, really exists in the domestic domain. Often the way this is done is to give the characters a semi-domestic relationship. As a result the charge of incest is courted but dispelled by the questionable status of the relationship and by the asexuality which is asserted by the domestic domain. Goethe's production of Lotte as virgin mother and Werther as cousin and stranger is but one example. I have already quoted Tanner's insightful analysis of *La Nouvelle Héloïse*, where he suggests that what Julie really wants is an extended family house. The work which most self-consciously concentrates on this problem must, however, be Bernardin de St Pierre's *Paul et Virginie*, published shortly before the French Revolution. In this novel Paul and Virginia (the symbolism of her name is obvious and apt) are brought up by their mothers in isolation on Mauritius. The domestic environment has no sexual male to threaten it. The mothers combine forces and set up a joint household even, so St Pierre tells us, suckling each other's child. There is, needless to say, no suggestion of any sexual behaviour between the two mothers. The mothers, after a short period, hope and expect that the affection which the two children show one another will be replicated in marriage at a later stage. St Pierre is not writing a Gothic novel—the reader is expected to sympathise with the characters and be distressed when Virginia dies. We have St Pierre's word for it that many to whom he read the manuscript shed tears. Brown and Jordanova have pointed out in respect of *Paul et Virginie* that it is Virginia's 'awakening sexuality' which sets the scene for the ensuing tragedy.[57] (Children are regarded by bourgeois society as asexual.) It comes as no surprise then when St Pierre makes Virginie fall in love with Paul shortly after puberty. Puberty becomes the signifier of the entrance into the charged world of sex and love. St Pierre's problem is to keep Virginie 'natural' and yet acknowledge her as sexualised; her rejection of bourgeois marriage and entrance into society does not in itself provide a solution. The fact is that in the bourgeois novel, with adult bourgeois readers, she is, inevitably, already sexualised. There is no solution to St Pierre's problem and so Virginie is made to die in a shipwreck as she returns to her family, having rejected French society, *le monde*. She dies because she refuses to take off her clothes in order to swim to land, drowning, one imagines, in the weight of them. It is a truly bourgeois death to end a bourgeois idyll. Paul, by the way, dies two months after Virginie, having never recovered from her death. The deaths of Paul and Virginie while, for St Pierre, symbolising the destruction of goodness which for him is implicit in bourgeois society, also mark the impossibility of his ideal society. Virginie (and Paul) cannot be both asexual and sexual. St Pierre's idyll is the same as Rousseau's and Charlotte Brontë's. However the Gothic preoccupation with incest is a concern with the articulation of repression as an aspect of the primary, creative displacement. The success of Goethe's presentation of Lotte as natural may be measured against the ease with which the scene of their first meeting may be given a Freudian analysis.

Modern society has a preoccupation with incest far in excess of earlier society. I have, elsewhere, noted Raymonde Testanière's regard for incestuous intercourse in Montaillou. She, however, was religious, and she claimed that the shock of the attempted incestuous rape was the reason for her renunciation of Cathar beliefs. Quaife is probably correct when he writes that 'Incest did not cause the horror that it did in later centuries.'[58] Little is known about incestuous intercourse in medieval Europe, but from the very fact that it was not written about we might surmise that its later horror was not present. By contrast Freud, reinterpreting a Greek myth concerned with kinship problems, places incest as the foundation of the Oedipus complex and at the very basis of the bourgeois family.

Unfortunately, little modern sociological research has been done on the subject of incest, but it is becoming increasingly apparent that transgressive intercourse between father and daughter is much more prevalent in bourgeois society than was previously thought. In earlier society where sex was not eroticised nor the female body fetishised, we might also surmise that the power relation inherent in the transgression of bourgeois domestic and kin taboos would not be present— hence the desire to commit incest as we understand it would not exist. I am not suggesting that incest did not occur in medieval society but rather that there was less of it and it was regarded with less horror. William of Auvergne (1180–1249), for example, in his *Summa de poenitentia* claimed that conscious masturbation was a worse crime than incest.[59] Moreover, the preoccupation in medieval society seems to have been with mother/son incest rather than father/daughter or brother/sister incest. I am, here, ignoring same-sex incest as it comes within the proscription of homosexuality. I can think of no example of same-sex incest in Gothic novels, and this may have something to do with the voyeuristic potential of father/daughter or brother/sister incest, although probably more to do with the fact that it is different sex intercourse which is the locus of bourgeois erotocised sexuality. Mother/daughter incest would have been inconceivable because of the inability to believe in female homosexuality and father/son incest would simply heighten the unnaturalness of the act without activating a sexualised threat or voyeurism. As far back as St Augustine's *De bono coniugali* mother/son incest was the form singled out. Goodich in *The Unmentionable Vice* cites two documented cases of eleventh-century incest—one with the male's mother, the other with the male's father's wife.[60] Without a recognised domestic domain and with marriage an institution of such low status, the most clear-cut relationship must have been mother/child. Hence, if any sexual relationship were to be proscribed it would have been mother/son. In the clearly delimited and sexually fraught domestic domain of bourgeois society where blood kinship is supplemented by the social kinship invoked by marriage, Freud raised the significance of the act to a new level of importance. In bourgeois society the horror of incest cannot be underplayed. Freud's work was the product of, and (re)presented, fully fledged bourgeois repressions.

In the eighteenth century the concern seems to have been much more related to brother/sister incest. In the Romantic writers themselves we find not only the extraordinarily close relationship of Wordsworth and his sister but the notorious relationship between Byron and his half-sister Augusta. They felt the relationship to be so threatening that it was decided that Byron should marry. We should remember that Shelley, an acquaintance of Byron, wrote a play about father/son incest, *The Cenci*. These relationships may have owed much to the sexual repression underlying the new ideology of love. In the fully developed bourgeois family the Oedipal structure is expressed in its inversion as a practice of power and sexuality by the father. The repression of the son as child is counterpointed by the expression of the adult as father.

To get the full sense of horror we must return to the Gothic novel *The Monk*. Lewis, when the novel was first published, was accused by Coleridge of trying to 'inflame the fleshly appetites', and the journal *Monthly Review* claimed that a vein of obscenity ran through the work which made it unfit for general circulation.[61] The story opens with Antonia going to hear the monk speak and reaches its climactic finale with

Ambrosio's abduction of Antonia, her confinement in a catacomb, her rape, Ambrosio's murder of her and the subsequent revelation that they were long-lost brother and sister. The incest, then, which is the eroticised revelation of the confining nature of the domestic sphere here confines the novel, and Antonia is confined within it. The end of *The Fall of the House of Usher* recognises, as I have shown, a similar preoccupation. The ambiguity of brother/sister love in a society based on sex(ualised) repression is made more obvious in *Frankenstein*, however, where Elizabeth has been brought up as Frankenstein's sister but is, in fact, no relation. It is a similar situation to that of Paul and Virginia. Elizabeth is adopted into the family as a child and, once again, we find the image of the expanded household.

The overtones of incest in *Frankenstein* are reinforced by the dream which Frankenstein has immediately after the monster has been given life:

> I thought I saw Elizabeth, in the bloom of health, walking in the streets of Ingolstadt. Delighted and surprised, I embraced her, but as I imprinted the first kiss on her lips, they became livid with the hue of death; her features appeared to change and I thought that I held the corpse of my dear mother in my arms; a shroud enveloped her form, and I saw the grave-worm crawling in the folds of the flannel.[62]

Elizabeth, the sister/fiancée, is transformed into the dead mother who had died from catching scarlet fever from her foster daughter. Moreover, it is suggested that that mother herself was a different generation to the father for she was the daughter of the father's business associate. It is Frankenstein who gives order to this bourgeois domestic confusion. As the first-born of the marriage he provides the permanent realisation of the domestic sphere called into being by marriage/intercourse. It is he whose material existence keeps all the others placed in the kinship structure. The chaos which his un-human creation implies for the family structure is echoed in his dream where sex intrudes into the forbidden sphere and the (just) acceptable slippage between sister/non-sensual love and fiancée/sensual love is metamorphosed into son/mother incest. Simultaneously, death becomes eroticised.

I have discussed the bourgeois connection between intercourse and death. Here we find the two overlapping in a dream just as they do in Clarissa's dream. We must remember that Freud's work and his recognition that dreams express (bourgeois) repression. While the kiss which suggests the more repressed and desired sexual experience (this representation is common to *Dracula* and bourgeois love iconography in general) takes place, the person he kisses changes from live sister/fiancée to dead mother. *Frankenstein* has called the bourgeois family into question by making, without intercourse/marriage, the monster who is his non-natural son. In his dream he calls reality into question by the lack of fixity of the person he is kissing/having intercourse with. The death which affirms the end of the individual and his/her bourgeois reality also affirms the generational cycle of the family. Analogously, death pervades the family structures of *Dracula*, including Lucy's mother and Arthur's father as well as Jonathan Harker's associate, who treats him as a son, Mr Hawkins. As marriage/intercourse becomes the site of the production of the domestic domain, so death becomes the moment of its dissolution. The removal of death provides an idyllic but illicit continuation of the domestic domain. The only acceptable way of stabilising the domain is by the use of names. In *Wuthering Heights* the Gothic eruption of Heathcliffe is framed by the two Catherine Earnshaws while in *Dracula* the domestic domain is reaffirmed—and the Gothic negated—by the giving of the name Quincey to the Harker's child.

We should now be able to understand better the ambiguities inherent in Werther's and Lotte's relationship and the reasons for the characterisation of Lotte as sister and mother. It is the repression of what I have just described which is entailed in the novel's Romantic realism and which generates the emotional involvement of the reader. If Lotte is sister, then she is also daughter; if she is mother she is also wife. Goethe wisely keeps Magistrate S., Lotte's father, away on business a great deal so these problems do not have to be confronted. Nevertheless, the representation of Lotte as the perfect bourgeois woman, as daughter, sister, wife and lover, demands their existence. It is only as the story proceeds that the union desired by Werther is gradually revealed as predicated upon physical union—intercourse. For example, on 16 July, Werther writes, 'She is sacred to me. All lust is stilled in her presence. I can't explain how I feel when I am with her. It is as if every nerve in my body were possessed by my soul.'[63] His awareness of lust, physical desire, and his repression of it is made more obvious a month later when on 21 August he writes, 'I stretch out my arms for her in vain when, troubled by my dreams, I awaken in the morning; at night I seek her in my bed when a happy, innocent dream has deceived me into imagining I am sitting beside her in a field and holding her hand and kissing her.'[64] Here we have the juxtaposition of Werther's private bed with his perception of the innocence of pastoral nature. The desire he feels is manifested in his dream reality as non-sexual. However, this idyllic inversion is itself a *mythos*. The asexuality of the text is (re)presented to the reader by the asexuality of Werther's love for Lotte. However, when he does finally kiss Lotte, it is in anything but a non-sexual way. The moment when Werther finally accepts the impossibility of the satisfaction of his desire is the moment when the sexual basis of his love is finally fully revealed:

> In his despair he threw himself on his knees before Lotte, took her hand, pressed it to his eyes, his forehead, and a hint of the terrible thing he was planning seemed to brush Lotte's soul. She became confused and pressed his hand tightly against her breast, and with a plaintive motion, moved closer to him. Their burning cheeks touched and the world ended for them. Werther wound his arms around Lotte, pressed her to him, and covered her trembling stammering lips with passionate kisses.[65]

They do not have intercourse; to the best of the reader's knowledge nobody has intercourse in the book, though one assumes that Lotte and Albert, once married, indulge. Goethe, however, as a good bourgeois, does not tell us. Werther's suicide appears to be the product of his inability to consummate union with Lotte. In this passage a transition is effected; that terrible thing suicide is in equilibrium with that other terrible thing sexual intercourse. The one partakes of the other as their cheeks touch and the world ends for them.

However, Werther's suicide, as I have already noted, is the ultimate assertion of his individuality, and his final onanistic act is a rearticulation of his desire, not just for union with Lotte but a union which is, in fact, possession of her. Interestingly, Werther himself never articulates his attitude towards Lotte in terms of possession. This is reserved for the rational capitalist Albert: 'Albert has come back, and I shall leave. He might be the best, the most noble man in the world ... but I would find it insufferable to see him take possession of so much perfection. To take possession ... let it suffice, William ... her betrothed has returned'.[66] Albert, the bourgeois, marries Lotte and, in doing so, establishes her as commodity within the capitalist social structure. She becomes a possession. Goethe's use of terminology here is quite clear (it even survives translation), but if he/Werther acknowledges the commodity/marriage-linkage, what kind of union is Werther after? If, as one assumes (for he never suggests she should marry him rather than Albert), he does not wish for marriage, then why should he be so disturbed when she does marry Albert?—'her husband! O God, Who didst make me as I am, hadst Thou but granted me this bliss my whole life would have been a praise to Thee! But I shall not remonstrate, and I beg Thee to forgive my tears and my vain desires. Lotte ... my wife!'[67] Werther's Romantic rebellion against the capitalism embodied by Albert is doomed to failure because its premises are those of capitalism. Werther, in fact, asserts the fetishistic structure of capitalism while claiming to be reacting against it. In his inability to articulate an alternative to the crucial duality of marriage/intercourse Werther describes his essential harmony with capitalism. It is only after her marriage to Albert, when it is impossible for him to achieve such a union, that he desires it. Barthes has suggested, in his discussion of the lover, that 'The amorous subject sees everyone around him as "pigeon-holed", each appearing to be granted a little practical and affective system of contractual liaisons from which he feels himself to be excluded; this inspires him with an ambiguous sentiment of envy and mockery.'[68] He goes on to illustrate this with specific reference to Werther. This demonstrates Werther's marginal existence well. However, it is not an explanation. Werther *requires* Lotte and Albert to get married so that he can be envious. He needs there to be the practice of bourgeois life so that he can assert his individualism in opposition to it while at the same time desiring the security (Lotte) which it offers.

This is one aspect of the structure of the book. Werther has known, from before he met Lotte, that she was engaged. The success of the book is dependent upon Werther's failure to consummate his desire. The structure of the book is Werther's desire; the lack of fulfilment of that desire enables Werther to assert, in the most absolute manner, his reality/individuality.

Women, by being made the primary focus of the fetishistic construction of the bourgeois world, become Other. Otherness, indeed, might be said to be the prerequisite for their construction as fetish. However, the fact that as fetish they are also confined does not also mean that they are assimilated. Quite the reverse is the case. The idyll of the unity to be achieved through Romantic love is counterpointed by the vision of woman as essentially Other, different and able to entrap men and lead them to their doom. Women become the ultimate threat as well as providing absolute reality. If, from one point of view, women confirmed and fixed as such by intercourse, ensure the existence of the bourgeois world then, from another, they may also be seen as calling into question the man's individuality. The idyll of Romantic love asserts the bourgeois ideal of the domestic family group at the same time as confirming the participant's individuality. An alternative theme is that intercourse should not emphasise unity but disunity. What this theme celebrates is the man as individual, essentially so because essentially independent—intercourse is in this context an affirmation of division not communion. Man above all is affirmed as different and as patriarchally dominant. Werther's Romantic love is a representation of a doomed striving for unity. Intercourse/marriage are fundamental to the bourgeois order, but they link the male with an Other with whom he strives to be united. Its importance lies in the sexualised ambiguity which surrounds the bourgeois woman.

With this in mind, it becomes understandable that an

alternative bourgeois reading of *The Sorrows* would see Lotte as stringing along both Werther and Albert, deciding on bourgeois safety and, through her cruelly ambiguous treatment, driving Werther to suicide. Lotte is now to be seen as a strange threat, like the voluptuous female vampires in *Dracula*. This is from the scene from that book when the male Van Helsing finally overcomes the female threat:

> She lay in her Vampire sleep, so full of life and voluptuous beauty that I shudder as though I have come to do murder. Ah, I doubt not that in old time, when such things were, many who set forth to do such a task as mine, found at last in his heart fail him, and then his nerve. So he delay, and delay, and delay, till the mere beauty and fascination of the wanton Un-dead have hypnotise him, and he remain on, and on, till sunset come, and the Vampire sleep be over. Then the beautiful eyes of the fair woman open and look love, and the voluptuous mouth present to a kiss—and man is weak.[69]

Here the horror is not so much in any reversal of the position of the female, though she is portrayed as at night being more powerful than the male, but lies in her ability to stop the male acting in a dominant, patriarchal and individual manner. Van Helsing becomes hypnotised by her sensual Otherness and is almost unable to perform his role. Indeed, he imagines a past in which men were unable to resist a combination of the look of love and the tempting mouth (the displaced vagina?) and succumbed to this female threat. In *Dracula* this does not happen. The male wins through and domestic harmony is established once again. Nevertheless, a part of the novel's Gothic horror is its portrayal of the sexualised female who is a threat to the male as independent individual. The male here is trapped in a paradox where he is both sexualised and individualised but, by virtue of his sexualisation, is in need of another for completion. The premise which underlies *Dracula* is the horror of the absence, the unknown, which is the expression of the essential displacement articulating bourgeois society. The expression of sexuality in *Dracula* is predatory. In the first place it is placed in a male, Count Dracula. Its feminine form is secondary just as the theme of the woman-as-threat is dependent, in the end, on the fundamental notion of woman as repository of the Real, but in a situation where the female is constructed, fetishised by the male. *Dracula*, as I have remarked before, is written as conservative. From this point of view the illicit pleasure experienced by the bourgeois reader makes *Dracula* one more incarnation of another bourgeois myth—that of the Don Juan figure.

To give in to female sexuality is to lose one's essential masculinity, here allied with individuality. Keats's poem 'La Belle Dame sans Merci' gives us such a man. The 'knight at arms, Alone and palely loitering' is the victim of 'a lady' he met 'in the meads, Full beautiful a fairey's child'. For the bourgeois male, women are both a source of reality—the male's individuality is confirmed through and within the confirmation of bourgeois social structures focused on the female—and also something to be feared because of their naturalness, a naturalness which includes the sexuality on which bourgeois society is founded. This fear is well expressed by Rousseau:

> Women so easily stir a man's senses and fan the ashes of a dying passion, that if philosophy ever succeeded in introducing this custom (that the first to feel desire should be the first to show it) into an unlucky country, especially if it were a warm country where more women are born than men, the men, tyrannised over by the women, would at last become their victims, and would be dragged to their death without the least chance of escape.[70]

For the male bourgeois, and for the female given that she partakes of the dominant ideology, there are two formulations of the male. One as the 'hero' figure, individualised and capable, the other as part of a Romantic marriage union. The alternatives are a function of the production of woman as fetish. It is this system which produces the plot line of much modern cultural production where the male proves himself as strong and individualised, subsequently falling in love with a woman who loves him. In Werther's case, his suicide affirms his individuality.

Lotte not only gets a 'hint' of his intention in their final scene together. She also hands his servant Albert's guns, one of which he will use on himself. Lotte (and Albert, who tells her to give the servant the guns) may be said to connive in

Werther's suicide. It is Werther's desire and his letters, which structure the book. It is his fetish, Lotte-as-object, which aids Werther's apotheosis, and unlike that of Clarissa or Julie, death is of the male signifier. The assertion of essence through death marks the coming-of-age of bourgeois society which exists fully displaced. Moreover, whereas Clarissa's and Julie's deaths form the basis for an escape from confinement, Werther's death preserves, ossifies, the structure of displacement, through desire, in which he dominated. Werther's death does not close off the structuration of desire as do those of the fetishised women-as-objects, rather it makes his signifying power permanent.

Albert, the rational male, does not have command of *The Sorrows*. Goethe has given this to Werther, and it is Werther's impossible quest to unite the public domain of social life and the private domain of his own emotional life, creating a world in which his individuality would be realised—in which the displacement on which the problem was founded would have been transcended. The irony is that such transcendence would only reinforce the displacement, not remove it. This is the same irony as exists in Rousseau's *Emile*. The success of *The Sorrows* is the success of this transcendence for the reader. This success may be measured simply by its impact on Europe after its publication. However, the degree to which Werther is able to assert his Romantic individuality is the degree to which the epistolary style is no longer relevant— indeed, is no longer workable. The individuality of the character reflects the reality of the world, a world no longer constructed by letters. It is an already constructed world where individuals, characters and their readers exist as real and essentially unique and alienated, structured only by displacement, the creator of desire and fetish.

Conclusion

All conclusions are also beginnings, and in this conclusion I want to explore some of the implications of the argument I have set out in this book. Critics tend to write about the novel as if the category has some taken-for-granted ontological existence. It has not. Traditionally, it has been argued that the novel developed during the eighteenth century, and literary critics have tended to assume that their concern has been with a form of the written. However, the novel not only refers to a form of the written but to a form of reading also. Other texts may be read as if they are novels—and evaluated accordingly. Herodotus's history, for example, or the Koran, may be appropriated as novels. The novel is a form of reading as well as a form of the written, for reading is a practice which determines a certain mode of apprehension.

In bourgeois society reading is a sexualised practice, as is the practice of writing. The consequence of this, as we have seen, has been a movement towards a certain form of written object determined by this sexualisation. This has generated a particular constructed written form which offers itself as objective and contained. The novel in bourgeois society may be described as a reified—and fetishised—object. But such a description might equally be applied to other textual products of bourgeois society. The novel, however, is produced in the context of the distinction between 'fiction' and 'fact'. One important element in a definition of the eighteenth- and nineteenth-century novel would be that it is a form of 'fictional' writing which seeks to disguise its own fictionality in its relations with the reader. If we recognise that the categories of fact and fiction are also historically specific, then we can also appreciate that the novel, as a form of reading as well as of the written, can only exist in a society in which the category of fiction exists, for the novel requires that category in order to appear to deny it.

The category of fiction exists through the strategic reproduction of the conditions under which something is regarded as fact. The category of fact claims to represent reality. The philosophical assumptions on which the 'fact'/'fiction' dichotomy is based are those of Descartes, Bacon, Hobbes, Locke and others whose work forms the underpinning of the philosophical articulation of bourgeois ideology. This reality, which is considered to exist elsewhere, exterior and Other to the reflexivity of thought, is constituted as interior, constant and unchanging. Fiction is a negative category; it is recognisable only for what it is not. Fiction is production masking itself as reproduction. Its existence is dependent on the claim of fact to present an existent world and, in this context, to be an accurate representation. Both the categories of fact and fiction, then, are in the end unprovable because both depend on the assumed existence of a metaphysically unprovable material reality. The existence of fiction is dependent on the legitimacy of fact. But both fiction and fact are dependent on the assumption not only that a material reality which can be meaningfully apprehended exists but that the presentation of that reality is productive *only* in the sense of being reproduction.

Fiction is meaningful to the extent that the fictional work denies the conditions of its own production. Such a project requires the connivance of the reader. The bourgeois reader reads in such a fashion as to appropriate the text. This, as we have seen, is a product of the libidinized nature of the text. It is no coincidence that Leavis, Watt and the bulk of critics trained in the traditional ways of literary criticism have assimilated the realist novel genre to be the 'only' form of the novel. It is equally not to be wondered at that those critics who have attempted to distinguish the realist genre from the Gothic have run into significant problems of criteria. Such a distinction cannot be made, ultimately, on the writing alone. Successful fiction is always realistic in the sense that the reader, as a product of bourgeois society, finds him/herself able to suspend his/her disbelief and 'enter' the text. Such a process is dependent on the perception of the text as a reified object. From this point of view it is more correct to think of the text as appropriating the reader. Once the text is produced as Other it is able to assimilate the reader. At the point where the reader refuses a sense of his/her own existence he/she is assimilated into the text.

The traditional bourgeois novel hides the mechanisms of its own existence. This is not a question of content but rather one of narration. Reading, then, appears as a passive process, but again this is a governing illusion. Reading in bourgeois society is dependent upon the production of the text as fetishised. Correspondingly, reading is also dependent upon the assumption of textual presence, the idea that the text contains immanent meaning. This idea is the cornerstone not only of bourgeois reading practices in general but also of traditional literary criticism. This assumption corresponds to the notion that the text bears a single meaning. The process of reading is the assertion of that meaning and the project of criticism is to ensure that the meaning is correctly formulated. The reading process in bourgeois society is, then, fundamentally hermeneutic. It is a hermeneutic in which the individual objectifies him/herself as a part of the project to produce meaning.

Because the fictional text offers itself both as a production of reality and as a reproduction of reality, it might be described as a manifestation of difference in which legitimacy (which is experienced as a singular unity) is gained by the acceptance of the illusion that production and reproduction are the same thing. This acceptance may be said to be a result of the constituting excessive libidinal fixation which Freud argues is the basis of fetishism. For Freud the occurrence of fetishism is located in the male fear of castration. The horror of the visual recognition that females do not possess penises is repressed and another object substituted for the non-existent female penis.[1] Fetishism is a form of constituting over-determination grounded in desire experienced as excess which, in bourgeois society, gives meaning to the object. It realises the world and enables the reader to 'believe' the text as realistic. Fetishism, as a process, denies (represses) the dual articulation of the text and replaces its potential (unstable) excessiveness with an apparent single, immanent meaning. At this point we may appreciate the links between Derrida's critique of the logocentric understanding of the text as a totalising system which, he argues, always excludes an excess of meaning, and the Lacanian notion of the text as always produced in terms of repression, repression which denies the excess of meaning which is always present in the text.[2]

The text, as a consequence of its grounding duality as production and reproduction is, itself, always potentially excessive in bourgeois society. Its meanings may be infinite. Hillis Miller, whose thinking about literature owes much to Derrida's critique of logocentrism, has described the French concept of *mise en abîme* like this:

> This is a cascade of expressions describing a twoness resting on the ground of a oneness which then subdivides once more to rest on a still deeper ground which ultimately reveals itself to be, if it exists at all, the abyss of 'annihilation'.[3]

Hillis Miller's priorisation of the text produces an image of an increasingly subterranean dialectic. As we have seen the fetishism of the text as object generates it as a container. In, however, taking the existence of the text for granted, Hillis Miller turns the constituting dualism inwards and, in doing so, recognises the excess which lies at the heart of the problem of textual meaning. But excessive, plural meaning is simply the mirror of single meaning. The text as reproductive argues for a singularity of (referential) meaning. The text as productive argues for a plurality of (immanent) meaning. The argument of conventional literary criticism, and the assumption behind the bourgeois, fetishistic reading process, is that meaning is both singular and immanent. This linkage is made possible, as I have already argued, through the denial of difference between production and reproduction. This, in turn, is based on a claim of equivalence between representation (mimesis) and reproduction. Such a claim asserts the world as a constant reality and makes the genre of realism the highpoint of fiction through its claim to (re)present/(re)produce the world, in the process for the reader who desirously, fetishistically, consumes the text, apparently reconciling not just this dichotomy but all the proliferating dichotomies into a single immanent meaning, a meaning which Hillis Miller has inverted as an excessive annihilation.

In order to understand the text as a fetishistically constituted site of meaning, we need, then, to recognise the text as a fetishistically constituted object. The movement, in the novel, from the epistolary form to the dominant third-person form relates to the latter. The specialisation of 'content' into the two genres of realism and Gothic (and, of course, the special—let us say revealing—case of pornography) relates to the former and is applicable to all 'fictional' texts. The instantiation of text as a fetishistic object produces it, as we have seen, in the position of 'female' in bourgeois society. The female in bourgeois society, as we have also seen, is constructed as apparently asexual. Her desire, when it is admitted, is limited to that of a single partner. Alternatively, there is the 'respectable' fear of the sexually uncontrollable woman. The textual content duplicates this production. The determined, patrolled and limited meaning of the realist text which measures itself, referentially, against the world—as domestic wife against worldly husband—is matched by the Gothic, fantasy text which offers a plurality of other worlds, though not, in terms of the conventional bourgeois reading practice, a plurality of meanings.

Perhaps the type of the truly feminist, and radical, novel might be Jean Rhys's *Wide Sargasso Sea*, which not only constitutes itself as a feminist commentary on *Jane Eyre* but is also a metaphysical commentary on the always already-positioned text. *Wide Sargasso Sea* is constructed on Hillis Miller's abyss of annihilation. The book is written in the form of two stories, that of Bertha Mason, Rochester's first wife, and that of Rochester himself. The meaning of the novel lies in the abyss between parts one and two. The text may be already constituted as female, indeed it could be argued to be realist. It nevertheless confronts the reader with its own processes of determination as meaning is reconstructed as the misrecognition, the misunderstanding, of female and male. The real abyss in the novel images the abyss between the two major characters and, in turn, asserts the abyss between this (re)writing and Charlotte Brontë's text. Simultaneously, the abyss in the novel replicates the abyss between text and reader, forcing the reader not to connive in the production of meaning, as in the epistolary novel, but actually to produce the 'meaning' of the text. Rhys's novel might be understood as a commentary on its own fetishistic production. It may also be read as a fitting commentary on the meaning of this text.

Notes

Introduction

1. M. Poster, *Critical Theory of the Family* (London: Pluto Press, 1978). M. Foucault, *The History of Sexuality* trans. R. Hurley (London: Allen Lane, 1979).

2. We may compare this understanding of sexuality as a social construction with the view put forward by Shorter in an early paper ('Illegitimacy, Sexual Revolution and Social Change in Modern Europe', *Journal of Interdisciplinary History*, vol. 2, no. 2, 1971) that 'Sexuality in traditional society may be thought of as a great iceberg, frozen by the command of custom, by the need of the surrounding community for stability at the cost of individuality and by the dismal grind of everyday life. Its thawing in England and Western Europe occurred roughly between the middle of the eighteenth and the end of the nineteenth centuries, when a revolution in eroticism took place' (p. 237).

3. See, for example, Poster.

4. J. Baudrillard, *For a Critique of the Political Economy of the Sign*, trans. with an introduction by C. Levin (St Louis: Telos Press, 1981), p. 92.

5. E. Showalter, *A Literature of Their Own* (Princeton: Princeton University Press, 1977).

6. F. R. Leavis, *The Great Tradition* (London: Chatto & Windus, 1948).

7. I. Watt, *The Rise of the Novel* (London: Chatto & Windus, 1957).

8. Todorov's book *The Fantastic* was published in translation in 1973: T. Todorov, *The Fantastic*, trans. R. Howard (Cleveland: Press of Case Western Reserve University, 1973). See also R. Jackson, *Fantasy* (London: Methuen, 1981) and this book's bibliography.

9. In a conservative but insightful article Aram Vartanian discusses the maleness of the Marquise. A. Vartanian, 'The Marquise de Meurteuil: A Case of Mistaken Identity', *L'Esprit créateur*, vol. 3, no. 4 (1963), 172–80.

10. N. Miller, *The Heroine's Text* (New York: Columbia University Press, 1980), p. 138.
11. In the day-to-day life we also find an increasing preoccupation with the letter as object. This is exemplified in a concern with style. See for example, H. Barnwell (ed.), *Selected Letters of Madame de Sévigné* (London: Dent, 1960).
12. The pun here of letter as letter of the alphabet implying writing and letter as epistle is now revealed, and revealed in its sexualised nakedness.
13. The eighteenth century saw the rapid expansion of a postal system in both France and Britain. While most of the letters in the novels under discussion appear to have been delivered by personal messenger, it is an interesting sidelight that throughout this period, with the brief exceptions of Velayer's short-lived system in Paris (1653) and Dockwra's in London (1680), letters were paid for on delivery *not* by the sender. In general on the British postal system, see H. Robinson *The British Post Office: A History* (Princeton: Princeton University Press, 1948).
14. The only article of which I am aware, which concentrates on the problem of the end of *Les Liaisons dangereuses* is D. A. Coward, 'Laclos and the Dénouement of the Liaisons Dangereuses', in *Eighteenth Century Studies*, vol. 5, no. 3 (1971–71), pp. 431–49. Unfortunately, Coward discusses the end only as an aesthetic problem. A. Vartanian, 'The Marquis de Meurteuil: A Case of Mistaken Identity', *L'Esprit créateur* vol. 3, no. 4, (1963), pp. 172–80 is useful on the problem of the end of the novel.
15. We should note here the pun on 'Lie' (1) as dissimulation (2) as sexual intercourse.
16. T. Castle *Clarissa's Ciphers* (Ithaca: Cornell University Press 1982).
17. T. Eagleton *The Rape of Clarissa* (Oxford: Basil Blackwell, 1982).

Chapter 1

1. M. Foucault, *The History of Sexuality*, trans. R. Hurley (London: Allen Lane, 1979), vol. 1.
2. G. Deleuze and F. Guattari, *Anti-Oedipus*, trans. R. Hurley, M. Seem and H. Lane (New York: The Viking Press, 1977).
3. See S. Marcus, *The Other Victorians* (London: Weidenfeld & Nicholson, 1966), chs. 1, 2 and 4, *passim*.
4. J. Baudrillard, *For a Critique of the Political Economy of the Sign*, trans. C. Levin (St Louis: Telos Press, 1981), p. 93.
5. A general discussion of the capitalist history of the family may be found in E. Zaretsky, *Capitalism, the Family and Personal Life* (New York: Harper & Row, 1976), ch. 3, *passim*.
6. H. Garfinkel, *Studies in Ethnomethodology* (Engelwood Cliffs: Prentice-Hall, 1967), p. 122.

7. V. Bullough, *Sexual Variance in Society and History* (New York: Wiley, 1976).
8. St Augustine, *De bono coniugali* (*The Good of Marriage*), in *The Writings of St Augustine* (New York: Cima Publishing Company, 1955), vol. 15, p. 12.
9. Gen. 1:28. St Augustine uses this reference in *Good of Marriage*, p. 10.
10. St Augustine, *Good of Marriage*, p. 17.
11. St Thomas Aquinas, *Summa theologica*, trans. the Fathers of the English Dominican Province (New York: Benziger Bros., 1947), vol. 2, pt 11. Q. 153, second article, p. 181.
12. *Ibid.*, third article, p. 1812.
13. *Ibid.*, fourth article, p. 1813.
14. *Ibid.*, Q. 154, eleventh article, p. 1815. Bullough, in *Sexual Variance*, p. 380, implies that Aquinas describes the correct position. I can find no point at which he does so.
15. Aquinas, *Summa theologica*, twelfth article, p. 1826.
16. A. Karlen, *Sexuality and Homosexuality* (New York: W. W. Norton, 1971), p. 415. This is a summation of the results of Beigel's investigation reported in H. Beigel 'The Meaning of Coital Postures', in *Sexual Behaviour and Personality Characteristics*, ed. M. De Martino (New York: Citadel, 1963).
17. Aquinas, *Summa Theologica*, Q. 154, twelfth article, p. 1827.
    18. M. Goodich, *The Unmentionable Vice* (Santa Barbara: ABC-Clio, 1979), p. 59.
19. Goodich, *Unmentionable Vice*, p. 64. On the penalties—and the degree to which they were enacted—for female/female sexual relations in the medieval period, see L. Crompton, *The Myth of Lesbian Impunity*, capital laws from 1270 to 1791, *Journal of Homosexuality*, vol. 6, nos. 1, 2 (1980–81), pp. 11–25.
20. J. Boswell, *Christianity, Social Tolerance and Homosexuality* (Chicago: University of Chicago Press, 1980), pp. 174–5.
21. Goodich, *Unmentionable Vice*, p. 83, following R. Davidson, *Geschichte von Florenz*, vol. 4, (Berlin, 1927).
22. Bullough, *Sexual Variance*, pp. 416–17.
23. Goodich, *Unmentionable Vice*, p. 82.
24. *Ibid.*, p. 83.
25. Quoted in L. Stone, *The Family, Sex and Marriage in Britain 1500–1800* (London: Weidenfeld & Nicholson, 1977), p. 541. Stone infers that homosexuality was on the increase.
26. Quoted from D. Defoe, *The True Born Englishman*, in Stone, *Family, Sex and Marriage*, p. 492.
27. Stone, *Family, Sex and Marriage*, p. 36.
28. *Ibid.*, p. 34.
29. L. Faderman, *Surpassing the Love of Men* (New York: Morrow, 1981), p. 419, n. 16. Faderman cites J. Gagnon and W. Simon's *Sexual Deviance* (New York: Harper and Row, 1967); M. Laner ' "*Personals*" Advertisements of Lesbian Women', *Journal of Homosexuality*, vol. 4, no. 1 (1978), pp. 41–61.

30. Baudrillard, *Political Economy of the Sign*, p. 92.
31. F. Henriques *Prostitution in Europe and the New World*, MacGibbon and Kec, (London: 1963), vol. 2, p. 160, discusses this. Karlen, *Sexuality and Homosexuality*, p. 140–1, also writes about this with reference to a male homosexual club called the Mollies. Karlen writes of 'an apparent increase in homosexuality' which 'was only part of a general efflorescence of psychosexual deviation' (p. 14).
32. Stone, *Family, Sex and Marriage*, p. 541, mentions this but without, unfortunately, giving a reference.
33. R. Pearsall, *The Worm in the Bud* (London: Weidenfeld & Nicolson, 1969), p. 235.
34. See G. Davis and H. Goss, 'Sexual Stereotyping of Black Males in Inter-racial Sex', *Archives of Sexual Behaviour*, vol. 8, no. 3 (1979), pp. 259–79.
35. R. Reiche, *Sexuality and the Class Struggle*, trans. S. Bennett (London: N. C. B., 1970), p. 40–1, discusses the Renaissance beginnings of a concern with male potency. We may note here that the argument put by E. Shorter, *The Making of the Modern Family* (New York: Basic Books, 1975), p. 98–102, that the eighteenth century saw a massive increase in male masturbation. Unfortunately, the majority of the evidence comes from medical literature, so it is possible that we are talking about a discursive as opposed to empirical phenomoneon. However, what empirical evidence does exist would suggest that the commentaries on masturbation (*Onanice* published about 1710 was the first in English to have a significant readership) were occasioned by empirical developments. The pattern, moreover, in which urban middle-class youth was considered to masturbate more than rural peasant youth, bears out my argument about the bourgeois enhancing the sexual desire.

    The increase in importance given to masturbation is another reflection of the shift from a medieval Christian to a bourgeois attitude to sexuality. The spread of the ideology of the individual was a precondition for the subsequent critiques of masturbation in terms of loss of (sexual) innocence, self-abuse, madness and personal physical debilitation. The acceptance of masturbation in the transitional phase is well-shown by ideas such as that of Fallopius, who in the sixteenth century recommended masturbation as a means of penis enlargement (noted in J. H. Plumb, 'The New World of Children in Eighteenth Century England', *Past and Present*, no. 67 (1975), pp. 64–93.

    I should add that my argument concerning the eroticisation of the world agrees more closely with Shorter's premises than with those of J. C. Flandrin, who in 'L'attitude à l'égard du petit enfant et les conduites sexuelles dans la civilisation occidentale: structures anciennes et l'évolution', *Annales de demographie historique* (1973), pp. 143–210, assumes the human libido as a constant.
36. Reiche, *Sexuality and the Class Struggle*.
37. Henriques, *Prostitution*, pp. 139, 144; Thomas in 'The Double Standard', *Journal of the History of Ideas*, vol. 20 (1959), p. 198,

following G. Scott, *A History of Prostitutes from Antiquity to the Present Day* (London, 1954), writes that in 1841 the Chief Commissioner of Police estimated that there were 3,325 brothels in the London Metropolitan district. It is enlightening to note that until 1875 the age of consent was twelve years.

38. R. Utter and G. Needham, *Pamela's Daughters* (London: Lovat Dickson, 1936), p. 33.
39. Henriques, *Prostitution*, p. 148.
40. Aquinas, *Summa Theologica*, Q. 152, first article, p. 1806.
41. *Ibid.*, p. 1805.
42. Gerson, *De confessione mollicei*, quoted in P. Aries, *Centuries of Childhood*, trans. R. Baldick (London: Cape, 1962), p. 107.
43. D. Berger and M. Wegner, 'The Ideology of Virginity', *Journal of Marriage and the Family*, vol. 35, no. 4 (1973).
44. D. Peters, 'The Pregnant Pamela', *Eighteenth Century Studies*, vol. 14, no. 4 (1980–1), pp. 437–8.
45. W. Fielding, *Strange Customs of Courtship and Marriage* (London: Souvenir Press, 1961), pp. 17–18.
46. Karlen, *Sexuality and Homosexuality*, p. 141, notes this without unfortunately, saying which book. I. Bloch, *Sexual Life in England Past and Present*, trans. W. Forstern (London: Atco, 1958), p. 176, discusses the eighteenth century English male's obsession with defloweration. I am presuming that we are talking of the middle and upper classes here, as the reference is in the context of London brothels which were frequented, predominantly, by people of these classes.
47. Sister J. Sassus, *The Motif of Renunciation of Love in the Seventeenth Century French Novel* (Washington: The Catholic University of America Press, 1963), p. 189. The *locus classicus* for this alliance of virtue with marriage is Madame de Lafayette's *La Princesse de Clèves*.
48. C. de Laclos, *Les Liaisons dangereuses*, trans. P. Stone (Harmondsworth: Penguin, 1961). This episode is recounted by the Marquise in letter 85.
49. I. Origo, *The Merchant of Prato* (London: Cape, 1957), p. 227.
50. L. Alberti, quoted in Aries *Centuries of Childhood*, p. 395.
51. L. Wright, *Warm and Snug: The History of the Bed* (London: Routledge & Kegan Paul, 1962), p. 48. This is a useful, if at times idiosyncratic, book.
52. La Salle, *Les Règles de la bienséance et de la civilité chrétienne* (Rouen, 1729), p. 55, quoted in N. Elias, *The Civilising Process*, trans. E. Jephcott (Oxford: Blackwell, 1978), p. 162.
53. S. Richardson, *Pamela*, ed. M. Kinkead Weekes (London: Dent, 1962), p. 369.
54. E. Showalter, *A Literature of Their Own* (Princeton: Princeton University Press, 1977), p. 33.
55. M. Wollstonecraft, *The Vindication of the Rights of Women*, p. 23.
56. *The Complete Tales and Poems of E. A. Poe* (New York: Modern Library, 1938), p. 232.

57. Showalter, *Literature*, p. 150.
58. Poe, *Complete Tales*, p. 237.
59. C. Herman and N. Kostis, ' "The Fall of the House of Usher" or The Art of Duplication', *Sub-stance 26* (1980), pp. 36–42.
60. Poe, *Complete Tales*, p. 235.
61. Madeleine's death images the repression of her sexuality and her own confinement in the domestic domain.
62. Poe, *Complete Tales*, p. 240.
63. *Ibid.*, p. 245.

Chapter 2

1. Some background to the development of the body as the site of sexuality may be found in F. Mort's 'The Domain of the Sexual', *Screen Education*, no. 36 (1980), pp. 69–84. This includes an interesting discussion on the emergence of 'sexuality' in official (state) discourse in Britain in the early century. With reference to eighteenth-century British novels, we may note M. Doody's *A Natural Passion: A Study of the Novels of Samuel Richardson* (Oxford: Clarendon Press, 1974), p. 106, who writes: 'The heroes of Defoe, Fielding, and Smollet have strong egoes, but their extrovert egotism does not try to create a world, but to find a place in it, success not absolute power, is their primary aim. There is much sexual activity, but not much sexuality. For the heroes of Fielding and Smollet, sex is an activity and a pastime, like fighting, a sequence of incidents and not, any more than their religion, a governing principle of life. Richardson is the first major English novelist to present sexuality as a constant vital principle of human life, both conscious and subconscious.'
2. Compare J. Derrida, 'Freud and the Scene of Writing', *French Freud: Structural Studies in Psychoanalysis*, ed. J. Mehlman, *Yale French Studies*, no. 48 (1972): pp. 73–117.
3. R. Day, *Told in Letters* (Ann Arbor: University of Michigan Press, 1966).
4. N. Miller, *The Heroine's Text* (New York: Columbia University Press, 1980), p. 150.
5. The full title goes on to relate together the real, the true, and the natural: 'A Narration which has its Foundation in Truth and Nature; and at the same time that it agreeably entertains, by a Variety of curious and affecting incidents, is entirely divested of all those images, which in too many Pieces calculated for amusement only, tend to inflame the Minds they should instruct.' In *Les Liaisons dangereuses* Laclos continues the tradition of confusing real and fictional by giving two prefaces, one from the 'publisher' and one from the 'editor' of the letters. V. Mylne discusses the debate about the reality of many of the

epistolary novels of this period from a rather empiricist viewpoint in *The Eighteenth Century French Novel* (Manchester: Manchester University Press, 1965), ch. 8.

6. H. Fielding, *Shamela*, ed. S. Baker (Berkeley: University of California Press, 1953), p. 14.
7. See B. Kriessman, *Pamela-Shamela: A Study of the Criticisms, Burlesques, Parodies and Adaptions of Richardson's Pamela* (Lincoln: University of Nebraska Press, 1960).
8. S. Richardson, *Pamela*, ed. M. Kinkead Weekes (London: Dent, 1962), p. 3.
9. *Ibid.*, pp. 9–10.
10. *Ibid.*, p. 239.
11. *Ibid.*, p. 283.
12. Fielding, *Shamela*, p. 31.
13. *Oxford English Dictionary*.
14. This point is noted in J. L. Flandrin 'Repression and Change in the Sexual Life of Young People and Medieval and Early Modern Times', in *Family and Sexuality in French History*, ed. R. Wheaton and T. Harevan (Philadelphia: University of Philadelphia Press, 1980), p. 32.
15. Perhaps I should also remark here on the British slang expression used by men that they 'made' a woman, meaning they have had sexual intercourse with her. Here the idea of the woman in bourgeois society being positioned by the male is given discursive confirmation. In this society there is an important sense in which man makes/creates woman. The etymology of this expression is uncertain.

    On the development of the bourgeois notion of love, see L. Stone, *The Family, Sex and Marriage in Britain 1500–1800* (London: Weidenfeld & Nicolson, 1977), pp. 274–6, 282–7.
16. A. Capellanus, *The Art of Courtly Love*, trans. J. Parry (New York: Ungar, 1941), p. 208.
17. Richardson, *Pamela*, p. 17 (original emphasis).
18. *Ibid.*
19. On de Sade it is time well spent reading R. Barthes's *Sade, Fourier, Loyola*, trans. R. Miller (New York: Hill & Wang, 1976), particularly Barthes's second section on de Sade. We might also usefully compare de Sade's materialist obsession with the body as the site of power to Masoch's work which reflects the decay of the importance of desire as the moment of social structuration. G. Deleuze makes this comparison well in *Masochism: An Interpretation of Coldness and Cruelty*, trans. A. Willon (New York: Doubleday, 1971).
20. G. Quaife, *Wanton Wenches and Wayward Wives* (New Brunswick: Rutgers University Press, 1979), p. 183.
21. J. Milton, *Paradise Lost*, Book IX, lines 1027–33.
22. For an expansion of this argument, see U. Cassuto, *A Commentary on the Book of Genesis*, trans. I. Abrahams (Jerusalem: Magnes Press, 1961), vol. 1, pp. 110–15.
23. C. Hill, *Milton and the English Revolution* (London: Faber, 1977), and bibliography.

24. D. Rogers, *Matrimonial Honour 1642*, p. 7, quoted in W. Haller, 'The Puritan Art of Love', *Huntingdon Library Quarterly*, vol. 5 (1940–1), pp. 246–7.
25. C. Hill, *Society and Puritanism* (London: Secker & Warburg, 1964), p. 443.
26. Compare with P. Laslett, *The World We Have Lost* (London: Methuen, 1965).
27. Quoted in K. Thomas, 'The Double Standard', *Journal of the History of Ideas*, vol. 20 (1959), p. 213.
28. J. Richetti, *Popular Fiction before Richardson 1700-1739* (Oxford: Clarendon Press, 1969), p. 90.
29. An outline of the contents of the pamphlet may be found in V. Bullough, *The History of Prostitution* (New York: University Books, 1964), pp. 161–3. Thomas in 'Double Standard' also writes about this pamphlet and talks in terms of the recognition of male lust.
30. Quoted in Thomas, 'Double Standard', p. 202.
31. Montesquieu, *The Spirit of the Law*, trans. T. Nugent (New York: Hasner Press, 1949), p. 101.
32. C. Hill, *The World Turned Upside Down* (London: Temple Smith, 1972), p. 249. See also L. Schucking, *The Puritan Family*, trans. B. Battershaw (London: Routledge & Kegan Paul, 1969).
33. Haller, 'Puritan Art of Love', p. 264.
34. In general, see Hill, *World Turned Upside Down*, passim. On the Ranters, see A. Morton, *The World of the Ranters* (London: Lawrence & Wishart, 1970).
35. C. Hill, 'Clarissa Harlowe and Her Times', in J. Carroll (ed.) *Samuel Richardson A Collection of Critical Essays*, (Englewood Cliffs: Prentice-Hall, 1969), pp. 102–23.
36. Fielding, *Shamela*, p. 52.
37. Quoted in Thomas, 'Double Standard', p. 210. Thomas also notes that in the sixteenth century Vives in *The Instruction of a Christian Woman* described a maid who loses her virginity as 'unthrifty'.
38. Fielding, *Shamela*, p. 46.
39. Aristotle, *Generation of Animals*, trans. A. Peck (London: Heinemann, 1942), p. 729, a25–34. For a discussion of medical (as opposed to popular) views of women in medieval Europe, see V. Bullough, *Medieval Medical and Scientific Views of Women*, Viator 4 (1973), pp. 485–501.
40. H. Ellis, *Studies in the Psychology of Sex*, vol. 5 (Philadelphia: Davis, 1928).
41. See Peters, 'The Pregnant Pamela'. The Term 'obstetrician' first appeared in 1828.
42. This is commented on in Steven Marcus's discussion of *My Secret Life* in *The Other Victorians*, (London: Weidenfeld & Nicolson, 1966), p. 113.
43. In 'Timon: A Satire'.
44. Quoted from S. Gilbert and S. Gubar *The Madwoman in the Attic* (New Haven: Yale University Press, 1979), p. 3. Gilbert and Gubar

are extremely good on the exclusion of women from writing. However, their book tends towards a literary ahistoricism.

45. E. Showalter, *A Literature of their Own* (Princeton: Princeton University Press, 1977).
46. E. Moers, *Literary Women* (New York: Doubleday, 1976) p. 139.
47. N. Miller, *The Heroine's Text* (New York: Columbia University Press, 1980), p. 150.
48. *Ibid.*, p. 155.
49. Gilbert and Gubar, *Madwoman in the Attic.*

Chapter 3

1. The idyllic quality of *Pamela*, the articulation of the bourgeois love myth, is reinforced by Richardson's use of the British tradition of the pastoral, a tradition he does not draw on in either *Clarissa* or *The History of Sir Charles Grandison*. On this see M. Doody, *A Natural Passion: A Study of the Novels of Samuel Richardson* (Oxford: Clarendon Press, 1974), ch. 3.
2. D. Defoe, *Conjugal Lewdness* (London, 1727). This facsimile edition ed. M. Novak (Gainsville: Scholars Facsimiles and Reprints, 1967), p. 68.
3. R. Barthes, *The Pleasure of the Text*, trans. R. Howard (New York: Hilland Wang, 1976), p. 19.
4. *Ibid.*, p. 61.
5. I. Watt, *The Rise of the Novel* (London: Chatto & Windus, 1957), p. 144.
6. L. Stone, 'Literacy in Britain during the Industrial Revolution', *Past and Present (1969).*
7. On this see L. Wright, *Middle Class Culture in Elizabethan England* (Ithaca: Cornell University Press, 1958), pp. 111–12.
8. *Ibid.*, p. 106.
9. Watt, *Rise of the Novel*, p. 44.
10. R. Day, *Told in Letters* (Ann Arbor: University of Michigan Press, 1966), p. 75.
11. *Ibid.*
12. J. Richetti, *Popular Fiction before Richardson 1700–1739* (Oxford: Clarendon Press, 1969), pp. 125–6.
13. Wright, *Middle Class Culture*, p. 109.
14. Watt, *Rise of the Novel*, p. 45.
15. Wright, *Middle Class Culture*, p. 112.
16. Day, *Told in Letters*, p. 77.
17. Barthes, *Pleasure of the Text*, p. 10.
18. Edward Copland has brought out well the similarities between *Clarissa and Fanny Hill* in his 'Clarissa and Fanny Hill: Sisters in Distress', *Studies in the Novel*, vol. 4, no. 3 (Fall, 1972), pp. 343–52. For a history of British 'pornography' in this period, see D. Foxon,

Libertine Literature in England, 1660–1745, (London: Book Collector, 1964).

19. W. Epstein, *John Cleland: Images of a Life* (New York: Columbia University Press, 1974), p. 88. For a history of the development of the legal notion of obscenity in Britain (one Edmund Curl, celebrated as the dunce in Pope's Dunciad in 1727, became the first Englishman to be convicted of publishing erotica), see G. Robertson, *Obscenity* (London: Weidenfeld & Nicolson, 1979).

20. S. Marcus, *The Other Victorians* (London: Weidenfeld & Nicolson, 1966), ch. 7.

21. On Victorian literary expurgation see R. Pearsall, *Public Purity, Private Shame* (London: Weidenfeld & Nicolson, 1976), ch. 8 *passim.*

22. Foxon, *Libertine Literature,* pp. 7–14.

23. Quoted in Foxon, *Libertine Literature,* p. 9.

24. J. Donne, *Complete Poetry and Selected Prose,* ed. J. Haywood (London: Nonesuch Press, 1929), p. 441.

25. Quoted in D. Thomas *A Long Time Burning* (London: Routledge & Kegan Paul, 1969), p. 337.

26. These Societies are discussed in greater depth in a later chapter.

27. Quoted from R. Weste, *The Book of Demeanor and the Allowance and Disallowance of Certain Misdemeanors in Companie,* in N. Elias, *The Civilising Process,* trans. E. Jephcott (Oxford: Blackwell, 1970), pp. 131–2.

28. Elias, *Civilising Process,* p. 139.

29. *Ibid.,* p. 131.

30. Quoted in Foxon, *Libertine Literature,* p. 19. Foxon gives a translation of the entire dedication.

31. P. Aretino, *Dialogues,* trans. R. Rosenthal (New York: Stein and Day, 1971), pp. 43–4.

32. A. Kinsey *et al. Sexual Behavior in the Human Female* (Philadelphia: Saunders, 1953), pp. 662–3.

33. Foxon, *Libertine Literature,* p. 27.

Chapter 4

1. L. Goldmann, *The Hidden God,* trans. P. Thody (London: Routledge & Kegan Paul, 1964), p. 108.

2. I. Watt, *The Rise of the Novel* (London: Chatto & Windus, 1957), p. 31.

3. R. Barthes, *Critical Essays,* trans. R. Howard (Evanston: North Western University Press, 1972), p. 224.

4. P. Brooks, *The Novel of Worldliness* (Princeton: Princeton University Press, 1969), p. 79.

5. Watt, *The Rise of the Novel.*

6. C. de Laclos, *Les Liaisons dangereuses,* trans. P. Stone (Harmondsworth: Penguin, 1961), letter 175.

7. D. Erasmus, *De civilitate morum puerilium*, trans. P. Aries, *La Civilité puérile* (Paris: Editions Ramsay, 1977), p. 59–60.
8. On the links between courts and bourgeoisie in the context of behaviour, see W. Woodward, *Studies in Education during the Age of the Renaissance, 1400–1600* (New York: Russell & Russell, 1965), ch. 12.
9. Brooks, *Novel of Worldliness*, p. 79.
10. *Ibid.*, p. 82–3.
11. Quoted in J. Lough, *An Introduction to Eighteenth Century France* (London: Longmans, 1960), p. 292.
12. P. Clark, *The Battle of the Bourgeois; the Novel in France, 1789–1848* (Paris: Didiet, 1973), ch. 2.
13. Quoted in F. Funck-Brentano, *The Old Regime in France*, trans. H. Wilson (London: Arnold, 1979), p. 155.
14. *Ibid.*, p. 154.
15. *Ibid.*, p. 194.
16. P. Aries, *Western Attitudes Towards Death*, trans P. Ranum (Baltimore: Johns Hopkins University Press, 1974), p. 12.
17. S. Padover, *The Life and Death of Louis XVI* (New York: Taplinger, 1963), p. 4.
18. Funck-Brentano, *Old Regime*, p. 162.
19. *Ibid.*, p. 184.
20. Quoted in F. Henriques, *Prostitution in Europe and the New World* (London: MacGibbon and Kee, 1963), p. 131.
21. Quoted from *Le Président mystifié*, p. 1475, by Clark, *Battle of the Bourgeois*, p. 44.
22. Clark, *Battle of the Bourgeois*.
23. R. Darnton, 'The High Enlightenment and the Low-Life of Literature in Pre-Revolutionary France', in *French Society and the Revolution*, ed. D. Johnson (Cambridge: Cambridge University Press, 1976), p. 79 and *passim*.
24. J. Lough, *Writer and Public in France* (Oxford: Clarendon Press, 1978), pp. 142–5.
25. This is how Brooks, *Novel of Wordliness*, p. 36, describes Crébillon's last novel: 'the Lettres de la Duchesse de ... au Duc de ..., was published in 1767. It is a curious work, 470 pages of letters from a Duchesse to a Duc who would have her love him, but never obtains permission to appear on the scene. Perilously close to the Flaubertian ideal of a 'book about nothing', the novel is the purest of lessons in listening to tones of voice, of penetrating to the truth about a character from the slenderest, most fragmentary evidence.' What better description of the true novel of worldliness could one wish for?
26. Duclos quoted in Brooks, *Novel of Worldliness*, p. 40.
27. L. Braudy, 'Penetration and Impenetrability, in *Clarissa*', in *New Approaches to Eighteenth Century Literature*, ed. J. P. Harth (New York: Columbia University Press, 1974).
28. V. Lee, *The Reign of Women in Eighteenth Century France* (Cambridge, Mass.: Schenkman Pub. Co., 1975), p. 106.

29. *Ibid.*, p. 37.
30. Brooks, *Novel of Worldliness*, p. 38.
31. Laclos, *Les Liaisons dangereuses*, p. 181.
32. *Ibid.*, p. 183.
33. The importance of the play of the love/desire/intercourse combination in bourgeois society is easily demonstrated by a cursory examination of the terminology of popular music.
34. See C. F. Brooks, *Novel of Worldliness* and Braudy, 'Penetration and Impenetrability', on penetration as a term used in *ancien régime* worldliness and bourgeois English society, respectively.
35. Laclos, *Les Liaisons dangereuses*, p. 315.
36. *Ibid.*, p. 181.
37. *Ibid.*, p. 303.
38. Crébillon fils, '*Ah, quel conte*', in *Complètes Oeuvres*, vol. VI, p. 177. A more complete discussion including this quotation (p. 29) may be found in C. Cherpack, *An Essay on Crébillon fils* (Durham: Duke University Press, 1962).
39. See once again Laclos, *Les Liaisons dangereuses*, letter 81. For the purposes of my argument this is the most important letter in this book.
40. Crébillon fils, '*Les égarements du coeur et de l'esprit*', in vol. I, p. 13. Quoted in Cherpack, *Crébillon fils*, p. 17.
41. Laclos, *Les Liaisons dangereuses*, letter 2.
42. J. Sassus, *The Motif of Renunciation of Love in the Seventeenth-Century French Novel*. Dissertation (Washington D.C.: The Catholic University of America Press, 1963), p. 72, discusses the decline of 'indecent' passages in seventeenth-century French novels.
43. This is why all the 'great' love stories are of lost love (and usually death). *Differance*, the impossibility of resolution, is thus itself made a part of the resolution. Compare R. Barthes, *A Lover's Discourse*, trans. R. Howard (New York: Hilland Wang, 1978).
44. Quoted in R. Sennett, *The Fall of Public Man* (Cambridge: Cambridge University Press, 1977), p. 185. The emphasis on the naked female body is reflected also in developments in Fine Art. K. Clarke in *The Nude: A Study of Ideal Art* (Harmondsworth: Penguin, 1960) notes that: 'The predominance of the female nude over the male, of which Raphael's Judgement of Paris is the first example, was to increase during the next 200 years, till by the 19th century it was absolute' (p. 343). Clarke argues that: 'no doubt in the eventual establishment of the female model the tug of normal sensuality must have a place' (p. 344). I would argue that, far from being normal, the sensuality of which Clarke speaks is the product of the development of a particular articulation of sexuality in which the female—denoted by physical signs visually perceived—is at one and the same time both the repository of reality and the occupier of an inferior position in the male-controlled world of signs thus realised.
45. J. McManners, *The French Revolution and the Church* (London: SPCK, 1969), p. 113.
46. The *Encyclopédie*, ed. D. Diderot, section on 'marriage'.

47. L. Stone, *The Family, Sex and Marriage in Britain 1500–1800* (London: Weidenfeld & Nicolson, 1977), p. 536.
48. Quoted in E. Ewing, *Underwear: A History* (New York: Theatre Art Books, 1972), p. 43.
49. Ewing, *Underwear*, p. 43.
50. Quoted in Ewing, *Underwear*, p. 45.
51. Quoted in R. Pearsall, *Public Purity, Private Shame* (London: Weidenfeld & Nicolson, 1976), p. 71.

Chapter 5

1. J. Tompkins, *The Popular Novel in England 1770–1800* (London, 1932; repub. Lincoln: University of Nebraska Press, 1961), p. 243.
2. *Ibid.*, p. 175.
3. I. Watt, *The Rise of the Novel* (London: Chatto & Windus, 1957), p. 32.
4. G. Levine, *The Realistic Imagination* (Chicago: University of Chicago Press, 1981), n. 25, p. 331.
5. S. Marcus, *The Other Victorians* (London: Weidenfeld & Nicolson, 1966), p. 45.
6. M. Goldstein, H. Kant and J. Hartman, *Pornography and Sexual Deviance* (Berkeley; University of California Press, 1974), p. 22.
7. E. Moers, *Literary Women* (New York: Doubleday, 1976), p. 100.
8. Of course, the internalised repression of realism and the social repression involved in pornography shade into one another in works such as D. H. Lawrence's *Lady Chatterley's Lover*, which precipitated a celebrated British court case in 1964.
9. N. Holland and L. Sherman, 'Gothic Possibilities', *New Literary History*, vol. 8 (1976–77), p. 285.
10. A similar reading may be given of Charlotte Brontë's *Jane Eyre*. 'Eyre' is an Old English word meaning 'journey', and the book reads as a morality tale in which Charlotte Brontë is commenting on another famous morality tale about a servant and her master, *Pamela*. Jane's journey is from governess to wife, but it is also from a place of female inferiority to a position of idyllic equality—more pragmatic, in this sense more 'real', but nevertheless still similar to that mapped out for Catherine and Hareton. Just as Thrushcross Grange has its Gothic equivalent in Wuthering Heights so Thornfield Hall has its equivalent in Jane's dream of it as a ruin—its final ruin destroyed by the expression of the repressed sexuality of the domestic environment. Bertha Mason is to Thornfield Hall what Madelaine Usher is to the House of Usher. In each case the liberation of female sexuality destroys the bourgeois domestic environment. It might also be argued that Charlotte Brontë gives Jane a male birth. The Red Room may not only be a womb image—it is a shine to Jane's protector Mr Reed. It is

only after swooning in the room that Jane leaves the Reed home to start her journey through life—a journey completed for the reader by her marriage.

11. M. Foucault, *The History of Sexuality*, trans. R. Hurley (London: Allen Lane, 1979), vol. 1.
12. T. Todorov, *The Fantastic*, trans. R. Howard (Cleveland, Ohio: Press of Case Western Reserve University, 1973), p. 126.
13. See R. Jackson, *Fantasy* (London: Methuen, 1981), p. 112.
14. On these see B. Kriessman, *Pamela-Shamela: A Study of the Criticisms, Burlesques, Parodies and Adaptions of Richardson's Pamela* (Lincoln: University of Nebraska Press, 1960).
15. D. Punter, *The Literature of Terror* (London: Longman, 1980), p. 27.
16. D. Punter, 'Social Relations of Gothic Fiction' in D. Aers *et al.*, *Romanticism and Ideology* (London: Routledge & Kegan Paul, 1981), p. 104.
17. Jackson, *Fantasy*, p. 25.
18. This point is made in C. Wolff, *Samuel Richardson and the Eighteenth Century Puritan Character* (Hamden, Conn.: Archon Books, 1972).
19. C. Hill, 'Clarissa Harlowe and Her Times' in J. Carroll (ed.), *Samuel Richardson: A Collection of Critical Essays* (Englewood Cliffs: Prentice Hall, 1969), pp. 102-23.
20. P. Laslett, 'Introduction' to P. Laslett, K. Oostervaan and R. Smith *Bastardy and Its Comparative History* (Cambridge, Mass.: Harvard University Press, 1980), p. 10.
21. Laslett *et al.*, *Bastardy*, p. 9.
22. L. Stone, *The Family, Sex and Marriage in England 1500–1800* (London: Weidenfeld & Nicolson, 1977), p. 502.
23. G. Deleuze and F. Guattari, *Anti-Oedipus*, trans. R. Hurley, M. Seem and H. Lane (New York: The Viking Press, 1977).
24. M. Foucault, 'Préface à la transgression' in *Critique* (1963), quoted in translation in Jackson, *Fantasy*, p. 79.
25. J. Lacan, 'The significance of the phallus', in *Ecrits*, trans. A. Sheridan (New York: Norton, 1977), p. 287.
26. J. Lacan, 'The subversion of the subject and the dialectic of desire in the Freudian unconscious' in *Ecrits*, p. 311.
27. J. Lacan, *The Language of the Self*, trans. A. Wilden, quoted in Wilden's notes (New York: Dell pub., 1975), p. 106.
28. J. Lacan, *Ecrits*, p. 2.
29. J. Lacan, 'Anamorphosis' in *Four Fundamental Concepts of Psychoanalysis*, ed. J. A. Miller, trans. A. Sheridan (New York: W. W. Norton, 1978).
30. A. Lavalley, 'The Stage and Film Children of *Frankenstein*: A Survey', in *Frankenstein*, ed. G. Levine and U.C. Knopfelmacher (Berkeley: University of California Press, 1979). The British Penguin edition went through seven reprints between its first publication in 1968 and 1978.
31. P. Brooks, 'Godlike Science/Unhallowed Arts' in *Endurance of Frankenstein*, p. 207.

32. D. Cottom, '*Frankenstein* and the Monster of Representation', *Substance*, vol.28 (1981), p. 61.
33. Watt, *Rise of the Novel*, ch. 3.
34. H. Cixous, 'The Character of "Character" ', trans. Keith Cohen, *New Literary History*, vol. 5, no. 3 (1974), p. 385.
35. W. Warner, *Reading Clarissa* (New Haven: Yale University Press, 1979).
36. Watt, *Rise of the Novel*, p. 20.
37. There is also a certain irony here in the close similarity between Clarissa's and Sinclair's names.
38. L. Braudy, 'Penetration and Impenetrability, in *Clarissa*', in *New Approaches to Eighteenth Century Literature*, ed. J. P. Harth (New York: Columbia University Press, 1974) has a great deal to say about Richardson's repeated use of this term in the novel.
39. See, for example, P. Berger and T. Luckman, *The Social Construction of Reality* (New York: Doubleday, 1966).
40. J.-L. Flandrin, *Families in Former Times*, trans. R. Southern (Cambridge: Cambridge University Press, 1979), pp. 11–14.
41. J. McManners, *The French Revolution and the Church* (London: SPCK, 1969), p. 104.
42. Stone, *The Family, Sex and Marriage*, p. 329.
43. We may usefully compare the naming of *Clarissa*—and also of course Pamela's name—with the naming in French works such as Laclos' *Les Liaisons dangereuses*, where the names, as in British realist novels, 'mean' nothing except as signifiers of particular individuals.
44. M. Doody, *A Natural Passion: A Study of the Novels of Samuel Richardson* (Oxford: Clarendon Press, 1974).
45. The motif of confinement figures very prominently in Gothic fiction because confinement is the realisation of displacement. See, for example, the Chinese box structure of Charles Maturin's *Melmoth the Wanderer*.
46. For a brief account of this development see E. J. Burford, *In the Clink* (London: New English Library, 1977), ch. 1.
47. See M. Gluckman, *Politics, Law and Ritual in Tribal Society* (Oxford: Blackwell, 1965).
48. M. Foucault, *Madness and Civilization*, trans. R. Howard (London: Tavistock, 1967), p. 43.
49. See M. Foucault, *Discipline and Punish*, trans. A. Sheridan (New York: Pantheon, 1977), pp. 76–8: 'A general movement shifted criminality from the attack of bodies to the more or less direct seizure of goods; and from a "mass criminality" to a "marginal criminality" ' (p. 76).
50. I should refer here to G. Bennington, 'From Narrative to Text', *Oxford Literary Review*, vol. 4, no. 1 (1970): p. 66. This briefly discusses rape in the context of M. Foucault, 'Un si cruel savoir', *Critique* (Juillet 1962) pp. 597–611.
51. S. Richardson, *Clarissa* (London: Chapman & Hall, 1902), vol. 6, letter LXIX, p. 325.

52. *Ibid.*, vol. 2, letter XL, p. 282: Methought my brother, my uncle Antony, and Mr. Solmes, had formed a plot to destroy Mr. Lovelace; who discovering it, and believing I had a hand in it, turned all his rage upon me. I thought he made them all fly to foreign parts upon it; and afterwards seizing upon me, carried me into a churchyard; and there, notwithstanding, all my prayers and tears, and protestations of innocence, stabbed me to the heart, and then tumbled me into a deep grave ready dug, among two or three half-dissolved carcases; throwing in the dirt and earth upon me with his hands, and trampling it down with his feet.' This dream, in its sensual use of death and Christianity, required only the transitional step from dream to reality, to be placed on a par with scences in such Gothic works as M. Lewis's *The Monk*.

53. *Ibid.* For a developed psychoanalytic interpretation of Richardson's works, see G. Levin, *Richardson the Novelist: The Psychological Patterns* (Amsterdam: Rodopi, 1978).

54. P. Aries, *The Hour of Our Death*, trans. H. Weaver (New York: Knopf, 1981), p. 370.

55. *Ibid.*

56. Todorov, *The Fantastic*, p. 135.

57. W. Warner, *Reading Clarissa* (New Haven: Yale University Press, 1979), p. 76.

58. Richardson, *Clarissa*, vol. 1, Preface, p. xi.

59. M. Zirker, jr., 'Richardson's correspondence: the personal letter as private experience', *The Familiar Letter in the Eighteenth Century*, ed. H. Anderson, P. Daghlion and L. Ehrenpreis (Lawrence: University Press of Kansas, 1966), pp. 77–8.

60. Zirker, *Richardsons's Correspondence*.

Chapter 6

1. A. Kinsey *et al.*, *Sexual Behaviour in the Human Male* (Philadelphia: Saunders, 1948), p. 580.

2. Quoted in R. Pearsall, *The Worm in the Bud* (London: Weidenfeld & Nicolson, 1969), p. 236.

3. Quoted in R. Pearsall, *Public Purity, Private Shame* (London: Weidenfeld & Nicolson, 1976), p. 38.

4. M. de Sade in 'Yet another Effort Frenchmen, If you would become Republicans'. This is the fifth dialogue of de Sade *La Philosophie dans le boudoir*.

5. Quoted in E. Showalter, *A Literature of Their Own* (Princeton: Princeton University Press, 1977), p. 130.

6. N. Elias, *The Civilizing Process*, trans. E. Jephcott (Oxford: Blackwell, 1970), p. 117.

7. J.-L. Flandrin, *Families in Former Times*, trans. R. Southern (Cambridge: Cambridge University Press, 1979), pp. 210–11.

8. E. J. Burford, *Bawds and Lodgings* (London: Owen, 1976), p. 178.

9. E. Le Roy Ladurie, *Montaillou*, trans. B. Bray (London: Scolar, 1978), p. 151.
10. *Ibid.*, p. 150.
11. S. Richardson, *Clarissa* (London: Chapman & Hall, 1902), vol. 6, letter X, p. 62.
12. R. Sennett, *The Fall of Public Man* (Cambridge: Cambridge University Press, 1977), p. 112.
13. Richardson, *Clarissa*, p. 62.
14. *Ibid.*, vol. 6, p. 3. As an aside, Mandeville had been dead some fifteen years at the time of the publication of *Clarissa*.
15. A useful introduction to this debate is in M. M. Goldsmith, 'Public Virtue and Private Vices', in *Eighteenth Century Studies*, vol. 9 (1976), pp. 477–510.
16. La Rochefoucauld, *Maximes*.
17. On these societies, and Mandeville's relation to them, see T. Horne, *The Social Thought of Bernard Mandeville* (New York: Columbia University Press, 1978), ch. 1.
18. B. Mandeville, *The Fable of the Bees*, ed. P. Harth (Harmondsworth: Penguin, 1970), p. 127.
19. A Hirschman, *The Passions and the Interests* (Princeton: Princeton University Press, 1977), p. 41.
20. Quoted in M. Seymour-Smith, *Fallen Women* (London: Nelson, 1969), p. 152.
21. F. Harrison, *The Dark Angel* (London: Sheldon Press, 1977), p. 22.
22. C. Terrot, *The Maiden Tribute* (London: Dutton, 1959), p. 14.
23. *Ibid.*, p. 19.
24. Richardson, *Clarissa*, vol. 3, letter LV, p. 385.
25. *Ibid.*, p. 384.
26. J. Goethe, *Elective Affinities* trans. E. Mayer and L. Brogran (Chicago: Regnery Co., 1963), p. 52.
27. On the history of English sumptuary laws see N. B. Harte, 'State Control of Dress and Social Change in Pre-Industrial England', in *Trade, Government and Economy in Pre-Industrial England*, ed. D. Coleman and A. John (London: Weidenfeld & Nicolson, 1976). Sumptuary laws continued to be of importance in France throughout the *ancien régime*. Twelve edicts, for example, were passed between 1661 and 1683.
28. L. Gabel, ed. *Memoirs of a Renaissance Pope*, trans. F. Grogg (London: Allen & Unwin, 1968), p. 35.
29. J.-L. Flandrin, 'Repression and Change in the Sexual Life of Young People in Medieval and Early Modern Times', in *Family and Sexuality in French History*, ed. R. Wheaton and T. Harevan (Philadelphia: University of Philadelphia Press, 1980), pp. 31, 43–5.
30. Flandrin, *Families in Former Times*, p. 97.
31. *Ibid.*, p. 99.
32. Le Roy Ladurie, *Montaillou*, p. 150.
33. B. Castiglione, *The Book of the Courtier*, trans. T. Hoby (London: Dent, 1974) p. 180.

34. *Ibid.*
35. *Ibid.*, p. 181.
36. Richardson, *Clarissa*, vol. 3, letter XCVII, p. 273.
37. G. Bennington in 'From Narrative to Text', *Oxford Literary Review*, vol. 4, no. 1, (1979) suggests, following an argument of Foucault's, that 'Virtue can be valorized only *outside* the closure of worldliness'— that is to say, by rape. This, however, misunderstands the already sexualised nature of rape in bourgeois society.
38. C. de Laclos, *Les Liaisons dangereuses*, trans. P. Stone (Harmondsworth: Penguin, 1961), p. 264.
39. J. Cleland, *Fanny Hill* (London: Mayflower, 1964), p. 34.
40. N. Miller, 'Novels of Innocence, Fictions of Loss', *Eighteenth Century Studies*, vol. 11, no. 3 (1977–8), p. 335.

Chapter 7

1. M. Abrams, *The Mirror and the Lamp* (New York: N.W. Norton, 1953), p. 142.
2. R. Friedenthal, *Goethe: His Life and Times* (London: Weidenfeld & Nicolson, 1965), p. 128.
3. By the way, I am not ignoring the other bourgeois fantasy about prostitutes, which is that they are all homosexual, frigid and hate men. This myth is a combination of male fear of the sexualised woman compounded by the perception of their male position in the society which produces them as a male/female anomaly. This is rationalised by making them homosexual.
4. Mrs Haywood, *Love in Excess*, quoted in J. Richetti, *Popular Fiction before Richardson* (Oxford: Clarendon, 1969), p. 283.
5. See L. Stone, *The Family, Sex and Marriage in England 1500–1800* (London: Weidenfeld & Nicolson, 1977), pp. 282–7.
6. A useful history of this kind of fiction, although it does not cover the seventeenth century, is R. Anderson, *The Purple Heart Throbs* (London: Hodder & Stoughton, 1974).
7. E. Shorter, *The Making of the Modern Family* (New York: Basic Books, 1975) p. 60.
8. *Ibid.*, p. 58.
9. *Ibid.*, pp. 5–6.
10. *Ibid.*, p. 7.
11. F. Goldin, *The Mirror of Narcissus in the Courtly Love Lyrics* (Ithaca: Cornell University Press, 1967), p. 40.
12. B. Castiglione, *The Book of the Courtier*, trans. T. Hoby (London: Dent, 1974), p. 306.
13. *Ibid.*
14. *Ibid.*, p. 313.

15. *Ibid.*, p. 304.
16. See for example, A. Lovejoy, *The Great Chain of Being* (New York: Harper, 1960).
17. Richetti, *Popular Fiction*, pp. 187–8.
18. *Ibid.*, p. 187.
19. J. Cleland, *Fanny Hill* (London: Mayflower, 1964), p. 188. L. Braudy discusses this aspect of *Fanny Hill* in '*Fanny Hill* and Materialism', *Eighteenth Century Studies*, vol. 4 (1970–71), pp. 21–40.
20. T. Tanner, *Adultery in the Novel* (Baltimore: Johns Hopkins University Press, 1979), p. 178.
21. J. J. Rousseau, *La Nouvelle Héloïse*, trans. and abr. J. McDowell (Pennsylvania: Pennsylvania State University Press, 1968), p. 25.
22. J. Goethe, *The Sorrows of Young Werther*, trans. C. Hutter (New York: Signet, 1962), p. 33.
23. *Ibid.*, p. 41.
24. S. Freud, 'Mourning and Melancholia', in *Complete Psychological Works*, ed. J. Strachey *et al.* (London: Hogarth Press, 1964), vol. 14, p. 257.
25. A. Alvarez, *The Savage God* (New York: Random House, 1972), p. 50.
26. For the figures for seventeenth- and eighteenth-century London, see S. Sprott, *The English Debate on Suicide*, (La Salle, Ill.: Open Court, 1961), Appendix. These show clearly that there was a new long-term level achieved in the early part of the eighteenth century.
27. Both D. Punter, *The Gothic in Literature* (London: Longman, 1980), p. 118, and R. Jackson, *Fantasy* (London: Methuen, 1981), pp. 118–22 comment on this.
28. B. Stoker, *Dracula*, London, 8th edn (Westminster: Constable, 1904), p. 40.
29. Quoted from S. Weir Mitchell, 'Fat and Blood' in R. Pearsall, *The Worm in the Bud* (London: Weidenfeld & Nicholson, 1969), p. 427.
30. Stoker, *Dracula*, pp. 91–2.
31. Quoted from J. Michelet, *L'Amour* (1859), in F. Harrison, *The Dark Angel* (London: Sheldon Press, 1977), p. 59.
32. R. Friedenthal, *Goethe: His Life and Times* (London: Weidenfeld & Nicholson, 1965), p. 128.
33. Goethe, *The Sorrows*, p. 25.
34. *Ibid.*, p. 33.
35. *Ibid.*, p. 99.
36. *Ibid.*, p. 125.
37. I should add that the length of time we are told it took Werther to die (six hours), coupled with the description the editor/Goethe gives us, not only adds to the Gothic horror but also emphasises the importance of the physical, the fetish of the body.
38. The history of this debate is well outlined in Sprott, *Suicide*.
39. Goethe, *The Sorrows*, p. 30. It is interesting to compare the attitudes to literary activity and sketching in *The Sorrows* with those in Virginia Woolf's *To the Lighthouse*.
40. Goethe, *The Sorrows*, p. 30.

41. We might add to this a reminder of Keats's description of his work: 'I live in the eye'.
42. See (4).
43. Goethe, *The Sorrows*, p. 35.
44. *Ibid.*, p. 65.
45. *Ibid.*, p. 74.
46. *Ibid.*, p. 26.
47. J. J. Rousseau, *Emile*, trans. B. Foxley (London: Dent, 1911), p. 7.
48. *Ibid.*, p. 9.
49. *Ibid.*, p. 321.
50. J. J. Rousseau, *The Confessions*, trans. J. Cohen (Harmondsworth: Penguin, 1953), p. 28.
51. *Ibid.*
52. Goethe, *The Sorrows*, p. 37.
53. *Ibid.*, p. 38.
54. From Byron, 'The Waltz: An Apostrophic Hymn', *The Poetical Works of Lord Byron*, ed. H. Frowde (London: Oxford University Press, 1909), pp. 142–6. A history of the waltz may be found in F. Rust, *Dance in Society* (London: Routledge & Kegan Paul, 1969), ch. 9. Rust misunderstands Byron's poem and opines that he was genuinely outraged.
55. *The Sorrows*, p. 35.
56. *The Sorrows*, p. 35.
57. P. Brown and L. Jordanova, 'Oppressive Dichotomies: The Nature/Culture Debate', in The Cambridge Women's Studies Group, *Women in Society* (London: Virago Press, 1981).
58. G. Quaife, *Wanton Wenches and Wayward Wives* (New Brunswick: Rutgers University Press, 1979), p. 177.
59. M. Goodich, *The Unmentionable Vice* (Santa Barbara: ABC-Clio, 1979), p. 61.
60. *Ibid.*, pp. 24–5.
61. See D. Thomas, *A Long Time Burning* (London: Routledge & Kegan Paul, 1969), p. 181.
62. M. Shelley, *Frankenstein*, in *Three Gothic Novels*, ed. P. Fairclough (Harmondsworth: Penguin, 1968).
63. Goethe, *The Sorrows*, p. 51.
64. *Ibid.*, p. 64.
65. *Ibid.*, p. 118.
66. *Ibid.*, p. 54.
67. *Ibid.*, p. 84. The linkage between Lotte and writing is reinforced by Werther when he writes, on hearing of Lotte and Albert's marriage, that he was planning on burying his silhouette of her and 'some other papers' (p. 76). Werther never goes through with this fetishistic destruction of his fetish.
68. R. Barthes, *A Lover's Discourse*, trans. R. Howard (New York: Hill & Wang 1978), p. 45.
69. Stoker, *Dracula*, p. 381.
70. Rousseau, *Emile*, p. 322.

Conclusion

1. S. Freud 'Fetishism', in *The Standard Edition of the Complete Psychological Works of Sigmund Freud*, trans. and ed. J. Strachey (London: Hogarth Press 1961), vol. 21.
2. See, for example, J. Lacan 'The Agency of the Letter in the Unconscious of Reason since Freud', in J. Lacan, *Ecrits*, trans. A. Sheridan (New York: W.W. Norton, 1977) and J. Derrida, 'The Purveyor of Truth', *Yale French Studies*, no. 52 (1976), pp. 31–113. This article of Derrida's is a critique of Lacan's argument.
3. J. Hillis Miller 'The Critic as Host', in H. Bloom *et al.*, *Deconstruction and Criticism* (New York: CONTINUUM 1979), p. 245.

Index

Abrams, M.
The Mirror and the Lamp, 156
Acton, William, 3, 144
adultery, 43–5, 86, 132, 138,
185–6
Alien, 102, 108, 121
Aquinas, St Thomas, 7–8, 9–10,
17
Aretino, P., 15
Dialogues, 66, 67–8, 70
Positzione, 8, 9, 67, 70
Aristotle, 50
asexuality, xiii, 1, 158, 188
of domestic domain, viii, 13,
26–7, 147, 186–7
of females, viii, xiv–xv, 13, 28,
45–6, 61, 69, 132, 136, 147,
159, 203
of text, xi, 29, 34, 61, 99, 147,
193
Augustine, St, 6–7, 9, 17, 144,
162, 190
Austen, Jane, 52, 54, 89
Northanger Abbey, 100

Bacon, Francis, 105, 200
Novum Organum, 74
Balzac, Honoré de, 96, 105
Barthes, R.
Critical Essays, 74
A Lover's Discourse, 194
The Pleasure of the Text, 57, 61
bastardy, 110–11, 138

Baudrillard, J., xi, 3, 14, 28, 98,
113
beds, 20–2, 193
Bell, Currer. *See* Brontë,
Charlotte
Bentham, Jeremy, 124
Bersani, Leo
A Future for Asyntax, 98
birth, 50, 81–2, 101–2, 103–4
blood, 158, 169, 172–3
body, 71, 91–2, 124, 151, 162
confinement of, 129, 148
fetishisation of, 2, 30, 66, 69,
81, 93–4, 95, 129, 139, 148,
151
nakedness of, 41, 65–7, 69, 81,
93, 95, 137. *See also*
clothes
site of sexuality, vii, 30 n1, 39,
93
bourgeois society. *See* capitalism;
confinement; domestic
domain; females; fetishism;
males; marriage; morality;
reality, of bourgeois society;
repression; sexuality, bourgeois
Braudy, L., 86
Brontë, Charlotte, xii, 188
Jane Eyre, 22–5, 55, 103 n10,
104, 171, 173, 179, 203–4
Brontë, Emily
Wuthering Heights, 100, 102–3,
121, 165, 181, 192

226

Index

227

Index

Index

Index

Index

Index